Business Process Management within Chemical and Pharmaceutical Industries

Guido Grüne · Stephanie Lockemann
Volker Kluy · Stefan Meinhardt

Business Process Management within Chemical and Pharmaceutical Industries

Markets, BPM Methodology and Process Examples

With Contributions by
Petronela Barnáková, Carola Feind-Just,
Markus Pfannschilling-Zerbe, Ornulf Rexin,
Klaus Schölzel, Jürgen Schroth

Springer

Guido Grüne
Stephanie Lockemann
Volker Kluy
Stefan Meinhardt
SAP Deutschland AG & Co KG
Walldorf
Germany

ISBN 978-3-662-50627-1 ISBN 978-3-642-11717-6 (eBook)
DOI 10.1007/978-3-642-11717-6
Springer Heidelberg New York Dordrecht London

Softcover reprint of the hardcover 1st edition 2014

Printed on acid-free paper

Springer is part of Springer Science+Business Media (www.springer.com)

Preface

It was not until the early 1990s that the idea of process optimization began to shape the way companies operated. The concept of "business process reengineering," as defined by Michael Hammer and James Champy, shifted the focus of all processes to the customer and required organizational structures to be built around optimized processes.

This concept gave birth to numerous management methods that have become established in companies, including lean management, total quality management, and kaizen, to name just a few.

Properly defined and managed processes lead to increased customer satisfaction and—thanks to smooth internal processes—employee satisfaction, and allow businesses to develop new products and services more quickly. Customers with optimized business processes also have tighter control of their costs.

The ability to quickly adapt business processes within the framework of an ongoing process of adaptation represents a significant competitive advantage in a market environment that is constantly evolving to meet global requirements.

Business process management (BPM) is the method developed by SAP® Consulting to help companies optimize their processes. In addition to the methodology that addresses the optimization of processes, BPM offers a collection of best practice processes from the process manufacturing industry. This allows chemical and pharmaceutical companies to identify and implement improvements rapidly.

These approaches are underpinned by the development of service-oriented architectures in the area of IT. For example, the growing demand for reusable software modules in companies necessitates a high degree of process standardization. The work of the traditional IT department is moving toward process management. The identification of use cases and adoption of new technologies such as smartphones and tablet PCs or SAPs in memory database can be rapidly improved by a process management driven company. BPM offers a holistic approach to defining the IT architecture of the company on the basis of industry-specific business process knowledge.

We begin this book by describing the market environment and the particular challenges faced by companies in the process manufacturing industry. We then go on to explain the business process management method, which is illustrated using examples of industry-specific business processes.

We would like to thank our colleagues for their contributions to the content of this book and for their patience in handling the layout and all other formalities.

Walldorf, June 2012

Guido Grüne
Stephanie Lockemann
Volker Kluy
Stefan Meinhardt

Contents

Chapter 1
The Process Industry

Stephanie Lockemann and Petronela Barnáková

1.1 Segments of the Process Industries

Process industries cover a wide range of businesses, typically from the chemical, pharmaceutical or life science, oil, gas, steel, paper, and glass industries, but also from the consumer goods sectors like cosmetics and food. However, the literature on the subject does not provide a single common definition of the process industry.

The production processes used in process industries differ significantly from those used in discrete manufacturing. While discrete manufacturing is based on discrete unit production, that is, component-based production and assembly processes, process manufacturing is characterized by continuous or discontinuous (batch) production processes. This results in the production of quantities or volumes rather than units. In process manufacturing, products are manufactured in production networks linked to each other via a distribution network. Typical for the industry are also regulatory standards and quality management requirements, which present their own particular challenges for production and logistics.

This book does have a focus on the chemical and pharmaceutical industries. Other segments are not considered. There are significant differences between pharmaceutical and chemical industries: the introduction of different technologies, changes in downstream markets, growth perspectives, drivers of success, approaches to innovation and changing shareholder expectations (CEFIC 2004). Since these are the crucial factors for economic success, the chemical and pharmaceutical industries are examined separately in this book.

1.1.1 The Chemical Industry and its Share in the Economy

The chemical industry refers to companies that, in the widest possible sense, are dealing with the processes of transforming natural and manufacturing synthetic raw materials. These materials are typically used by other industries to create products mainly for the industrial and less for consumer products markets.

G. Grüne et al., *Business Process Management within Chemical and Pharmaceutical Industries*, DOI: 10.1007/978-3-642-11717-6_1,

Similar to process industries as a whole, there does not exist a common agreement which industry fields belong to the chemical industry. Therefore, a precise definition is not possible. Considering the official classifications throughout the world, there is also less convergence. Historically, the chemical producers have seen themselves belonging into one of the five main segments: basic chemicals, specialty chemicals, agricultural chemicals, pharmaceuticals, and consumer products. The differences apply to the structure, growth dynamics, markets, and other special issues, but in many cases a clear distinction is not possible (ACC 2011).

Generally, the chemical industry can be divided into two sectors:

Basic (*or commodity*) *chemicals* are produced in large volumes with no product differentiation. They are primary products for further processing. These include inorganic chemicals, bulk petrochemicals and organic chemical intermediates, petrochemical derivatives and other industrial chemicals, plastic resins, synthetic rubber, and synthetic fibers.

Basic chemicals are a mature business. Prices are highly correlated with capacity utilization and feedstock costs. Companies generally employ low-cost leadership strategies. The low profit margins and a strong sensitivity toward economic cycles are typical features. Availability of feedstock and large capital (plant size, technology) and energy requirements are strong barriers to entry (ACC 2011).

Specialty chemicals (*or specialties*) are differentiated and often technologically advanced products. They are manufactured in lower volumes than basic chemicals and are used for a specific purpose—basically as solutions to problems. A feature distinguishing specialties from basic chemicals is their large customer servicing or technical servicing component. That is, they are sold for what they do, rather than for what they contain. Included are for example coatings, adhesives, and sealants.

Specialty chemicals companies are generally niche players and fragmented along specialty market lines. Nevertheless the long-term growth prospects for specialties are mostly more dynamic than for basic chemicals. The customer industries needs are rising and the lower volumes allow easier transportation. Specialty chemicals prices tend to be set by "value-in-use", not by cost and historically their earnings have not been impacted as much by demand pressures. In general, specialty chemicals represent a small portion of customers total cost, but they are essential to enhancing productivity and performance. Innovation is critical there and producers of specialties typically spend 4–8 % of their revenues on research and development. Strong technical servicing, marketing and distribution competencies are a must. Patents and technology requirements are high barriers to entry (ACC 2011).

Agricultural chemicals can be seen as a part of specialty business. A distinguishing feature is that only one end-use customer industry—farming—clearly dominates. This sector produces primary fertilizers and crop protection.

Segments like food, cosmetics or detergents are often labeled as *consumer products* within the process industries, because they are manufactured in batch-type operations. Consumer products feature a high degree of differentiation along branding lines. Markets are segmented along distribution channels, price points, and customer demographic lines. Brand advantages and product development are extremely important, as is the management of distribution channels. The profit margins are higher than for basic chemicals although long-term prices are falling fast. This context makes the analogy to consumer products in other industrial segments clear. Since consumer products are subject to the book "Innovative Design of Business Processes in the Consumer Goods Industry", they will not be further discussed.

The world chemical turnover share by segments shows, that basic chemicals are predominant in the global business of chemistry (Fig. 1.1).

The chemical industry produces a high number of different products for all manner of applications. The products can be found in almost all manufactured goods. According to the American Chemistry Council, over 96 % of all manufactured goods in the US are directly touched by chemistry. Including indirect support, chemistry touches 100 % of manufactured goods (ACC 2011). This implies that the chemical industry has a great impact on the economy. The pricing and quality directly influence the downstream production. The scientific improvements enable better productivity, health, and safety. Longer lasting paints, stronger adhesives, better packaging materials, faster microprocessors, lightweight automobile parts, synthetic fibers and permanent-press clothing, health-improvement products are only a few examples. The commitment of the chemical industry to the goal of the sustainable world economy is essential for the success of the topic.

Vice versa, as chemicals are being a part of nearly any manufactured good the economic climate itself has a bearing on the sales and profits made by chemical companies. As a result, compared with the pharmaceutical industry, for example, the chemical industry is strongly influenced by economic cycles.

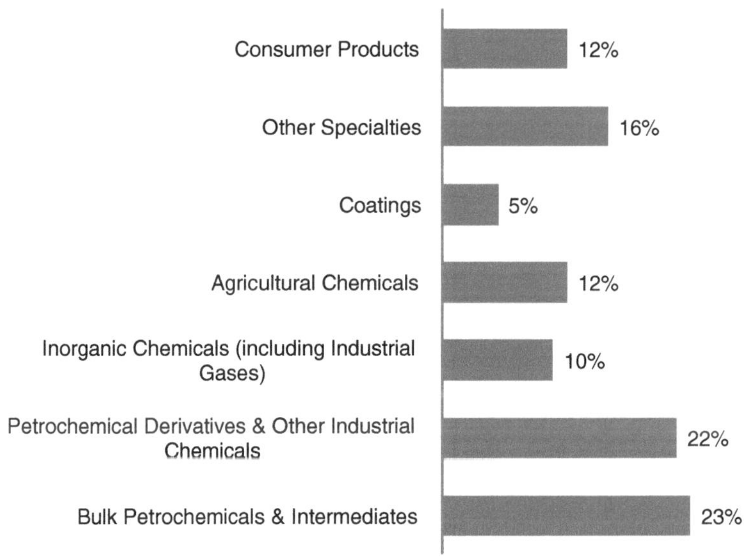

Fig. 1.1 Global chemical shipments by segment (2010, percentage) (ACC 2011)

1.1.2 *The Pharmaceutical Industry and its Share in the Economy*

The pharmaceutical industry refers to companies that produce and/or sell drugs. It is the main group in the life sciences industry next to the manufacturers of veterinary medical products, the diagnostics industry and the producers of medical equipment and dressing materials.

The products from the pharmaceutical industry fall into two categories: products available only on prescription (also known as ethical drugs) and products available over the counter (Fig. 1.2). While ethical drugs are sold on medical prescription, the OTC-products are available to purchase directly without prescription.

The manufacturers of pharmaceutical products can generally be divided into pharmaceutical research manufacturers (originators) and producers of generic drugs.

Research companies are pharmaceutical companies that develop drugs and apply to have them licensed. These companies then possess the patents for these drugs for a fixed period of 20 years. When the patent protection for a drug expires, the originator no longer has exclusive manufacturing rights and the product is opened up to the general manufacturing market. It is at this point that generic drug manufacturers come into play. Generic drugs are a copy whose active ingredients match those of the original product but whose galenics may vary and for which the manufacturing technology may differ. The therapeutic effects of the generic drug must match those of the original product.

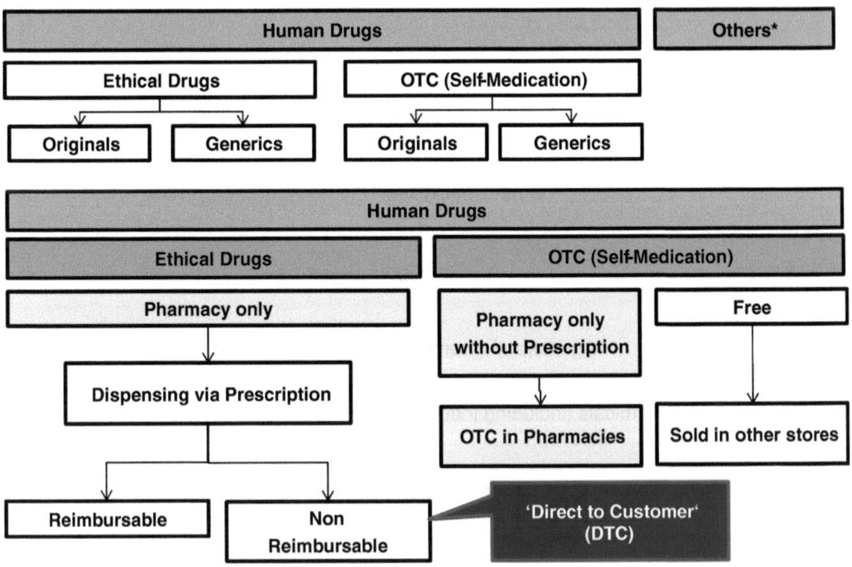

* Others: animal health, diagnostic, surgical and hygienic products

Fig. 1.2 Product differentiation in the pharmaceutical industry (in Germany)

Generic drugs are usually far less expensive than the original product because the level of spending required for research and development as well as for registration is either much lower or non-existent, which means this outlay does not have to be recouped through the sales price. A prominent example of a generic drug is the active ingredient acetylsalicylic acid. Developed and established under the name "Aspirin" by Bayer, this active ingredient is also available as a product from a wide range of other manufacturers besides Bayer under various different names.

Industry practice shows that there are often mixed forms, for example, originators with their own generic drug line or generic drug manufacturers who focus strongly on research.

1.2 The Global Chemical Market

1.2.1 Key Figures

Global Chemical Sales

Chemical products play a fundamental role in most of the countries in the world. However, more than 90 % of the world chemical output is provided only by 3 regions: Asia (48 %), Europe (25 %), NAFTA (19 %) (Fig. 1.3). It is also remarkable that the Asian (48 %) chemical production is higher that the European (25 %) and American (19 %) together. In 2008 the ratio was yet 38 % (Asia) to 51 % (EU-27+NAFTA). The world chemical sales amounted to 1,950 billion euro in 2008, two years later it was 2,353 billion euro. It is obvious, that the emerging countries essentially contributed to the recovery of the sector after the world financial crisis in 2009 (CEFIC 2011).

Considering the countries, the differences are even more apparent. Only four countries: USA, China, Japan, and Germany account for more than 50 % of the world chemical output (Fig. 1.4). In 2008 the US was the world leader with 374 billion euro chemical sales, in 2010 the US achieved a rise to 395 billion euro. However, China gained the first position in 2010 with 575 billion euro, which is more than a 70 % growth to 337 billion euro in 2008 (CEFIC 2011).

Global Chemical Growth

The long-term figures of the growth show a non-surprising lead of the Asian region (Fig. 1.5). In the five-year-period from 1999 to 2004, the European and North American chemistry achieved only moderate growth. In the next five-year-period until 2009 there were even negative growth rates. In contrast, the Asian-Pacific Region[1] was booming with average growth rates of about 5 % in both periods.

---

[1] Asian–Pacific Region includes Australia, Bangladesh, China, India, Japan, Korea, Malaysia, Pakistan, Philippines, Singapore, Taiwan and Thailand.

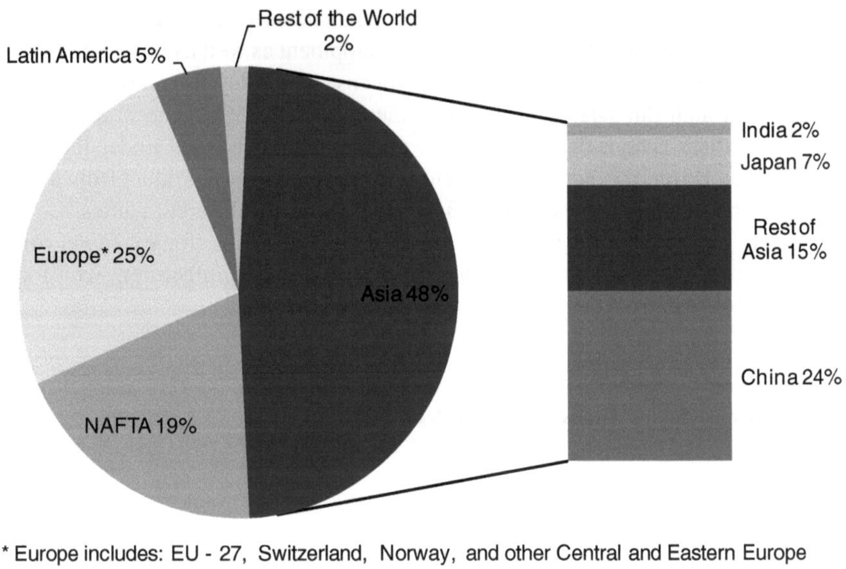

Fig. 1.3 Regional breakdown of world chemical sales (2010, percentage) (CEFIC 2011)

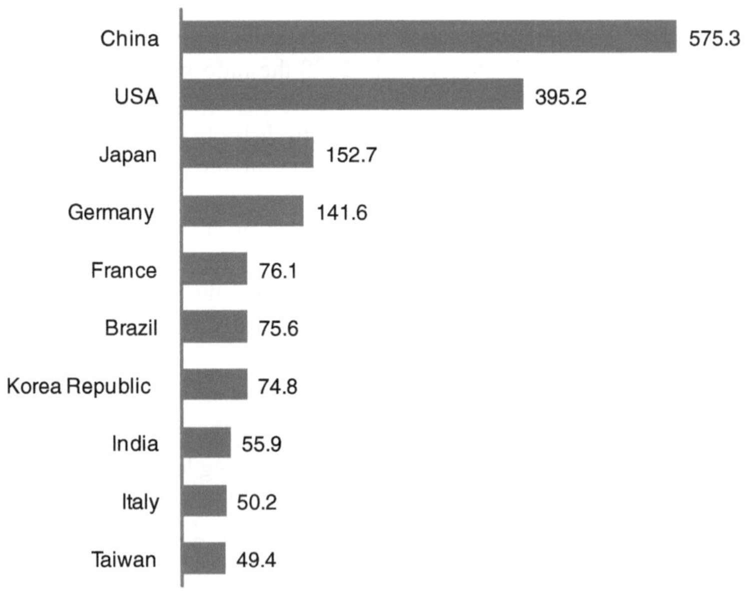

Fig. 1.4 World chemical sales by country (2010, billion euro) (CEFIC 2011)

Throughout the whole ten-year-period (1999–2009) the EU grew only by 0.1 % and the average growth rates of the NAFTA-region counterbalanced themselves to 0 %. Despite of the strong reduction in the second period, Latin America still

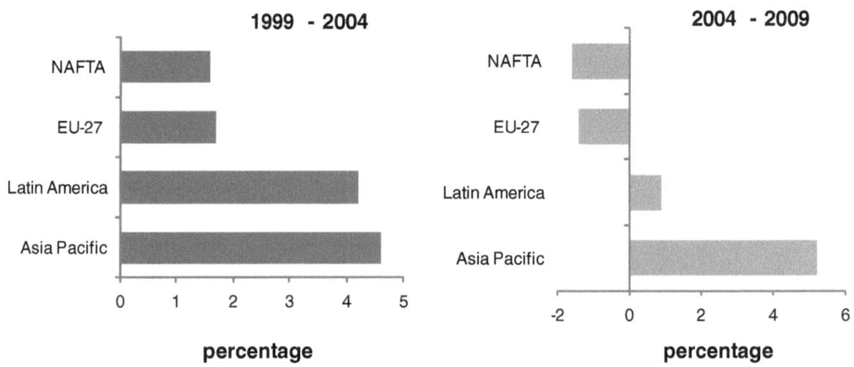

Fig. 1.5 International growth rate by region in two five-year-periods (1999–2004, 2004–2009, percentage) (CEFIC 2010)

achieved growth rates of 2.5 %. Asia–Pacific kept the growth rates at an average level of 4.9 %. Since Japanese growth rates are at a similar level as those of EU and NAFTA, it is primary the Chinese chemical market causing the rise (CEFIC 2010).

Already in the ten-year-period previous to the crisis (1997–2007) the average growth rate in China was 16.5 % (Fig. 1.6). The world average growth rate was 4.8 % in this period and the industrialized countries (Japan, USA, Canada, EU-27 and Switzerland) remained below that threshold (CEFIC 2009a).

In 2010—the year of the economic recovery—chemical sales (incl. pharmaceuticals) increased in all regions. The worldwide growth rate reached 21 % with the highest rate of 30 % in the Asia–Pacific region. Figure 1.7 shows the cumulated growth rates in the three regions with the largest production over the last ten years (ACC 2011).

Global Chemical Market Share

Following the trends in the growth, the chemical world market share has changed rapidly already in the years previous to the crisis. The United States, the European Union, and Japan have lost their market shares and China was the winner with 8 % within the five-year-period (2003–2008) (Fig. 1.8).

There is also one another factor fostering the change in the global market share. The world market as a whole was growing much faster in the last years. World chemical sales increased by almost 64 % in 2010 compared to 2000 (Fig. 1.9).

Global Chemical Trade

The chemical trading statistics[2] give a slightly different view as those of sales. In 2010 the European Union remains the largest trading block[3] (Fig. 1.10). It is losing

---

[2] Pharmaceuticals included.

[3] The intra-European trade is included, mainly for reasons of comparison with other regions. The European Union remains the largest exporter for chemicals even after eliminating the intra-European trade.

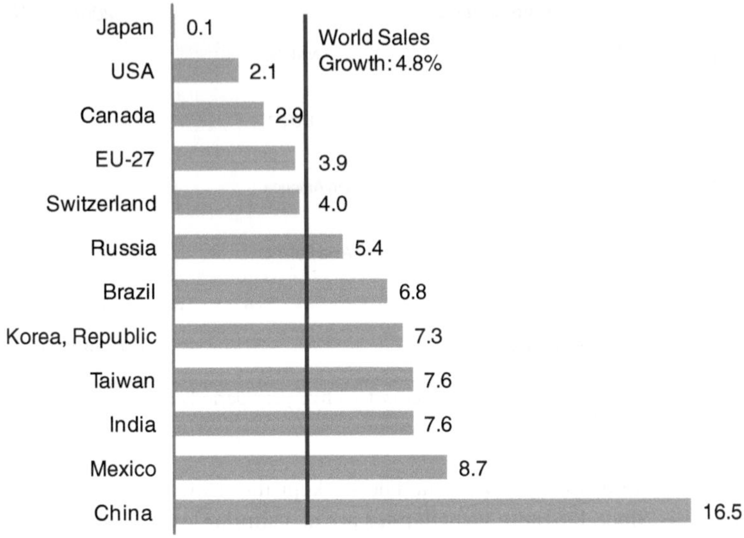

Fig. 1.6 Chemical sales growth rates of selected countries and regions (1997–2007, percentage) (CEFIC 2009a)

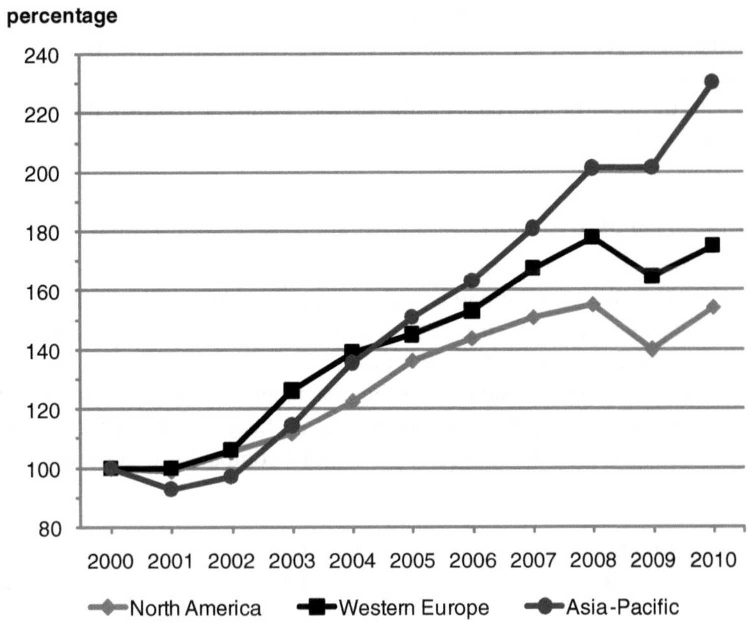

Fig. 1.7 International comparison of the sales growth (cumulated) (2000–2010, percentage) (ACC 2011)

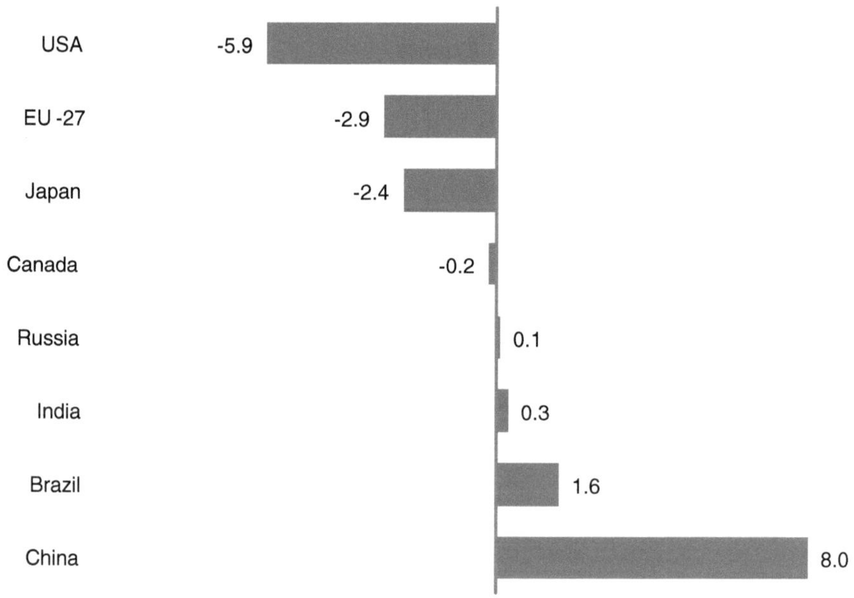

Fig. 1.8 Shift in the world market share in major countries (2003–2008, percentage) (VCI 2010)

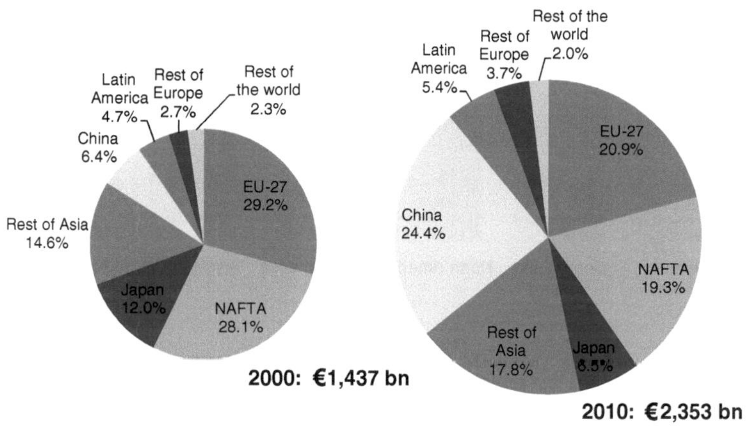

Fig. 1.9 World chemical sales by region (2000 vs. 2010, billion euro) (CEFIC 2011)

the trade share to Asia, but slowly. In 2000, Asia shared only about 22 % of the world exports, ten years later about 26 %. The EU-27 accounted for 54 % of the world chemical exports in 2000, in 2010 the export-share dropped to 50 %. Imports also only decreased from 45 to 44 %. In contrast, NAFTA reduced the exports and imports share by about 4 % each in 2010 comparing to 2000 (ACC 2011).

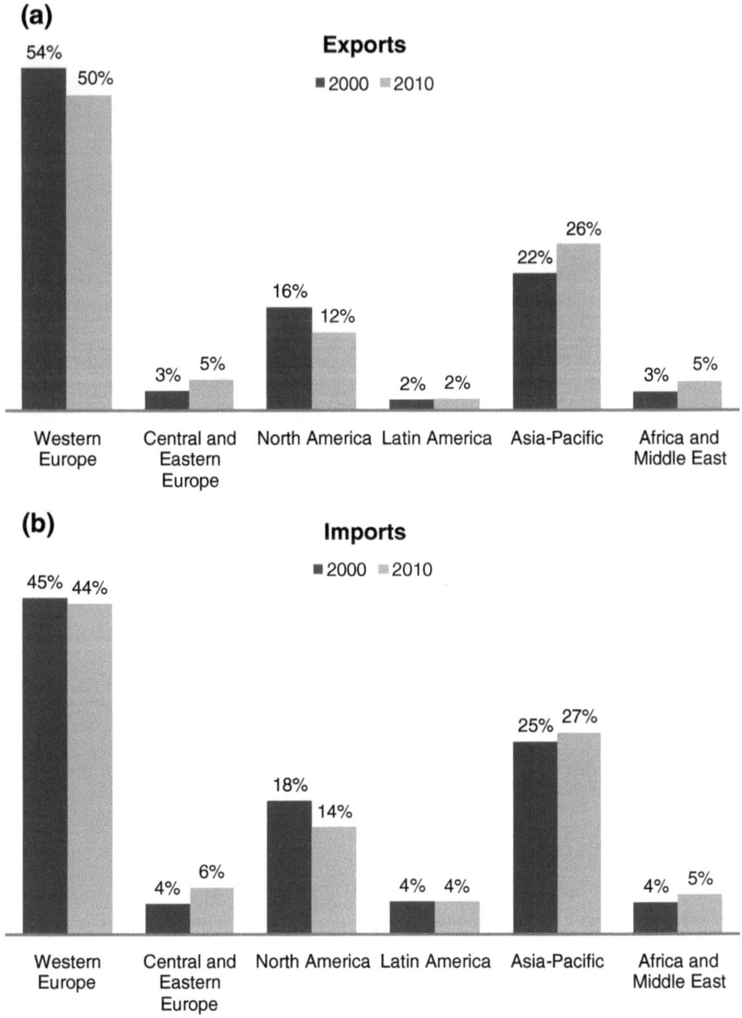

Fig. 1.10 Regional shares in world exports and imports of chemicals (2000 and 2010, percentage) (ACC 2011)

The main competitive disadvantage for the EU-countries was the USD/EUR exchange rate, which picked up rapidly. The exports became expensive and the threat from new imports on the own market higher. The European manufacturers could counterbalance this only by exports to booming parts of Asia (DBR 2008).

Demand for chemical products in China is strong. Both the demand from the major customer industries (construction sector, automobiles, electrical engineering, and textile industry) and the private consumption are growing rapidly. In the basic chemicals segment, the high speed of building new capacities does not suffice the even higher speed of increasing demand and also meets the shortage of raw materials (DBR 2008). In the special chemicals segment, China had a positive trade balance in the first half of 2009 (CPCIF 2009). There was a strong dependence on imports of high-tech specialty chemicals in the first booming years. Though China started own sufficiency plans in the recent years, thus we may expect a lower export opportunities for western companies in some sub-segments in the future (DBR 2008).

According to the statistics of American Chemistry Council the US had a trade deficit in chemicals in 2002 for the first time. Reaching the peaks in 2003 (9.5 billion US dollar) and 2005 (8.8 billion US dollar). Since 2010 the US has a positive trade balance again. China had an increasing trade deficit in chemicals in the past. In 1998 this was only 12.5 billion, in 2000 17.4 billion but in 2010 already 35.6 billion US dollar. In Western Europe and Japan, the chemical trade surplus has been steadily growing since 2001 up until the crisis in 2009 (Fig. 1.11) (ACC 2011).

Considering the trade balances in chemicals in 2008 between the four main regions: Japan had a trade surplus only with China. China had trade surplus with the US and the EU-27. The US had a trade surplus only with Japan. The EU-27 had a trade surplus with USA and Japan.

Global Chemical Companies

In 1960s chemical companies began to enhance their activities in foreign countries. In the following years the conditions for international trade were improving rapidly: reduction of tariffs and other barriers advances in telecommunications and

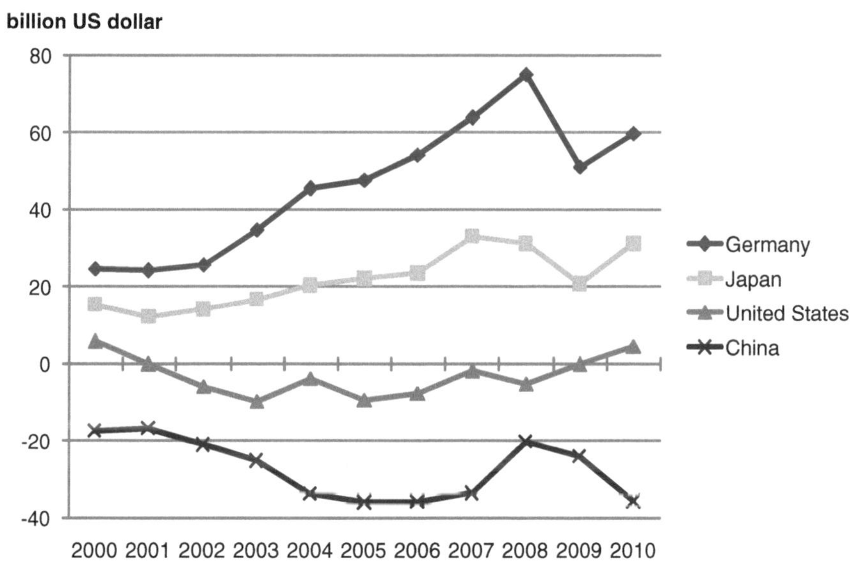

Fig. 1.11 Global chemical trade balances in Germany, Japan, United States and China (2000–2010, in billion US dollar) (ACC 2011)

transportation and increasing world economic growth. These movements established the world market with prices set by global supply and demand.

During the 1980s and 1990s the international investments of western companies grew even faster than in the years before. In 1990s companies originating in emerging countries also started to expand by abroad investments. Thus apart from the world market and worldwide spread of industry resources, also the emergence of multinational companies was enabled in the course of globalization (ACC 2009) (Fig. 1.12).

The Global Financial Crisis

During the years 2008 and 2009, the world economy was suffering one of the biggest crises in the history. In all world regions in parallel, the financial system broke down, all important industrial segments were struggling, the raw material prices became highly volatile and the deflationary pressures increased (CEFIC 2009b).

The chemical industry was hit hard by the global financial and economical crisis. The demand for chemical products dropped in all chemical end markets, especially in construction and automotive. The chemical companies had to face both falling the sales and the prices with the unelectable consequence of financial stress. Moreover, in the 4th quarter of 2008 and 1st quarter of 2009 all industries began destocking, because of a lack of capital, waiting for prices to drop down and to reduce stocks in general. The nonfunctioning banking system in all regions of the world made it impossible to obtain a credit to finance the depths or missing working capital. Many companies did not last the pressure (Dvorocsik 2010).

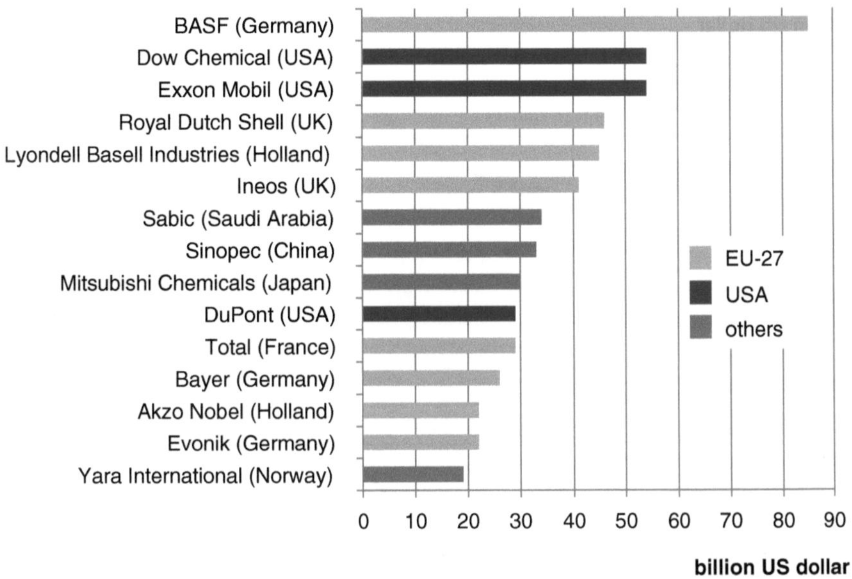

Fig. 1.12 Top 15 chemical companies in the world (2007, according to sales in billion US dollar, including pharmaceuticals) (CEFIC 2009a)

In 2009, governmental intervention helped the credit market to start working again. Since most of the chemical industry products are used for further processing, the demand is strongly linked to the changes in economic output. Statistics show that the gross domestic product (GDP) has been improving again passing the bottom in 2009 (Table 1.1). There are still two major concerns about the future progress: whether there is a serious risk of next crisis and how nations will cope with the financial burden of governmental support programs. However, among the experts prevails the positive attitude (Chang 2010).

1.2.2 The Market Environment of the Chemical Industry

The market environment of the chemical industry is shaped by three main issues: globalization, regulations and sustainability. There are manifold effects hidden behind each of these issues. Globalization is facilitating the rise of emerging markets, thus opportunities like new markets, investments or M&A-deals are opening up. On the other hand margin pressure, volatility of global prices, commoditization rate and market dynamics are increasing. Considering these changes as opportunities or threats is a matter of individual capability of each chemical company. The same is true for the impact of regulations protecting health, environment and intellectual-property-rights. The goal of sustainability also cannot be seen only as a restrain, it implies opportunities in form of demand on renewable energy sources and environmental friendly products. Other global mega topics like health and mobility have similar effects.

The following chapter gives an overview on the central trends in the world of chemistry. The topics have been divided into four groups: economical, technological, political and legal, and demographic market environment. A differentiation like this is only possible on the analytical level. The strong interdependencies between the issues and in some cases various implications make the situation much more complex.

The complexity is, indeed, the main issue chemical companies have to face. In the globalized environment each strategic or operational decision has to consider the world market. For instance in the supplier selection items like price, legal compliance, reliability get a whole new dimension. The globalized market also brings up issues of its own, such as new possibilities for investments, business-location, partnership, customer needs or innovation and also new restrains through new competitors and

Table 1.1 World economic activity: GDP growth in selected regions (outlook 2008–2010, percentage) (CEFIC 2009c)

	EU-27 (%)	North America (%)	South America (%)	Emerging Asia (%)	Japan (%)	Eastern Europe (%)
2008	0.8	1.0	5.4	6.1	−0.7	4.5
2009	−3.9	−3.2	−0.7	2.4	−5.5	−2.4
2010	0.0	1.4	2.9	5.6	0.5	1.8

regulations. The pressure for change in an increasingly dynamic environment makes it even more difficult. The obvious consequence of the globalized world is that the risk is rising. Controlling the complexity is the key to the success.

According to the recent Gartner study[4] 58 % respondents chose 'managing risk resulting from complex demand and supply chains' as one of the critical business drivers. It keeps the issue of complexity on the first place outplaying the innovation (56 %), regulatory pressures and costs (54 %) and operations (54 %). The results are even more evident considering the question about the most critical driver to overall success. Managing complexity scores 35 %. The second place took innovation with only 18 % (Lord et al. 2010).

This result is a clear implication of the economic downturn in 2009. Following the wake-up call chemical companies were forced to review their portfolios of customers, channels, products and suppliers in search for optimizing potential. Managing the complexity is seen as the key. A. T. Kerney Consulting states increasing margins by 2–5 % as a release of hidden earnings potentials due to controlling complexity. The executives of the industry believe, that the companies, which are able to manage complexity better than others are able to grow twice as fast with a 70 % higher profitability (Kerney 2010). Thus managing complexity enables both protecting margins and keeping resources focused on growth.

1.2.2.1 Economic Market Environment

Globalization is the superior factor for most aspects of the market environment, providing various opportunities and threats. Making no claim to be exhaustive, this chapter covers following main issues and their implications: rise of emerging countries and a changing competitive landscape.

The rise of emerging countries

In the 1980s many developing nations started to run programs to establish globally competitive chemical industries. The newly industrialized countries of Asia (NIC) (such as Singapore, South Korea, Taiwan and Thailand) and many economies of Latin America (Argentina, Brazil, Mexico and Venezuela) have made remarkable improvements on this field (ACC 2010). The advanced feedstock nations in the Middle East have been gradually expanding their advantageous position, meanwhile working on new investment strategies in order to reduce their dependence on oil and gas exports. Their amassed funds have been invested, among other industries, to chemical downstream production (refineries, petro-chemical plants and chemical end-products) (DBR 2008). The economic reforms in China started in the late 1970s. In 2001 joining WTO, China has been fully integrated in the world market. Since then only the international trade participation of China and the inflows of foreign direct investment have higher rates than the rapid economic

---

[4] Gartner conducted a research study of 100 US-based chemical companies through online surveys in February 2010.

growth (Greaney and Li 2009). Also India kept up with the developments. In 2010 India was on place eight among the countries with top chemical sales.

The direct impact of the rise of emerging markets can be reflected either from the demand or the supply side. The demand for chemical products has been strongly shifted to emerging countries, namely due to three interacting factors. The companies from matured markets recognized early the expanding opportunities and the benefits from low costs production. While the structural changes towards service oriented economy limited the growth opportunities on the matured markets, the emerging markets just entered the path. Despite of relatively high risk, the companies started to invest in the emerging countries and even to move their whole production in that area. This is true for chemical companies and for their customer industries, such as construction, textile, and electronics. Following the customer, even more manufacturers moved or opened their subsidiaries in emerging countries. And finally the demand for chemical products there increased through the growth of countries own manufacturing industries, facilitated by legal reforms and booming economy. Changes in the structure modify also the demand. For instance, China attracted investments in basic chemicals first. Today being a world major exporter for basic chemicals, China starts supporting programs for the specialties. The share of specialty chemicals in the chemical export increased from 6.2 % in 2006 to 12.5 % in 2010 (CPCIF 2011).

This strong expansion of chemistry and its customer industries, especially in China, cannot be caught up by production. For some chemical substances, there are still supply shortfalls, e.g. ethylene (DBR 2008). Since many chemical substances are used as preliminary products for further chemical processing, the chemical companies themselves have to face the shortage too. The supply disruptions are reflected in the prices. The same applies for the raw materials themselves.

In the globalized chemical market volatile prices of raw materials, energy, and end products became the common concern. Customers do not easily accept any price increase, thus margin pressures follow.

One another serious issue—the supply chain disruptions—is also clearly related to the growing dynamics. Apart from the supply shortfalls and relocations or bankruptcies of the business partners, the companies themselves have to look for better contracts consistently in order to win the competition, since the pressure has increased.

Changing competitive landscape

The price and margin pressures are the traditional drivers for change. In the globalized world with export oriented emerging countries, these pressures are stronger. However, this is not only because of the low-cost advantages in the emerging markets. The intense competition is fostering increasing technological dynamism, commoditization,[5] and decreasing product life cycles (Eisberg 2010).

[5] Commoditization is the process by which a product reaches a point in its development where one brand has no features that differentiate it from other brands and consumers buy on price alone.

The companies are forced to use all options they have, to stand the competitive pressure. The fast orientation on the markets, as well as continual search for hidden potential in companies businesses is essential.

Field research shows, that the following three areas became more and more important: meeting customer needs, fast reaction time through more flexible business models and portfolio consolidation. The anticipation of customer needs has been stepped up notably due to the crisis. Especially the customer driven innovation became much more important (Morawietz et al. 2009). However, the first steps such as bundling products with services or total quality management have been made already before the crisis as a reaction on the increased competition.

The second area: flexible business models, involves changes in internal organization and new forms of cooperation between companies. For instance integrated companies should consider how many different business models are able to coexist (CHEMIE.DE 2010). Examples for extended forms of cooperation are new partnerships regarding market, collaborations for development, joint ventures to penetrate new markets or to gain new technology. For example, Dow Corning was established as a joint venture equally owned by The Dow Chemical Company and Corning Inc. in 1943 specifically to explore and develop the potential of silicones. Today, there are many examples for joint ventures in order to provide synergies by vertical downstream integration between chemical and oil and gas industries. Crack products from crude oil refining are used for synthesis of polyolefines for instance, at the same time, the supply of energy for chemical manufacturing can be ensured. As examples, LyondellBasell, formerly Basell, originally arose from a joint venture between BASF and Royal Dutch Shell. The Dow Chemical Company and the Saudi Arabian Oil Company (Saudi Aramco) are currently establishing the worldscale Sadara Chemical Company joint venture.

Mergers and Acquisitions, as long as carried out properly, enable to follow the strategic goals more quickly or make changes more rapidly. The learning process of a company required to catch up with new technologies, new processes, and new products can be also reduced (Siu 1999). For example, DuPont acquired the Danish niche chemical company Danisco in order to gain access to Dansico's enzyme technology as well as its strength in cellulosic ethanol research. Both technologies can enrich DuPont's product range (Cassidy et al. 2011).

In the last twenty years, the portfolio consolidation has been one of the most important goals among the global chemical players. In consequence, the industry's competitive landscape has been extremely restructured. The traditional oil and gas players (such as Shell or BP) have largely sold their chemical businesses. The large integrated chemical players (BASF, Dow or Akzo Nobel) have dramatically changed their portfolios. Some of them have strengthened their main business with buyouts of similar businesses, for instance the disaggregation of former Hoechst. Its pharmaceutical business has been absorbed into Sanofi Aventis, the agrochemical business has been sold off to Bayer Crop Science and Celanese took over its basic chemicals and Clariant the specialty chemicals division. Other companies, such as BASF, Dow and Akzo Nobel, have enhanced their value chain by acquiring specialty producers. Additionally, new large players formed themselves through "buy-

and-build" strategies (Ineos, Hexion, Lyondell Basell), often using access to private equity. In the emerging countries, the fast growth was the stepping stone for the strong competitive position of the new global players, such as Saudi Arabia's SABIC and Sipchem or China's Bluestar (Morawietz et al. 2009).

The world financial crisis has reduced the Investment- and M&A–Activities to a minimum. On the other hand the companies facing an economic crisis are much more sensitized for their improvement capabilities. As soon as credit was available again, strategic investments became more important than ever. The producers of specialties are trying to sharpen the portfolio, basic chemical companies aim to downsize their overcapacities, private-equity-companies are looking for acquirers and investors from financial sector are ready to enter the market (Delloitte 2010).

In the medium term, the process of concentration in the global chemicals industry particularly in the basic chemicals sector continues, where the production costs per unit fall. A.T. Kearney estimates, in the future, there will be only one to three Western players per customer segment (DBR 2008). In the specialty chemicals segment the M&A activities may reach beyond the own industry to come closer to the end-customer or to extend the own know how (CHEMIE.DE 2010).

1.2.2.2 Technological Market Environment

In the context of technological environment the prime topic is the research and development (R&D) activity in the chemical industry. However, two other issues should also be discussed here: the infrastructure and the trend towards alternative feedstock, since nowadays these have a strong influence on the use of technologies.

A winning innovation is a critical factor for success in the R&D-driven industries, like chemicals. Successful innovations can produce 25–35 % return. For instance, according to the study of the Council of Chemical Research, in the US for public chemical companies every dollar invested in R&D returns as 2$ in operating income over six years (17 % return). However, the research intensity (R&D expenses as a proportion of sales revenues) in the industry has fallen, despite of the constantly rising R&D spending. According to the US-based consultancy Kline the research intensity achieved its maximum in 2004.[6] Considering the segments, the research intensity of specialty chemicals companies was 2.8 %, investments of basic chemical companies were 1.1 % and the diversified companies lay in between with 2 %. Kline also analyzed the geographical division. The research intensity was highest in Europe, corresponding with high representation of specialty and diversified companies in the region (Challenger 2008).

As the companies from matured markets move their activities to the markets with strong growing demand and lower costs, whole R&D sites are being relocated. In Asia centers of excellence arise, partly by foreign investments, partly by strong governmental support. Furthermore in China the steering of foreign

[6] Kline analyzed the R&D spending of the top 50 global chemical companies.

investments moves rapidly towards high tech production. However the relocation of the R&D sites does not match the relocation of the production. Since 2008 only high tech companies can take part on support benefits (Abele 2010). Since the scientifically relevant infrastructure and human resources as well as own scientific networks provide the basis for R&D allocation plans, the early developed countries still provide a favorable environment. BASF, for instance, still allocates its R&D investments as follows: 80 % in Europe, 17 % in USA and 3 % in Asia (Challenger 2008).

The traditional R&D with focus on product and technology innovation is increasingly been complemented by developing new ways of marketing, branding, cooperation and searching for new business models or targets. In 2007 BASF used 63 % of its R&D spending on product innovation, 19 % on process optimization, 16 % on new methods and 2 % on new applications (Challenger 2008).

However, it is not only the R&D spending by chemical companies, which reflects the image of technological improvement. The more the technology is advanced the cooperation between different academic fields appears necessary (CHEMIE.DE 2010). This can for example be seen in the area of bionic science and chemistry.

Another point is that in the Asia, the research sponsored by government is traditionally much stronger than in matured markets. A study on nanotech patents carried out by University of Muenster (Germany) shows the high importance of universities and research institutes in nanopatenting in China. As the governmental sponsorship decreases, universities begin to cooperate with industry, to set up science parks and spin-offs. The applied research in China is booming since the reforms of the national research system. The growing number of patents in nanotechnology since 2000 confirms this. In 2005 China ranked first ahead of the US and Japan, the generally perceived leaders in nanotechnology (Preschitschek and Bresser 2010).

The main targets of research within the chemical industry are the improvements of product features ("smart" materials and advanced composites) and alternative feedstock to oil-based products. The technologies in focus are bio-based processes, novel catalysts, sustainable chemistry and energy efficiency. BASF, for instance, has 5 areas with the highest attention: energy management, raw material change, nanotechnology, plant biotechnology, and white (industrial) biotechnology.[7] These clusters are expected to bring in annual sales between $2.6 and $5.2 billion by 2015 (Challenger 2008).

The infrastructure is crucial for the success of the chemical companies. The essential business activities such as communication, supply chain operations, funding, staffing, or sales all depend on a functioning infrastructure. Despite of high growth rates on the emerging markets, the infrastructure there does not

---

[7] White biotechnology uses biocatalytic processes (enzyme, cells and microorganisms) in the industrial production of chemicals. These can replace the conventional production processes as well as raw materials or energy sources.

Table 1.2 Quality of overall infrastructure (2011, weighted average) (WEF 2011)

Country	Rank	Score	Country	Rank	Score
Hong Kong SAR	1	6.71	Canada	11	5.88
Germany	2	6.35	Japan	15	5.69
Singapore	3	6.33	United States	16	5.68
France	4	6.30	Taiwan	20	5.62
Switzerland	5	6.15	Saudi Arabia	25	5.31
United Kingdom	6	6.09	Italy	32	5.01
Netherlands	7	6.02	China	44	4.63
United Arab Emirates	8	5.97	Brazil	64	3.99
Korea, Republic	9	5.94	Mexico	66	3.98
Denmark	10	5.89	India	89	3.60

achieve the level of matured markets. It implies the high level of risk, the companies have to anticipate. For instance, in the latest survey Banomyong shows, that the infrastructure in Asia is not improving quickly enough to enable a successful supply chain management (Banomyong 2010).

The World Economic Forum issues yearly the global competitiveness index[8] (GCI) for 133 countries. Infrastructure is one of the nine pillars for the evaluation. The Executive Opinion Survey shows how the infrastructure in the country meets the needs of the companies inside the country. The matured chemical markets and the Newly Industrialized Nations (Hong Kong, Singapore) approached the top positions in the ranking (Table. 1.2). China (44) and India (89) ended up rather poor. In contrast, the oil-rich Gulf States ranked in the first third (WEF 2011).

1.2.2.3 The Political and Legal Market Environment

Chemical companies have to act in a highly regulated market environment. Indeed dealing with many and various regulations is one of the characteristics of the chemical industry. It is essential for the success to follow the latest changes, because of the immediate consequences for the competitive position. The direct economical sanctions (fees, competitive disadvantages) are not the only reason for the efforts. The chemical industry has had strong public attention for the past

[8] The World Economic Forum postulates that as a nation is developing, the wages tent to increase, so the labor productivity must improve for the nation to stay competitive. As the productivity drivers differ depending on the stage of development the nation is in, the GCI distinguishes between three types of stages: factor-driven, efficiency-driven and innovation-driven. Thus the pillars are given different weights depending on the per capita income of the nation. The twelve considered pillars are: institutions (public and private), infrastructure, stable macroeconomic framework, good health and primary education, higher education and training, efficient good and labor markets, financial market development, technological readiness, market size, business sophistication, innovation. Approximately two thirds of the variables are identified through the Executive Opinion Survey and one third comes from statistical sources.

30 years. Pollution caused by technological defects, risks caused by low quality products or non-legal practices quickly become subject for the media. Particularly the goal of sustainability receives increasing attention.

In addition to common market regulations (e.g. laws against unfair competition), there are three areas of matter crucial for the chemical industry: human health and safety, environmental compliance and intellectual property rights.

However, the protection standards and compliance with the norms differ strongly between countries. Europe and the US have typically high levels of regulation. They have been confronted early on with the challenges of protecting human health and the environment as well as making the necessary investments to prevent accidents and increase safety measures.[9] Over the years, the regulations got intensified. Since the EU and the US are strongly innovation oriented, they took on the pioneering role in the protection of intellectual property rights too. The emerging markets despite of the pressure from matured markets can only slowly catch up with the standards.

On the field of environmental compliance, health and safety the latest challenge faced by chemical companies is the European REACH legislation (Nr. 1907/2006). It constitutes an entirely new approach of compliance addressing the production and use of chemical substances and affects also companies outside the EU to a large extend. REACH (Registration, Evaluation, Authorization and Restriction of Chemicals) came into force on the 1st of June 2007. It is a volume-based legislation which is being carried out in three phases. During the registration all substances (over 1 t/a) produced in the EU or imported have to attain a registration number. For the registration the proof of harmlessness and safety has to be provided by an in-depth description and evaluation of substance properties and usages. In the evaluation phase the danger status will be officially approved. The substances labeled as SVHC (Substances of Very High Concern) are subject to authorization or restriction procedures. The expected social profits of REACH are: an extensive monitoring of chemical substances, pressure to substitute dangerous substances and approach to the goal of establishing one international standard.

The significant differences to other similar regulations (e.g. TSCA in the US) are: the shift of burden of proof to manufacturer or importer of chemicals, the principle ‘no data no market’, as well as the compulsory data exchange along the value chain with suppliers and users. The sharing of data between the producers of the same substances attempts to reduce the testing effort. However, the additional communication presents a grave effort itself.

Indeed the most serious charge against REACH is the enormous effort the companies have to render. The costs of the required safety analysis can be critical for small and medium companies. On the other hand the international companies have to register various substances and intermediates from subsidiaries abroad as soon as imported for further proceeding. These costs can have a negative impact

[9] In the 1970s and 1980s a number of chemical accidents (such as Seveso, Bhopal and Schweizerhalle) put pressure on the chemical industry and politicians.

on the competitive position. A global relocation of specific production sites to less regulated countries might follow. If REACH as a quality feature can compensate the disadvantage, the further development will show.

Another point is that the producers abroad consider the regulation as a technical barrier for the market entry. As a result, the companies (local or importing), for which the legal procedures are too expensive, might decide to no longer supply the European market. However, the European Chemical Agency (ECHA) provides support for producers or importers outside the EU. And outside the EU are institutions being established, to help the producers to handle the requirements (e.g. REACH 24 h China).

In parallel to REACH another globally important legislation is being introduced: the GHS (Globally Harmonized System of Classification and Labeling of Chemicals). It has been initiated by United Nations and aims a globally standardized labeling system for chemicals. In the EU, the GHS for substances came into effect since 2010 and the GHS for procedures is set for 2015. In the US the GHS is scheduled for 2011. In China it has been implemented into three compulsory standards in 2010 and China is currently working on system coordinating the GHS adoption.

Next to REACH and GHS, there are some other legislations with single purposes the companies have to comply with: RoHS/WEEE and China RoHS legislation, TSCA (Toxic Substances Control Act), American Food and Drug Administration (FDA) and Clean Air/Water Act. Particularly for international companies, the complexity of legal environment covers a large part of the overall complexity problem.

A second challenge regarding the legal environment is the management and protection of intellectual property. For the chemical industry as one of the most innovative industries, a strong protection of knowledge is crucial. Therefore, an intelligent patent strategy is an important key success factor, not only to protect and defend the innovation itself, but also to build market entry barriers excluding new market players and to hinder competitors in their business.

Basically, a company tries to file patents for all products or methods, which shall be protected against imitators, thereby achieving technical, economical or salable advantages. The alternative strategy is to keep an invention protected by simple non-disclosure (company secret), however, there is always a risk of disclosure due to fluctuating employees for instance.

In very competitive research areas a large quantity of patent coverage enables a company to cross-license their patents with competitors, i.e. two companies allow each other to use specific inventions.

According to this strategy companies try to file as many as possible 'blocking patents', which either can be cross-licensed with other companies, or, which hinder competitors to file patents for a specific area of research. The economic usability of reserve patents is often not visible at the point in time, when they are filed.

Another intellectual property strategy is to publish an invention as 'defensive disclosure', so that it enters the public domain and becomes prior art. This prevents another party from obtaining a patent.

A critical challenge is the geographical range of protection as there does not exist any fully working global patent protection system yet. Regions like Russia, Latin America, the Middle East, and Asia (except Japan) still have gaps to close.

The OECD has worked on pursuing the worldwide attention to data protection for many years. In 1983 the economic value of certain data on chemicals has been introduced in broad terms in three resolutions. Apart from the OECD efforts, the WIPO (World Intellectual Property Organization) was established in 1967. Since 1974 WIPO belongs to the UN. Its aim is the worldwide guarantee of intellectual property rights. Among others the responsibility of WIPO is the enforcement of the PCT (Patent Cooperation Treaty) from 1970. Each patent approved to the company of one PCT member state is effective in all member states. Currently 145[10] states ratified the treaty (China in 1994, India 1998), but important chemical producers like Argentina, Saudi Arabia, Taiwan or Venezuela are not among them. In 1994 within the framework of GATT the TRIPS (Agreement on Trade-Related Aspects of Intellectual Property Rights) has been concluded. TRIPS is a set of requirements on member states, which can be enforced by WTO sanctions. However, TRIPS includes only minimal requirements, it lacks on the proper interpretation, which is often necessary.

One another important topic among the political and legal environment is the political stability as well as the reliability of the public institutions and the legal system. The investments into new assets in chemical industry are comparatively high, thus they are designed for long periods. The additional costs in disadvantageous political environment can increase rapidly. Therefore, the political situation must be taken into account in each choice of new location.

The World Economic Forum issues yearly a report on private and public institutions for 139 countries. The attributes of public institutions being examined are: property rights, ethics and corruption, undue influence, government inefficiency, and national security. In the category private institutions corporate ethics and accountability are being reviewed. Table 1.3 shows which position the major chemical players have attained (WEF 2011).

Table 1.3 Quality of institutions (2011, weighted average) (WEF 2011)

Country	Rank	Score	Country	Rank	Score
Singapore	1	6.11	France	28	5.00
Switzerland	6	5.78	Taiwan	31	4.94
Netherlands	10	5.61	United States	39	4.64
Canada	11	5.57	China	48	4.32
Saudi Arabia	12	5.47	Spain	49	4.27
United Kingdom	15	5.34	Korea, Rep.	65	3.89
Germany	19	5.27	India	69	3.84
United Arab Emirates	22	5.21	Brazil	77	3.72
Japan	24	5.18	Italy	88	3.61
Belgium	27	5.03	Mexico	103	3.44

[10] July 15th, 2011.

1.2.2.4 The Demographic Market Environment

The reflection of the demographic environment is essential for chemical companies, since various strong interdependencies exist. The chemical industry has a great social responsibility. First, many of the products have a direct positive or negative impact on health and safety of beings and their environment. Second, the chemical industry is an important employer. For example, more than 34 million people in the EU are working in the chemical industry. On the field of social standards for the employees, the chemical industry serves as a benchmark for other European industries (VCI 2010).

On the other hand, the chemical industry depends on skilled labor. Ageing of the world population, the quality of education, and the mobility of labor are serious issues for chemical companies. Population ageing is a result of two demographic trends: decreasing of fertility rates and rising of life expectancy. Most of the nations follow these trends. Still there are differences in the speed of the ageing process between the countries. There are great differences even within the industrialized countries. The population of the US is much younger than the European or Japanese are. And within the EU: France and Great Britain are ageing slower than Germany and Italy. However, in some countries, the changes are so dramatic, that their future labor, capital, and goods markets will be strongly affected (Börsch-Supan and Ludwig 2009). For example the rapid ageing in Asia causes the median age rise well above the world average in 2050 (Asher 2010). Since the ageing of the population is spread in both developed and developing countries, the consequences for the industry are inevitable. The shortage of labor force can lead to the increase of its price and more capital intensive production. Large international flows of labor, capital, and goods from the faster ageing countries to the slower ageing countries may follow (Börsch-Supan and Ludwig 2009). Ageing pushes the human resources strategies of the companies higher in the priority list. Considering this, new strategies including employment of older people and new approach in human resources development can be just as important as the right choice of the location and technology.

The level of education and the international mobility of labor have to be considered additionally to the ageing issue. Since only unskilled workforce has unlimited surplus, the surplus on skilled workers must be obtained. The activities a company itself must take depend strongly on the coverage the public sector provides. Table 1.4 shows the state of the higher education in the main chemical nations. The ranking is based on secondary and tertiary enrollment rates and the evaluation through the management representatives of the home industries (WEF 2011).

Table 1.4 Quality of higher education and training (2011, weighted average) (WEF 2011)

Country	Rank	Score	Country	Rank	Score
Switzerland	3	5.80	Japan	19	5.27
Singapore	4	5.77	France	20	2.24
Belgium	5	5.75	Spain	32	4.90
Germany	7	5.73	United Arab Emirates	33	4.84
Netherlands	8	5.66	Saudi Arabia	36	4.81
Taiwan	10	5.64	Italy	41	4.69
Canada	12	5.59	Brazil	57	4.35
United States	13	5.57	China	58	4.34
United Kingdom	16	5.47	Mexico	72	4.07
Korea, Republic	17	5.44	India	87	3.88

1.3 The Global Pharmaceutical Market

1.3.1 Key Figures

Global Pharmaceutical Sales and Production

One of the differences between the chemical and pharmaceutical market is the global market share. Asia plays rather an inferior role in the global pharmaceutical industry. From the 597,043 million euro (in ex-factory prices) worldwide sales in 2010, the three early industrialized regions North America, Europe, and Japan account for more than 80 %. Asia (excluding Japan) together with Australia and Africa come up to only 12.4 % market share (Fig. 1.13). On the production side the numbers look very similar. In 2007 the US accounted for 38.1 % of the world pharmaceutical production and Europe was the second largest producer with 36.1 % (Fig. 1.14). Considering individual countries, Japan ranks second with some distance to the US, followed by China, Germany, and France (Fig. 1.15) (EFPIA 2011). Within the Europe the largest sales volumes in 2010 were in France, Germany, Italy, and Great Britain (BPI 2011).

Global Pharmaceutical Growth

The pharmaceutical industry is becoming increasingly important all over the world. In the last ten years the pharmaceutical sales more than doubled (increase of 234 %). Figure 1.16 shows the year-to-year growth of the worldwide sales. The two strongest years were 2003 and 2010, where the growth exceeded 13 %. Even in the years of the financial crisis the pharmaceutical industry achieved positive growth rates (ACC 2011).

However, there are grave differences between the world regions regarding the growth rate. Figure 1.17 shows the growth in world regions for three consecutive years (2008, 2009, and 2010). The pharmaceutical market in North America, which already operates on a high level, grew in 2008 only by 1.7 %. One year later, even despite of the crisis, the growth rate there was more than doubled. This is attributed to the increased demand and launch of several innovative products on the US market

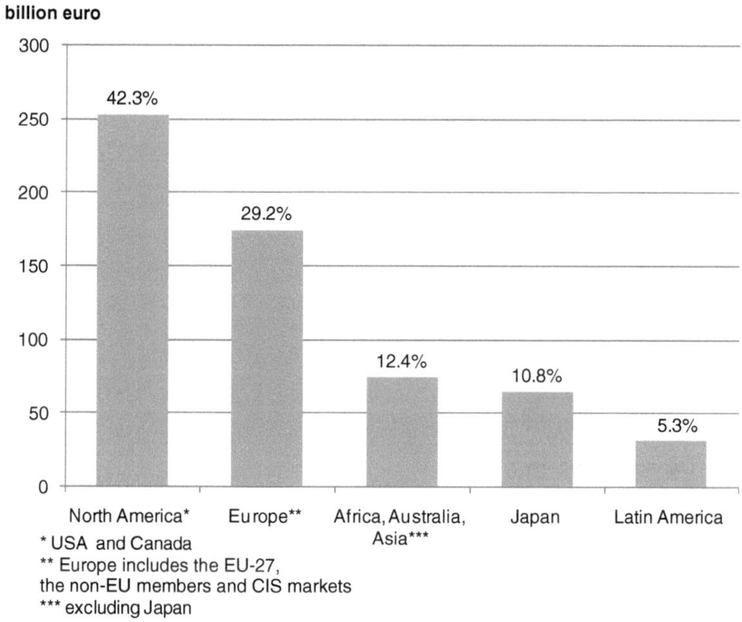

Fig. 1.13 The world pharmaceutical sales and market share (2010, billion euro and percentage) (EFPIA 2011)

Fig. 1.14 Regional breakdown of the pharmaceutical production (2007, percentage) (EFPIA 2010)

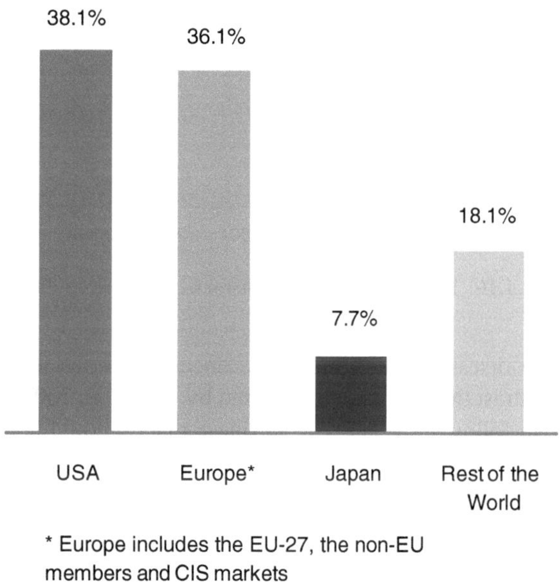

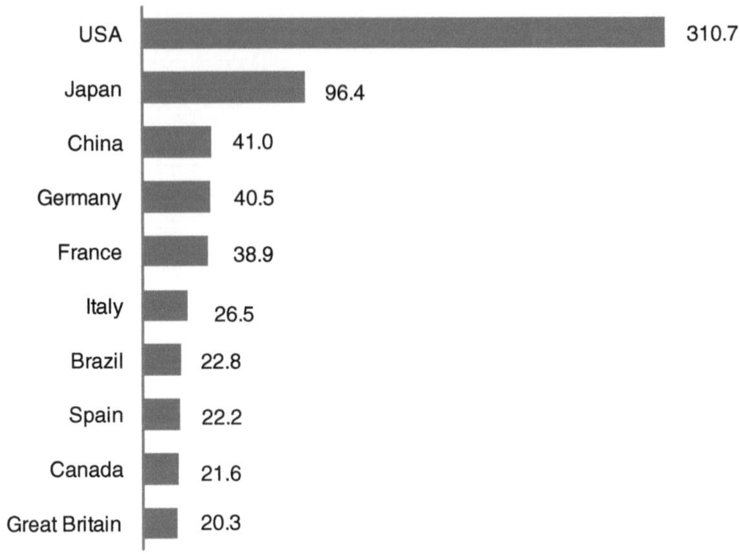

Fig. 1.15 The top ten pharmaceutical markets (2010, billion US dollar) (BPI 2011)

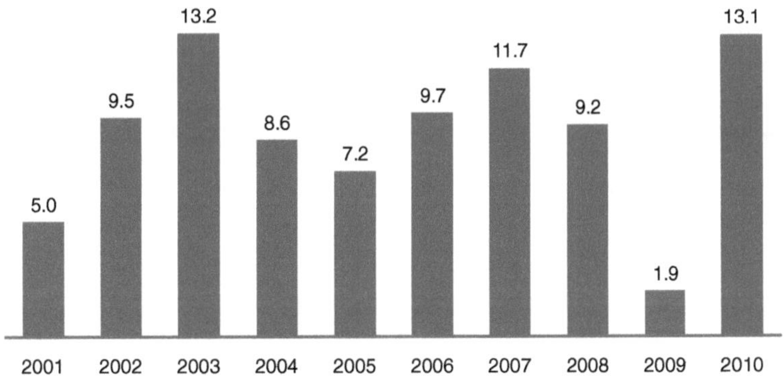

Fig. 1.16 The growth of global pharmaceutical sales (2001–2010, percentage) (ACC 2011)

(for diseases like thrombosis, cancer, and arterial fibrillation) (RNCOS 2010). In contrast the EU market increased by 10.5 % in 2008 and fell to negative rates in the two following years. The Japanese market could hold strong growth rates in 2008 and 2009 and decreased only in 2010. This shows clearly that the pharmaceutical markets in different regions develop differently and independently from each other. Furthermore the pharmaceutical industry sales are mostly independent from the general economic situation. Emerging regions of Asia and Latin America achieve high growth rates. The crisis strongly stressed the market in Latin America in 2009, but one year later the growth rates rose to a new record high. The growth rates in Asia remained high over the three years. This is attributed to the high growth rates in the booming regions of Asia. The growth rates in China were at 27 % in 2008 and 2009 and 22 % in 2010 (BPI 2009, 2010, 2011).

Following the trend in the five year period (between 2004 and 2009) the region which includes Asia, Australia, and Africa shows the highest growth of 13.9 % (Fig. 1.18). On the second place is Latin America with 10.9 %. The well developed regions are not able to keep up with these rates. Europe had slightly higher growth rates than the US and Japan in this period (EFPIA 2010). However, the figures of the year-to-year growth in 2009 and 2010 show that Europe experienced an upturn lately (Fig. 1.17).

Figure 1.19 shows the growth rates in the top ten countries. There it is obvious that the high growth rates in Asia and Latin America are caused by a few countries only, like China or Brazil. Within the EU the highest growth rates were achieved by the new EU members, thus not among the top players either (BPI 2011).

Global Pharmaceutical Market Share

The differences in the growth rates between the world regions have an impact on the pharmaceutical market share (Fig. 1.20). In the last five years the traditional market leaders, the US and Europe, slightly lost their shares to the emerging regions in Asia and Latin America. Japan could hold its position. In 2009 the high growth rate brought Japan even to 11.2 % market share (EFPIA 2006, 2010, 2011).

Global Pharmaceutical Trade

The pharmaceutical trade is clearly dominated by the EU (Fig. 1.21). With exports summing up to 308 billion US dollar and imports by 247 billion US dollar in 2010, the EU broadly overtakes the countries on the following positions. Even if the intra-European trade is excluded, the EU keeps the top position for exports. The extra-European exports account for 27 % of the worldwide exports. The imports slide to the second place with 13.3 % close behind the US. The US

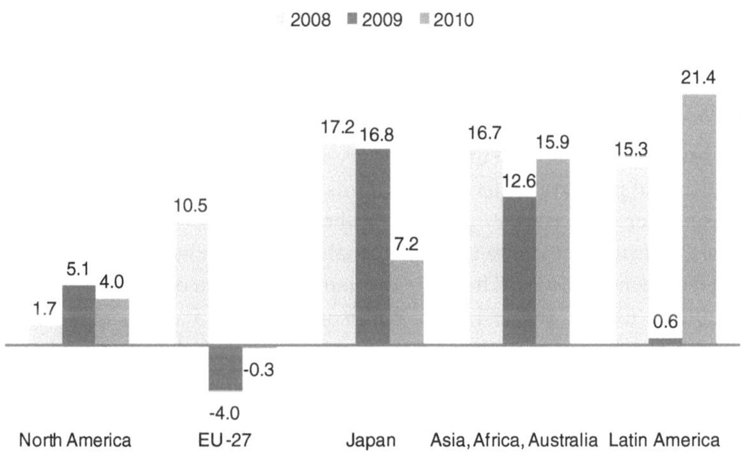

Fig. 1.17 Growth of pharmaceutical sales in world regions (2008–2010, percentage) (BPI 2009, 2010, 2011)

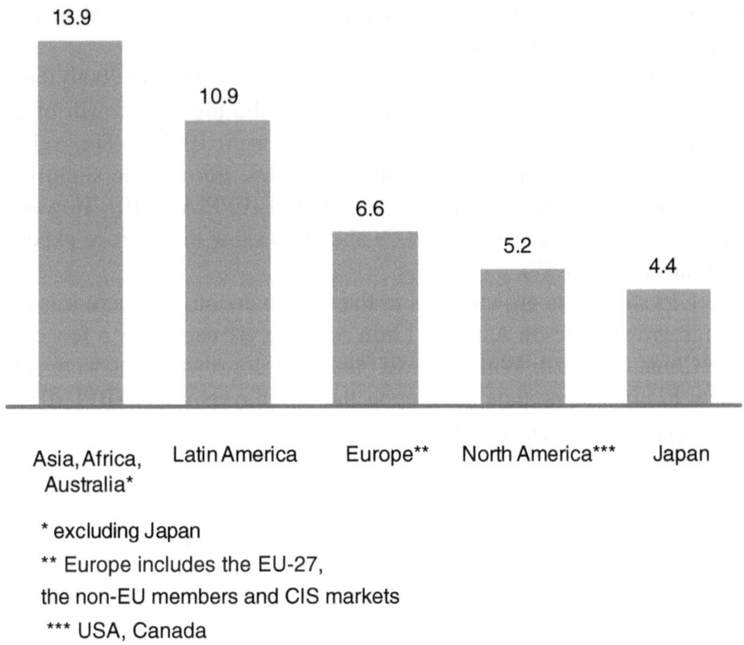

Fig. 1.18 Growth of pharmaceutical sales in the world regions (2004–2009, percentage) (EFPIA 2010)

account for 13.9 % of the worldwide pharmaceutical imports with the value of 66 billion US dollar. On the export-side the US are on the third position with 45 billion US dollar. The second largest exporter is Switzerland with 50 billion US dollar and an export share of 10.8 %. The fourth position on the export side gains China with 11 billion US dollar and the fifth India with 7 billion US dollar. As for the imports—with 19 billion US dollar Switzerland is on the third position followed by Japan with 17 billion US dollar (WTO 2011).

Global Pharmaceutical Companies

The structure of the pharmaceutical industry is shaped by national medical traditions, intellectual property protection standards, and industrial policy (EFPIA 2010). Since these differ from country to country, the global structure appears rather heterogeneous. For instance, there are many small companies in China that are mostly specialized on generic drugs. The top 3 companies in China occupy only 5 % of the pharmaceutical market there. For comparison, the top 3 companies worldwide account for more than 16 % of the global pharmaceutical market. Furthermore, there are more than 2,000 applications for approval of generic drugs registered yearly in China and only about 40 approvals for drugs, which have never been launched before (Achema 2010). In India, the business is also primarily oriented on generics, but India has more large producers of generics with a strong lobby position in the Indian government (Cipla, Ranbaxy, Hetero Drugs, Nacto Pharma).

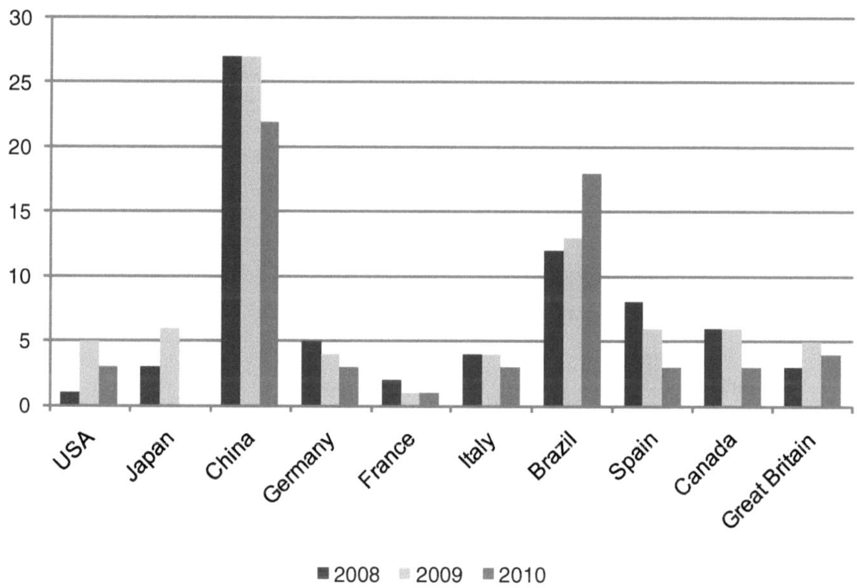

Fig. 1.19 The growth of pharmaceutical sales in the top ten countries (2008–2010, percentage to local currency dollar that is the currency fluctuations are not considered) (BPI 2009, 2010, 2011)

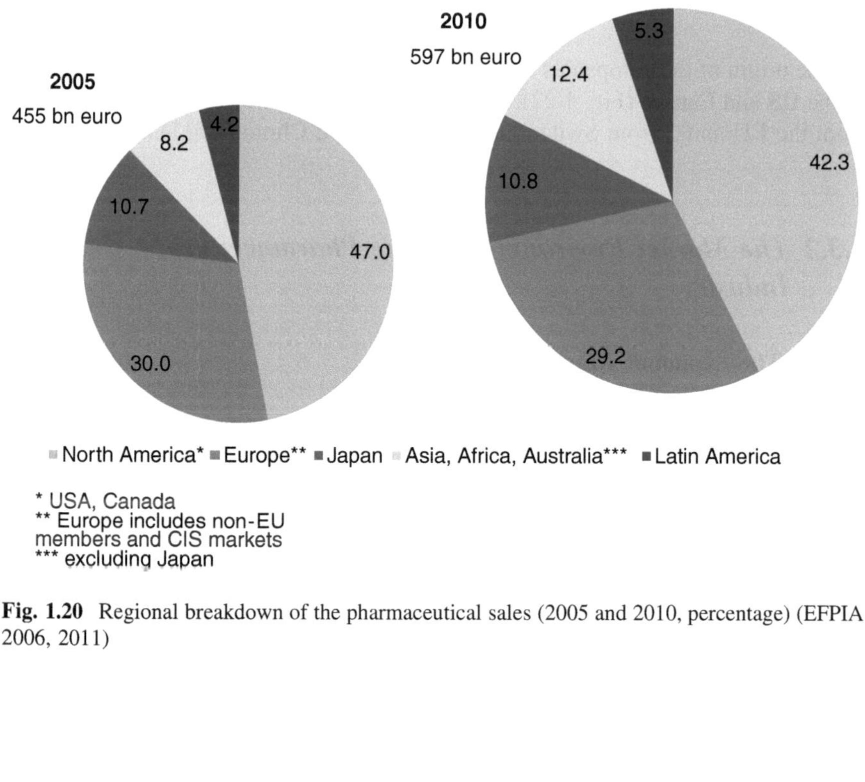

Fig. 1.20 Regional breakdown of the pharmaceutical sales (2005 and 2010, percentage) (EFPIA 2006, 2011)

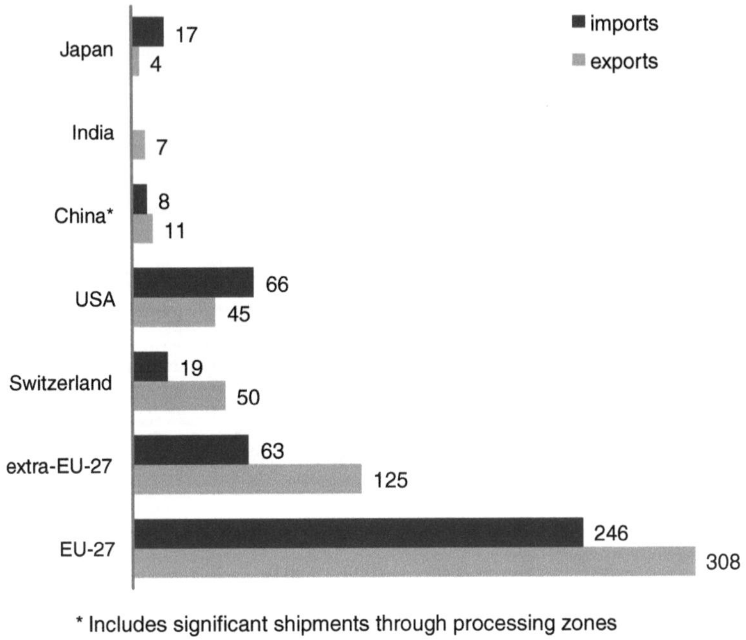

Fig. 1.21 Leading exporters and importers of pharmaceuticals (2010, billion US dollar) (WTO 2011)

The origin of the companies dominating the world market is almost exclusively in the US and Europe (Fig. 1.22). 7 of the top 15 companies come from the US, 4 from the EU and 2 from Switzerland (Cacciotti and Clinton 2011).

1.3.2 The Market Environment of the Pharmaceutical Industry

1.3.2.1 The Economic Market Environment

The pharmaceutical industry is one of the fastest growing industries with a high level of resilience to the volatility on world markets. Consequently it is one of the most important growing markets worldwide (PWC 2008a). On the other hand, the industry has to cope with particular economical issues which are attributed to the specific nature of healthcare products. This chapter gives an overview on the prospects for growth and the main economical threats the pharmaceutical companies are facing.

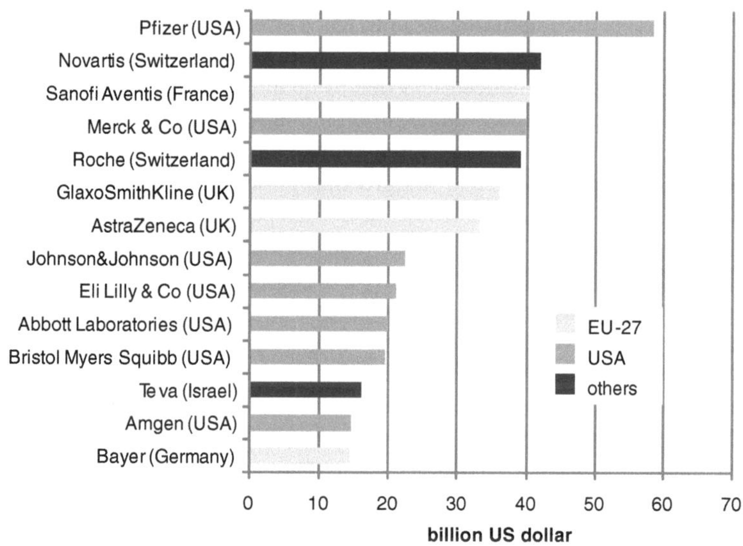

Fig. 1.22 The top 15 pharmaceutical companies worldwide according to the sales volume (2010, billion US dollar) (Cacciotti and Clinton 2011)

Growth Prospects

The growth perspectives are facilitated on both supply and demand side. The crucial importance of innovation in the pharmaceutical industry is a significant growth promoting factor. New technologies and product-innovations generally enable increase of production or profits. The production of drugs is also positively affected by the feature of many healthcare products to induce a supply-driven demand, i.e. the demand emerges only after the market introduction of the product. Pharmaceutical producers benefit less than others from new production facilities in low income countries and cheaper precursors due to the approval requirements, but indeed they derive the advantages. For example, the less sophisticated operations like packing are being often moved to low income countries. Their admission is requested right at the beginning of the pharmaceutical's registration. The advantages of globalization among the well established producers are rather on the side of the originators. The threat of new competitors from emerging markets is delayed in the in-patent sector, because of the high R&D investments and the know-how needed for the entry. The producers of biosimilars have often alike advantages as the originators, because imitation of the complex production process of biopharmaceuticals is much more difficult and thereby generates a higher barrier for the potential competitors. In contrast, the producers of generics have to anticipate a quick expanding of new competitors from low cost countries (PWC 2008a).

The growth on the demand side is attributed to even more factors. The worldwide improving of the income situation and opening up of the markets are very important opportunities for the pharmaceutical industry. Particularly in the emerging countries, the improving income has a stronger effect because there the elasticity of demand for pharmaceuticals is higher than one brackets. The growth in the matured markets is induced less due to quantitative than to the qualitative demand. New medication and product differentiation are the keys for the success there. The incipient trend towards individualization in diagnostics and therapy facilitates the differentiation. Also the growing public awareness towards health issues favors the development. Whole new therapeutic areas occur due to the intensified search for more quality of life and the broadening of the definition of health. It can be concluded, that especially the private spending will continuously increase on matured markets (PWC 2007).

Another trend positively affecting the demand for pharmaceutical products is the ageing and growth of the world population. The population is growing, if the birthrate exceeds the mortality rate. Despite of the fact that the birthrate in all industrialized and emerging countries is dropping, the world population is growing by about 78 million each year (PRB 2011). This is caused by remaining high birthrates in some parts of the world (Central and South Africa, South and East Asia) and growing life expectancy due to improved healthcare in most world regions.

The population ageing means that the proportion of the elderly population is increasing. It is a result of low birthrates in industrialized and emerging countries and high life expectancy. In more developed regions, the number of elderly people exceeded the number of children first in 1998. It is expected that after 2045 this will occur worldwide. In terms of figures, the population aged over 60 developed as follows: 200 million in 1950, 600 million in 2000, 700 million in 2009 and 2 billion are projected for 2050. Ageing applies to nearly all countries in the world. In more developed countries the elderly people account for 20 % and by 2050, the share will rise to one third. In less developed world regions the share is currently 8 %, but will increase to 20 % in 2050. Yet, the demographic change in the developing regions is faster. The countries have to face the changes on lower development stage and the time left for adjusting on the new demographic structure is shorter (UN 2010). Without appropriate programs, this might cause macroeconomic problems and have also consequences for funding of the health-care system. Thus the pharmaceutical companies might have to face the negative consequences of the demographic change, if the funding of the healthcare system will not be adjusted.

Apart from the opening of new markets and advantageous demographic trends, the growth perspectives for pharmaceutical industry include also the development of the diseases. Particularly in the emerging countries, the changes are grave. Along with the economic progress, the civilization or lifestyle diseases (cancer, diabetes, high blood pressure, allergies, asthma) spread. Meanwhile the disease burden there resembles the one of the developed world (PWC 2007). Moreover, the extremely swift urbanization and mobility increases the risk of the infectious diseases. The nature of strains to build up a drug resistance or mutated forms extends the risk. Another factor is the climate change. The global warming causes the expansion of infectious diseases (e.g. malaria, cholera, diphtheria, dengue fever) to more developed regions. The preventive measures in North America and

Western Europe are expected to be sufficient. The impact of global warming there involves rather worsening of respiratory illnesses, since the production of pollens and other common allergens increases. Another point is that, there are still diseases, which do not have therapy yet and also that new diseases can emerge. To find a new effective medication, especially for diseases like cancer, means to gain a large head start for pharmaceutical company (PWC 2007).

Thus the new fast growing purchasing power in emerging countries and the demand for new medicines in both matured and emerging markets as well as the anti-infectives markets represent enormous potential for pharmaceutical producers. The matured markets have much higher purchasing power but low growth rates. The pharmaceutical market in the emerging countries has huge growth prospects, particularly because of the fast growing economies, high ageing rates and social changes. China is predicted to be the second or third largest pharmaceutical market by 2020. India and Turkey might be upon the top ten. The decisive factor in less developed regions is the pricing due to the still low purchasing power. However, all the markets have one thing in common: the driving factor will be the innovation which is able to meet the various upcoming conditions (PWC 2007).

Figures confirm the positive trend. As already stated the healthcare expenditures grow with increasing GDP and also as proportion of the GDP. Consequently the increase occurs in most of the countries of the world. Figure 1.23 shows the growth of healthcare expenditures in Europe, the US, and Japan, presented as percentage of GDP. Since 1960 the proportion of expenditures has been tripled. The forecast for 2020 predicts even faster growth. In the US the expenses are expected to reach more than 20 % and the OECD-average shall rise from 9 to 15 %. In 2004 the worldwide healthcare expenses amounted to 4 billion US dollar, which is in average 639 US dollar per capita. The healthcare-expenses of the nation ranking first, the US, were 6,103 US dollar per capita. The average in the OECD[11] countries was 2,716 US dollar, indicating that the differences are huge. For instance the per capita expenses in Germany were 3,521 US dollar, whereas in China 70 and in India only 31 US dollar (PWC 2008a).

Considering only the prescriptive drugs, the E7[12] countries spent in average 0.94 % of their GDP in 2004 and accounted for 8 % of the world market. The G7[13] countries spent 1.31 % of their GDP accounted for 79 %. Even if all 14 countries spend the same proportion of their GDP for prescriptive drugs in 2020 the market would be, only due to the growth of GDP, worth 800 billion US dollar. The data of the whole pharmaceutical sales confirm this development. In 2010 the sales worldwide increased to 812 billion US dollar compared with 643 billion US

---

[11] The average is based on data from 30 OECD Members in 2007: Australia, Canada, Czech Republic, the EU-14 (Austria, Belgium, Denmark, Finland, France, Germany, Greece, Ireland, Italy, Luxembourg, Netherlands, Portugal, Spain, Sweden, and United Kingdom), Hungary, Iceland, Japan, South Korea, Mexico, New Zealand, Norway, Poland, Slovakia, Switzerland, Turkey, United States.

[12] The seven major emerging countries: China, India, Brazil, Mexico, Russia, Indonesia, Turkey.

[13] France, Germany, Italy, Japan, United Kingdom, Unites States, Canada.

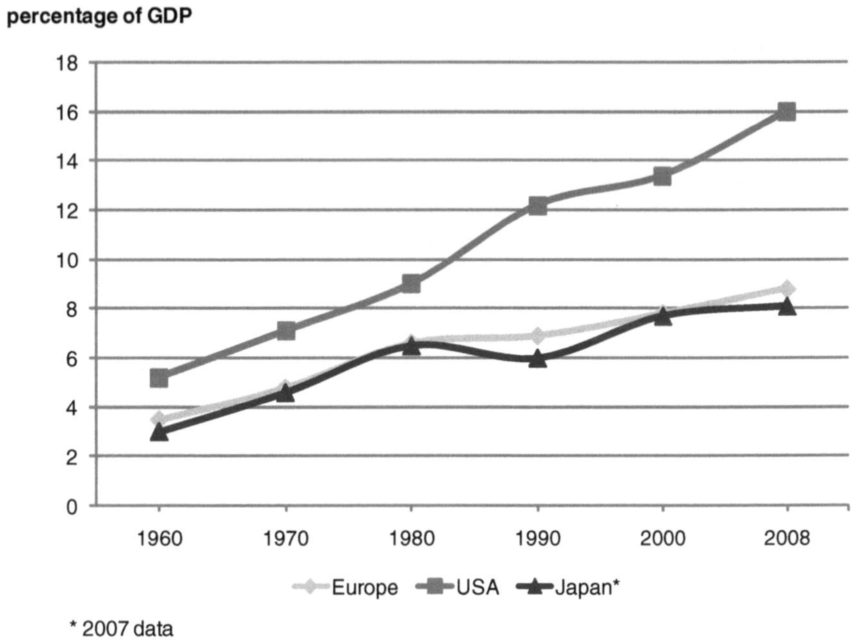

Fig. 1.23 Total spending (public and private) on healthcare as a percentage of GDP at market prices in Europe, the US & Japan (1960–2008, percentage) (EFPIA 2011)

dollar in 2006. The forecast for 2015 is 1.1 billion US dollar and for 2020 1.7 billion US dollar (PWC 2008a).

The Specific Challenges of the Pharmaceutical Industry

One of the crucial issues the top-pharmaceutical producers are facing is a lack of productivity in the lab. The originators are spending far more for R&D and produce far less molecules than 20 years ago. In 2007 Price Waterhouse Coopers indicated following reasons: (1) the targeted diseases need more complex medicines, (2) the demands for financial resources are higher but funding is more difficult due to higher risk and competition from other sectors like biotech, (3) many companies run a disadvantageous research-practice by concentrating on new molecules without sufficient knowledge of the disease, which is often responsible for late and expensive breakups (PWC 2007).

On the account of lack of sufficient innovation new problems occur: the financial situation is worsening, sales and marketing expenditures are rising, and the battered reputation does not improve. The bad reputation is a problem the pharmaceutical producers have been dealing with ever since. It refers to both the response of the medicines and the possible side effects of it. Specific sales practices (e.g. payments to medical practitioners for the preference of own products) in the recent years has also left its marks. Since improvement is not fast enough and public regard towards health is rising, the reputation is rather worsening.

The rising sales and marketing expenses were supposed to improve the financial performance, however, they had a negative impact eventually. Meanwhile sales and marketing costs are the biggest corporate expense. For instance, in 2005 R&D accounted for 17 % and sales for 33 % of the total corporate spending. There are several reasons for the growth of sales expenditures. Mostly it is due to the specific conditions for sales and distribution. In the matured markets the medical practitioners and the health insurance systems have a strong bargaining power. Also the complex healthcare system forced the companies to extend the sales channels. Through the fast expansion there are processes left which needs to be optimized. Lack of product improvements and bad reputation are contributive factors for difficulties. And last but not least the doubtful marketing practices towards healthcare practitioners do not cost only money but undermines the trust in the healthcare system. Many governments in the US and EU have already passed laws for more transparency in the promotion of medicines (PWC 2007).

Funding of pharmaceutical companies is a cyclical problem—adverse rating due to bad financial performance implies less money for further research. The deteriorated financial performance is caused by various reasons: (1) higher costs for R&D and higher break-offs, due to the higher complexity of the R&D process, (2) the absence of new TOP-sellers, (3) rising costs of market entry due to the difficult approval procedures, (4) high sales and marketing expenditures, (5) bad bargaining position with well organized customers and with highly specialized certificated suppliers, (6) overcapacity, (7) battered reputation.

For the big pharmaceutical companies, there is also another serious problem connected to the financial position. In 2006 more than 90 % of the revenues of the top-10 companies came from products which have been on the market for more than five years. Many of these patents are due to expire shortly. The US research company Sanford C. Bernstein has calculated, that the top-10-pharma companies will lose between 2 and 40 % (best and worst company) of the revenues to the producers of generics between 2008 and 2015 (Fig. 1.24). Since these are mostly blockbuster drugs, it makes for the top-10 together about 157 billion US dollar of sales. [e.g. in 2011: Pfizer's Lipitor cholesterol regulator ($9.1 billion), Eli Lilly & Co.'s Zyprexa anti-psychotic ($2.8 billion), Bristol-Myers Squibb Co.'s Plavix blood-thinning agent ($6.6 billion) and AstraZeneca Plc's Seroquel schizophrenia drug ($5.6 billion)]. Moreover, only 4 of them have sufficient pipelines to replace the loss (PWC 2008b). According to Standard and Poors, the expiration loss is unprecedented for both the number of drugs and the amount of sales (S&P 2010). This indicates the end of the blockbuster business model and of course downgrades the financial rating and eventually makes the funding of new R&D more difficult.

In addition to the internal problems, there are also movements happening outside the industry, which have a great impact on the pharmaceutical companies. Two of them should be discussed here: the funding of the healthcare system and globalization.

As the population in both the high developed and the emerging world is ageing, governments are under pressure to adjust the funding of the healthcare systems. One of the steps is to optimize the prescription of the paid medication. The aim is

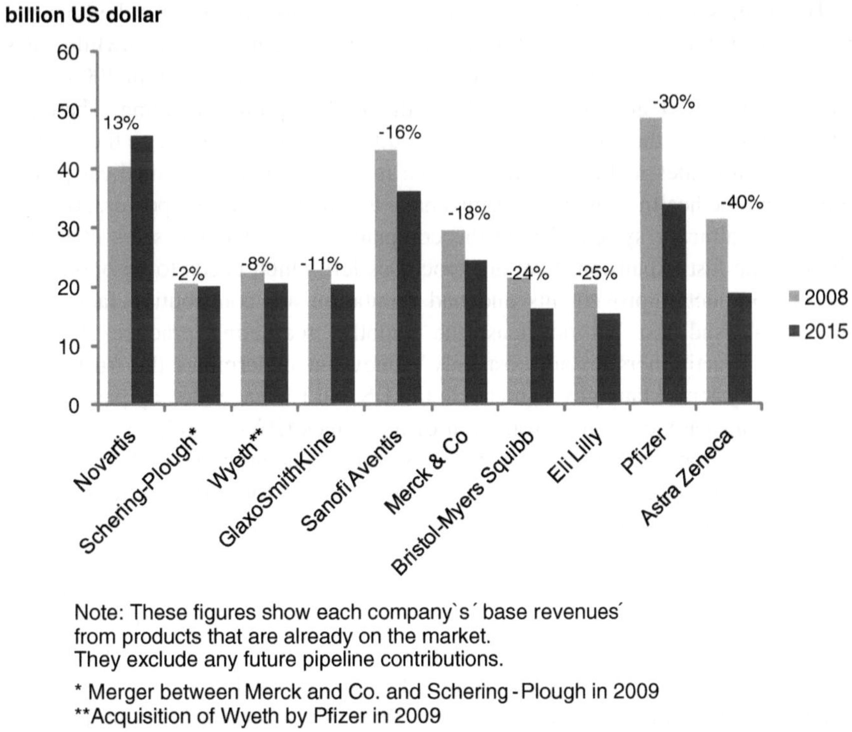

Fig. 1.24 The impact of generic erosion on big pharma revenues (2008–2015, billion US dollar, percentage) (PWC 2008b)

to ensure that prescribed drugs are effective and as low priced as possible. The US and the EU are already building systems for measuring the cost benefit ratios of medicines. The key should be the electronic medical records (EMR)—the data about effects of prescribed drugs gathered by medical practitioners and patients. The outcoming data provide best practice for further drug prescriptions and thus have a great economic impact on the pharmaceutical producers. In future only medicines, which are particularly safe, efficient, and cost-effective, will be included. It is estimated, that about 85 of the 273 big pharma major products might then fail. These make about 82 billion US dollar sales. In addition there is a higher risk in bringing new medicines on the market. On the other hand the EMR is a great data source for the originators too. Since different medicines often work for different people, the detailed records might lead to differentiated products with smaller outputs. This is positive not only for the patients, but also for the companies, since they would spread the risk much better. The clear winners are the producers of successful drugs, because also the prices will depend on the effectiveness.

There are also other ways of optimizing the healthcare system and although it falls to the responsibility of the governments, the pharmaceutical industry must establish a dialogue with politicians as well as support the finding of solutions to avoid unnecessary pressure on the margins. For instance in the US the administrative costs account for between 20 and 31 % of the healthcare costs. The prevention of the diseases is less expensive than the treatment. Pharma can help to shift the approach towards prevention. Also the legislative requirements on the pharmaceutical companies can be optimized and the costs and therefore the prices can be reduced (PWC 2007).

Globalization has been one of the biggest challenges of recent years. Each industry has to deal with an increasingly complex and a rapidly changing environment. The pharmaceutical industry is no exception there. New markets and wider choices of locations or partners are only one side of the coin. Tough competition, supply chain disruptions, and counterfeiting are the other side. The increasing competition and new markets force pharmaceutical companies to produce more diversified products, to use a differentiated pricing for different markets and cut costs to save the money for innovation (PWC 2007). The innovation involves not only new medicines, but new technologies, business models, and internal processes too (Illert 2009). The traditional supply chains also do not suit the situation anymore. The challenge is to find the best and most reliable suppliers, to coordinate the cooperation between globally spread subsidiaries and research centers, and to update sales strategies. Since the demand in the markets of the developing world rises and the infectious diseases can travel fast, the sales structure must be also globalized. The globalization is expected also to impair the parallel trading and counterfeiting. For instance the re-imports to the EU are worth about 4.2 billion euro and about 10 % of the medicines sold worldwide are counterfeit. The situation is much worse in the developing countries. For example one half of the malaria medicines in Africa are probably fakes (PWC 2007).

In order to meet the challenges pharmaceutical companies have to perform a fundamental transformation of their business. The aim is to change or optimize the business processes in order to fit the new terms as well as to last in the highly dynamic environment. In the course of transformation following stakeholders need to be considered: investors, politicians, and customers. The investors need positive messages about improved productivity in the lab and reduced costs. The governments struggling with funding of healthcare systems would engage the dialog with pharmaceutical representatives, when the reputation improves and the price-healing-ratio is reasonable. In return the pharmaceutical industry would have more influence on legislation, particularly on the expensive approval procedures, international IP-management or cooperation models. Considering the customers, better and cheaper sale structures targeting the end customer rather than the healthcare practitioner as well as differentiated pricing for different markets are recommended (PWC 2007).

Meanwhile most of the major players have taken action towards the recommendations of Price Waterhouse Coopers from 2007. Research is focusing on the specific therapeutic areas in which the company has its strengths and is also advancing by highly rising areas of biopharmaceuticals, vaccines, and in some cases even generics. The revision was accompanied by a boom in the M&A

activity (Most prominent: Merck/Schering-Plough and Pfizer/Wyeth). A strong downsizing of costs has also been started. The leading companies (Pfizer, Merck, GlaxoSmithKline Plc, Bristol-Myers Squibb and Eli Lilly) are all running multi-billion-cost-cutting programs. Sales expenditures have been already cut by 10–15 % from the peak in 2005 and are planned by more than 30 % by 2015. As further sources for cut backs the personnel costs, overcapacities, internal structures, and the R&D approach were addressed. For example, Pfizer was running $2 billion costs saving program and the additional savings of the merger with Wyeth were estimated at further $4 billion. As it seems the companies are again on the way towards a long term profit growth (S&P 2010). However, according to the experts many of the implemented costs saving programs are rather in a manner of a top down approach with only short-term effects thus improper to secure the competitiveness. The search for real internal potentials as well as external synergies (through M&A and partners), and finally the distinction from the competitors has to be the objective (Illert 2009).

1.3.2.2 The Technological Market Environment

R&D Expenditures in the Pharmaceutical Industry

The business of the pharmaceutical industry is strongly R&D oriented. The global average expenditures on R&D among pharmaceutical companies come to 16.5 % of net sales in 2008, which is more than in any other industry. In 2008 the expenditures on pharmaceutical research amounted to 71,409.8 million euro. Thus the pharmaceutical industry accounts for 19 % of global expenditures on R&D. By far the most important driver for innovation are the research based pharmaceutical companies from the US, Europe, and Japan. As Fig. 1.25 shows, their expenditures increase yearly. The US overtook the others in 1995 and expands its lead since then considerably (EFPIA 2010, 2011)

Figure 1.26 shows the differences between these three regions regarding the R&D expenditures in the main industrial sectors. The pharmaceutical sector has a leading position in the US with 25 %. In the EU it ranks second with 17 % and in Japan third with only 8 % (EFPIA 2010).

The leading nations in the pharmaceutical sector have also high levels of national research intensity, calculated as R&D expenditures of all industries as a percentage of GDP (Fig. 1.27). They are surpassed only by Sweden (3.75 %) and Finland (3.73 %). Japan ranks first with (3.44 %). The difference between the US and Switzerland is minimal. Only the average of the EU-27 countries is relatively low. Considering the major European players in the pharmaceutical industry, the differences are rather striking: Germany (2.63 %), France (2.02 %), and Great Britain (1.88 %). Not only economic activities are shifting in the emerging countries, but also research. China has still a moderate R&D investment level (1.34 %), but since the GDP growth rates are immense, China is becoming an important research location (EFPIA 2010).

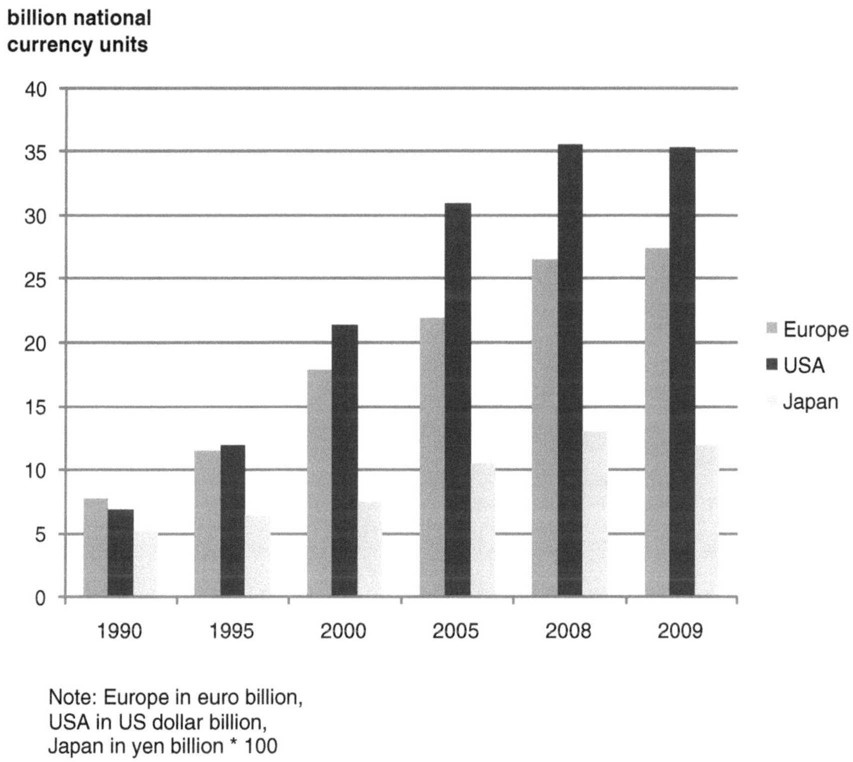

Fig. 1.25 Pharmaceutical spending on R&D in Europe, the US, and Japan (1999–2009, billion of national currency unit) (EFPIA 2010, 2011)

Next to the private research activities of the companies even more important research locations are the Chinese universities. These traditionally are the main resource of innovation in China and work closely with the private sector since the reforms of the education system (Preschitschek and Bresser 2010). The increase of research activities is also expected in other emerging countries like Brazil and India (EFPIA 2010). Considering the pharmaceutical industry, the emerging countries are becoming notably strong in basic research. Furthermore the labor costs there are still lower than in the mature countries. However, the companies from mature markets still do not have sufficient access to these new scientific areas. For the research based companies it is essential to establish a close cooperation or to move own resources there (PWC 2007).

The R&D process in the pharmaceutical industry is highly complex, risky, and expensive. In 2007, the expenses for development of one new chemical or biological entity were more than 1 billion euro, but the success of the medicine is not certain. After 12–13 years of R&D only two or three compounds out of 10,000 reach the market and of these only every fifth achieves the break-even (EFPIA 2009).

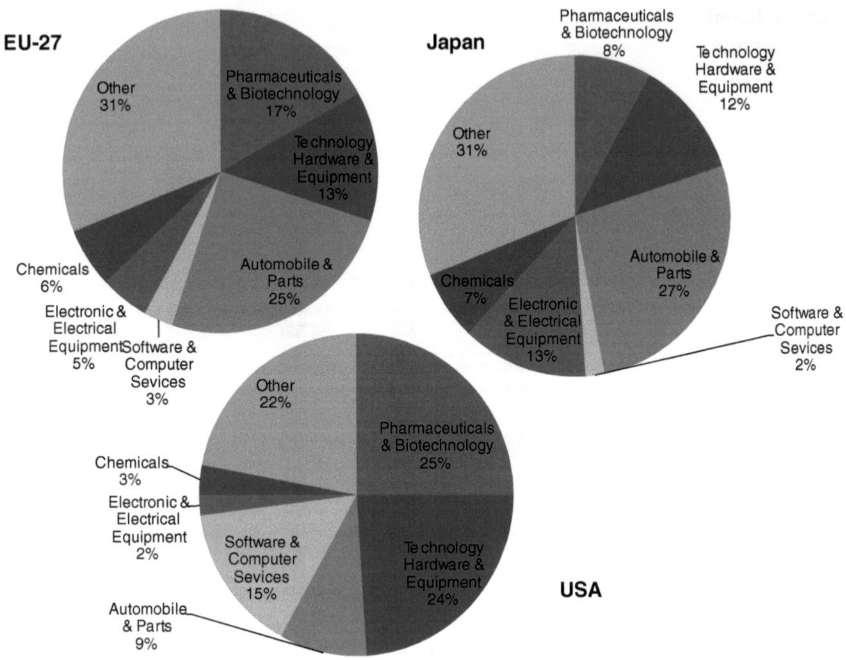

Fig. 1.26 Share of R&D investments in industrial sectors in the three main world regions (2008, percentage) (EFPIA 2010)

Fig. 1.27 R&D expenditures as a percentage of GDP (2008, percentage) (EFPIA 2010)

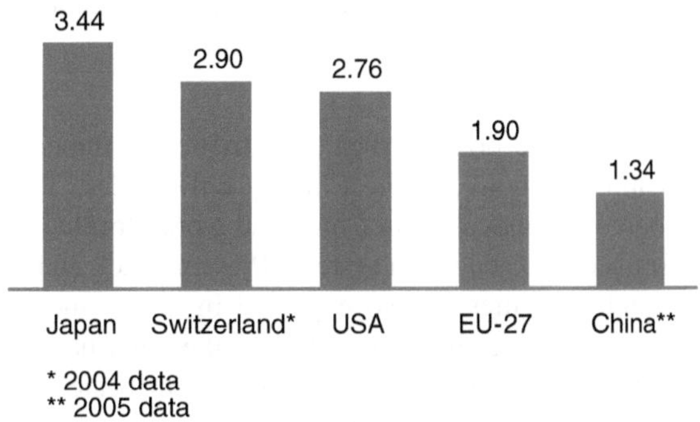

Figure 1.28 gives an overview over the process of development and commercial exploitation of new medicine. First the newly discovered compound is subject to the patent application. When granted, the preclinical testing of the chemical, biological and toxicological features, and healing qualities begins. If the results turn out satisfactory the company can start the clinical trials. These are tests on human beings and therefore, follow very strict technical and ethical rules. In phase I between 20 and 100 healthy volunteers receive the new medicine. In the second trials about 100–500 patients are being tested. The compound efficacy (the relation

between dose and effect) and safety (possible side-effects) are the main focus of this phase. In phase III between 1,000 and 5,000 voluntary patients are involved, which allows a much deeper understanding of the effects. Also the comparison with other treatments already in use and the long-term effectiveness are being examined. Finally the marketing authorization can be granted. The monitoring however, still continues. During pharmacovigilance medical practitioners and patients give feedback about the effects of the treatment. It is an important source for further information to effectiveness and long-term safety for a wide range of patient types. Based on these information improvements, new treatments but also withdrawals of the product from the market are possible (EFPIA 2010).

Until the market entry of the new treatment typically already 10–13 years of the patent protection (granted for 20 years) are elapsed. On average the pre-clinical development requires four years, phase I one year, phase II one or two years, phase III between two and four years. The R&D costs are distributed rather unequally. Figure 1.29 depicts results of the survey conducted by The Pharmaceutical Research and Manufacturers of America (PhRMA) among its members. In 2009 the clinical trials required about 59 % (phase I 8.1 %, phase II 15.4 %, phase III 35.1 %) of the R&D budget. The pre-clinical development accounted for

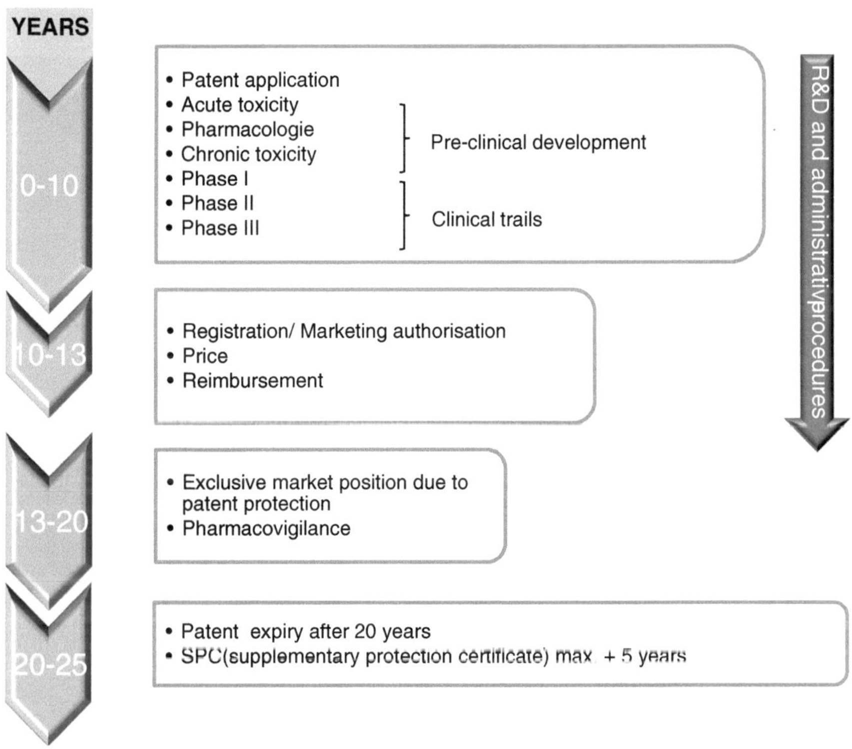

Fig. 1.28 The phases of R&D and sales of new medicine (EFPIA 2010)

25.5 %, the approval 4.4 % and the pharmacovigilance 11.4 % (EFPIA 2011). The costs for clinical trials have a rising trend. In 2008 clinical trials accounted for 53.6 % of the R&D expenditure and a year earlier for 49 % (EFPIA 2010, 2011).

The costs of R&D are rising not only due to more complex diseases, but to a large extend also because of the ever-more demanding legislative requirements. The pharmaceutical industry should engage in a dialog with legislative authorities in order to optimize the requirements for testing and approval procedures (PWC 2007). Figure 1.30 shows the evolution of the R&D costs between 1975 and 2006.

The Compound Crisis

In addition to the sharply rising costs also the number of new compounds reaching the market is sinking. Since the mid-90s the number dropped in all three leading regions (Fig. 1.31). The largest decrease suffered the EU, which has had a leading

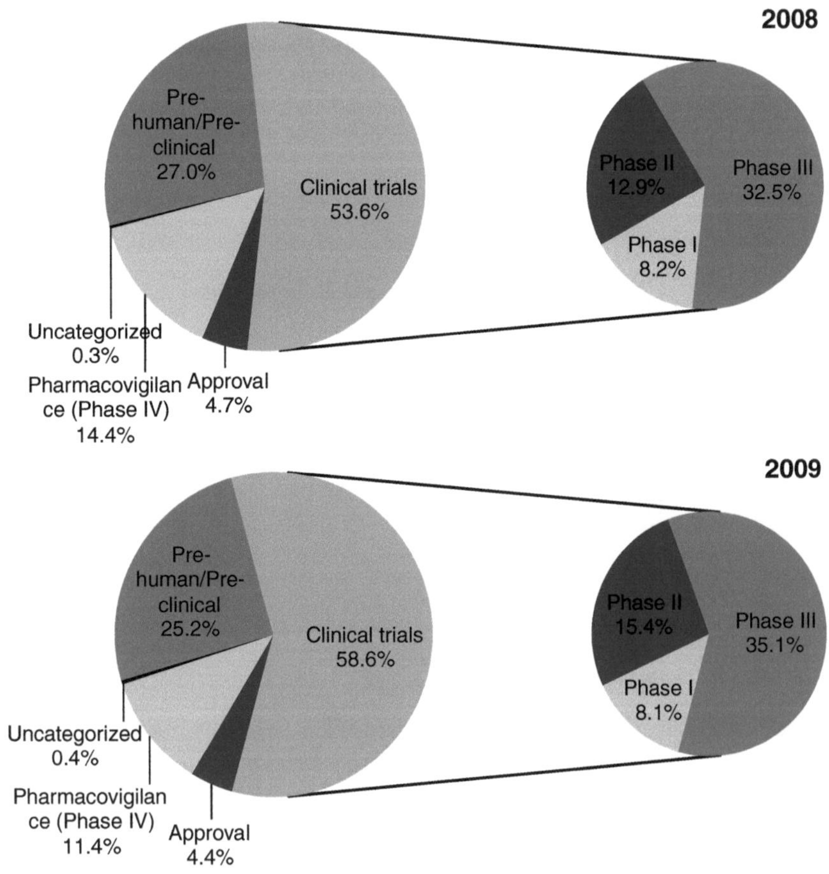

Fig. 1.29 The allocation of R&D investments by function (2008, 2009, percentage) (EFPIA 2010, 2011)

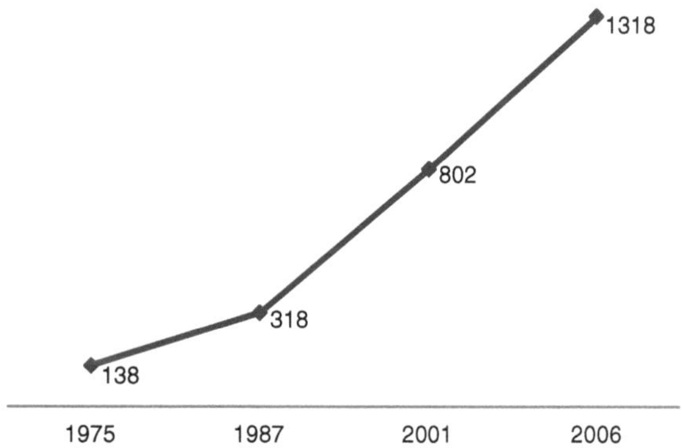

Fig. 1.30 Estimated full costs of bringing new chemical or biological entity to the market (1975–2006, million US dollar) (EFPIA 2010)

position until then. The US have become the major player. Particularly in the fields of biotechnology the EU needs to catch up.

Figure 1.32 shows a deeper insight in the share of new entities which reached the market in the last five-year period. Given the total number of compounds, which were in the trials or waiting for approval, an amount of 2,950 in 2009, the weak chance of any compound to be marketed becomes clear (EFPIA 2010). On the other hand the growth prospects for the industry seem favorable. For comparison, there were only 1,800 compounds in the pipeline in 1999. Many of the recently patented target the most pressing diseases like cancer (750), heart disease and stroke (277), rare diseases including immune system disorders (300), and HIV/AIDS (104) (S&P 2010). Any successful treatment of these would provide high revenues and possibly reach blockbuster rates. This explains the willingness of companies to put high bets in the R&D.

The R&D spending is rising and the amount of new compounds is sinking. In general terms, nowadays only two-fifths of new medicines are produced than ten years ago and the R&D costs are twice as large. The experts speak of a compound crisis. There are several reasons for the rising costs. Besides the increasing legal requirements (approval, trials, and other), many can be found in

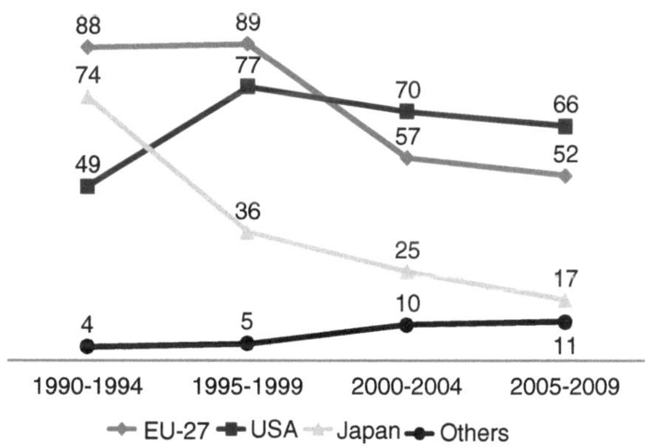

Fig. 1.31 Number of new chemical or biological entities (1990–2009) (EFPIA 2010)

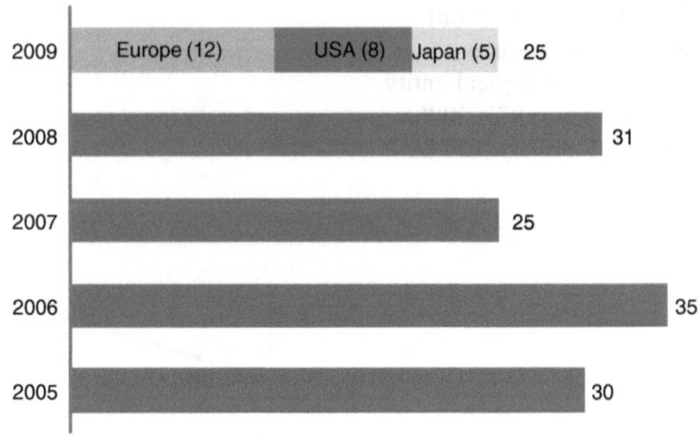

Fig. 1.32 Number of new chemical or biological entities (2005–2009) (EFPIA 2010)

the R&D process itself. In the search for new treatments the biotechnology looks much promising, but the retooling towards the biotech-revolution has also contributed to the increase of costs (EFPIA 2010).

Some of the cost drivers are based rather on the prevailing R&D process and can be optimized by the company itself. First the development of the compound is carried out often without a proper knowledge about the targeted disease. This partly explains the high rate of attrition in advanced stage of development, when already many resources have been spent. This strategy was successful when common diseases ware targeted and a chance for block-buster drugs was much higher. More complex treatments need more resources per se and the risk of dropouts is also higher. Furthermore it is expected that many of the new treatments would be oriented on specific patient subpopulations, thus even if successful, they cannot be turned to blockbusters (PWC 2007).

Since the statistics show that indeed for different groups of patients different medicines are effective and also that there are specific disease subtypes, the idea of targeted medicines seems to be the right approach. However, the strategy of developing new treatments according to specific patient subgroups proves to be more difficult than expected. The human genome is less approachable to mechanistic research than the scientists anticipated. For the past few years a new approach has been developed—the biomarkers. Within the framework of pharmacovigilance supported by databases founded by governments (EMR), better data about effects of the medicines matched with the patient data can be gathered. The evaluation shall help to identify the distinguishing marks of the patient subpopulations. As soon as the biomarkers are defined the patients can get the right treatment without having to try several others first. Also the pharmaceutical producer can save costs, since the number and size of the trials can be reduced and further research can be more targeted. The price of the therapy which has higher expectancy of success can be higher and the marketing costs much lower. The estimated savings of effective biomarkers are 50 %. Another cost saving potential delivers the pervasive healthcare—the monitoring of patients from remote and on real-time basis. With this a part of the clinical trials can be performed outside the clinical setting as well as data with higher quality can by collected and faster evaluated (PWC 2007). In the recent years the real-time technology is booming (hardware: RFID, software: SAP HANA™), only the legal basis must be established yet.

The low number of new compounds is ascribed also to the cautious R&D strategy. Due to the higher risk whether a compound reaches the market (the approval) or not and then whether or not the new treatment will be eligible for reimbursement (only if there is no other treatment or it proves much better for the therapy than other) the companies try to minimize the risk by 'playing it safe'. Indeed the achievement of minor improvements rather than breaking innovations became a characteristic of pharmaceutical industry in recent years. The standardized 20 years of patent protection, regardless the complexity of the research, facilitate this strategy. Possibly some additional years of patent protection for superior products would bring forward the true innovation. Price Waterhouse Coopers estimates higher cash-flows from truly innovative medicines by 50–100 % if patent protection for them rises from 20 to 25 years (PWC 2007).

Considering the grave organizational and cultural changes the pharmaceutical companies must undertake it might be in many cases more advantageous to buy the research results from small and highly specialized research companies. This reduces the complexity and allows much flexible business strategy (PWC 2007).

Products

The transformations in the pharmaceutical industry have an impact on new medicines. The combination therapies, biomarkers, and identification of disease subtypes imply product diversification. Thus the financial risk in case of failure can be reduced, but more complex technologies and also new manufacturing approaches (the return of economies of scale will drop) are needed first. The new manufacturing process must become more flexible to produce a wider range of products (PWC 2007).

The search for new treatments in order to differentiate own products from competitors resulted in a boom of biological-based medicines. These are more sophisticated than chemical-based medicines and are better suited to fit the individual needs of patients. Examples for the therapeutic areas are cancer, metabolic or immunological disorders. The molecules closely resemble their natural counterparts in the human body. They are also larger than chemical molecules and more complex in terms of manufacturing and administration (the exact function in the human body is difficult to determine). The production is not possible through chemical synthesis but only on biological materials (in bioreactors) (EBE 2008). As for biosimilars (biopharmaceutical generics)—the biopharmaceuticals are difficult to copy, even if the patent application of the process (natural product cannot be patented) is disclosed, because the right conditions in bioreactors are necessary.

The first biopharmaceutical treatment came to market in 1982. Since then over 160 biological drugs and vaccines have been approved and reached ca. 350 million individuals. There are still new products possible, not only among proteins, but

Table 1.5 The key biopharmaceutical companies ranked by sales in 2006

Rank	Company
1	Amgen
2	Genentech[a]
3	Genzyme[b]
4	UCB
5	Gilead sciences
6	Serono
7	Biogen idec
8	CSL
9	Cephalon[c]
10	MedImmune[d]

[a] Acquisition of Genentech by Roche in 2009
[b] Acquisition of Genzyme by Sanofi in 2011
[c] Acquisition of Cephalon by Teva in 2011
[d] Acquisition of MedImmune by AstraZeneca in 2007

also genes (gene-therapy) and tissue-engineering[14] (EBE 2008). In 2001 biopharmaceuticals accounted for 12 % of global market sales, by now they are an estimated 30 %. Among the new molecules launched on the market each year about one-fifth come from biotechnology. Although the sector is fast growing all around the world, the leading position with a sizeable head start has the US. For example among the public traded companies the US accounts for 73.8 % of global biotechnology revenues and 79.6 % global biotechnology R&D expenditures (EFPIA 2009). When having a look at the profitability there are only a few large leading companies. The top 10 companies ranked by sales are listened in Table 1.5. Some of the traditional big pharma companies, like Johnson & Johnson and Merck & Co., also have considerable biotech business areas. However, the market is dominated by small non-profit research companies. These depend on other sources of financing than sales. These include angel investors, venture capital firms, public offerings, partnership deals with big biotech and pharmaceutical companies. M&A plays an important part in this line of business. The big pharma companies made deals with biotech companies in order to improve their pipelines. For instance in 2006 and 2007 Novartis purchased Chiron, Merck & Co. acquired Sirna Therapeutics, and AstraZeneca merged with MedImmune (Hoovers 2010). In 2008 Eli Lilly & Co. purchased ImClone Systems Inc. In 2009 the acquisition of Wyeth by Pfizer and the acquisition of Genentech (remaining 44 %) by Roche also considerably strengthened the biotech lines of these two giants (PWC 2009).

The changes regarding the products are not restricted only to new technologies. Also new uses for long known treatments combined with new technologies are conceivable as vaccines show. As already stated the vaccines sector is growing rapidly (see Sect. 1.3.2.1). One reason is the rising demand, but there is also one

[14] Covers the applications that repair or replace tissues. The tissues are promoted to grow in vivo in bioreactors and than they are implanted into the living body.

other, the broader range of indications the vaccines are developed for. Many of the vaccines in the pipeline differ from the common approach. The largest proportion holds oncology with 90 vaccines in the pipeline (in 2007). Furthermore there are also vaccines for cocaine addiction, diabetes, hypertension, Alzheimer's disease, psoriasis, food allergies, rheumatoid arthritis, and nicotine withdrawal in development. There were traditionally the Big Five players, which dominated the sector (GlaxoSmithKline, Merck & Co., Sanofi-Aventis, Wyeth (now Pfizer), and Novartis via its acquisition of Chiron), but according to the pipelines many smaller pharmaceutical companies might be expanding (PWC 2007).

1.3.2.3 The Legal and Political Market Environment

On this field the pharmaceutical industry faces challenges very similar to those of chemical industry (see Sect. 1.2.2.3). The legal market environment is highly complex since the legislation involves detailed health and safety, intellectual property and approval regulations, which vary from one country to another. However, it is crucial for the success to manage the complexity, because each slip might be disastrous in the fierce competition. For example one gap in the patent application or wrong geographical patent range might lead to the loss of the patent right to a competitor. For pharmaceutical companies this situation is even more difficult than for chemical companies and that for more reasons. Due to higher R&D expenditures the refuse or loss of a patent right hurts more. Second the legislation is more penetrative on the pharmaceutical industry since the medicines are in direct contact with the human body. The R&D-process as well as sales conditions are highly regulated (see Sect. 1.3.2.2). The room for collaboration and the usage of the potential in the emerging countries is also restricted due to regulations. For instance the patent application includes also the suppliers of active ingredients and important auxiliaries. Therefore, the company cannot easily switch to a new supplier. Even the contracts on less important stages of the supply chain (e.g. packing) must fulfill rigorous requirements.

Another important topic is the public attitude towards the pharmaceutical industry and its research. This includes mainly the ethical questions of research (genetic engineering) and the approval of a pharma-promotive legislation among voters (PWC 2008b).

Indeed in the long-term it is expected that companies will relocate in the regions with better conditions—starting with application procedures and approval conditions, further the production and sales conditions, the range of international patent protection, and last but not least the governmental support and political stability. The US have a clear advantage due to the standardized regulations and single language. The EU attempted standardization for this field already in 2001, but it failed because of the different national implementations (PWC 2008b). Among the emerging countries India gained capital importance. The country joined WTO in 2005 and transformed its patent legislation and a huge growth of contract research and manufacturing services (CRAMS) followed. The analysts estimate that India has potential for 35–40 % of the global pharmaceutical CRAMS market. India has long term experience with R&D and production activities in chemicals as well as advantageous regulations and low labor costs (Goodall 2005).

Still according to the market share the world most important approval authorities are the American Food and Drug Administration (FDA) and the European Medicines Agency (EMEA). The companies evaluate the quality of approval procedures for both comparable, but they criticize the huge differences in the requirements between them. The efforts a company has to supply for the second application are almost double. All previous attempts to harmonize the systems have failed because of the high complexity and costs required (PWC 2008b). The regulators in the emerging countries become more and more important since the manufacturing and R&D activities are shifting away from their traditional locations. The Association of South East Asian Nations (ASEAN) countries, for example, already completely transformed their regulatory systems in order to adjust them to their patient population. The countries also attempt to harmonize the registration and control regulations, which would give them further competitive advantages besides low labor costs (PWC 2007).

Despite of the efforts to harmonize the systems, the pharmaceutical industry will in the future have to deal with more requirements than ever, since the authorities enhance their programs. First the regulators require communication on regular basis at a much earlier development point. For the FDA it is stated within the framework of the Critical Path Initiative with the aim to create new tools for improving safety and efficacy of new medicines. The EMEA intensified a similar goal through its Road Map to 2010. Second in order to improve the risk management, the companies are required to provide information not only on what they know but also what they do not know about the effects of the medicine (European Risk Management Strategy). And third the evidence that the new medicine is better that any comparable medicine becomes increasingly important. Furthermore in order to achieve more transparency all data must be submitted electronically, the prescribing doctors must have access to the evidence on adverse events as well as all business processes must be audited through a third party. The FDA is also running an initiative to improve the manufacturing process and several countries already passed pedigree laws, which apply to every contractor in the supply chain worldwide (PWC 2007). In the US also the Physician Payment Sunshine Act has been adapted. It aims to make the relationship between the pharmaceutical company and the healthcare practitioner transparent. For the pharmaceutical industry it means further reporting requirements and also a dramatic change in the sales process. In order to meet all these new requirements, the companies need to address actively following problem areas: data aggregation and reporting issues as well as process complexities and that in all operations (esp. R&D, finance, sales, and manufacturing).

1.3.2.4 The Demographic Market Environment

The demographic environment of the pharmaceutical industry regards to two strategic issues: the purchasing power of the population and labor market. As already discussed in the Sect. 1.3.2.1 the growth and ageing of the world population favors the pharmaceutical industry. The question on available labor resources and their educational level resembles the situation in chemical industry (see Sect. 1.2.2.4). Since the pharmaceutical industry is even more research oriented than the chemical industry and has also to meet more legislative requirements, its dependence on highly qualified employees is even higher.

On the other hand the research based pharmaceutical industry creates besides the direct employment also indirectly new jobs. Following the studies in different countries the indirect employment (upstream and downstream like wholesalers, pharmacies, pharmaceutical consultants, and suppliers of active ingredients) is three or four times higher than the number of own employees. A significant proportion of them are the positions with high value added. For instance in the EU the industry employs directly more than 633 thousand people and about 113 thousand work in R&D. Since R&D is being done with close cooperation with universities and hospitals, actually more thousand researches are involved (EFPIA 2010).

1.4 Process Areas and Process Groups of Process Manufacturing Companies

Looking at the environment in which the chemical and pharmaceutical industries operate and the market forces to which they are exposed makes clear that both industries are subject to a permanent change process that can only intensify with time. This is forcing existing companies to focus on their core competences and fields of business. In doing so, they must in particular observe, analyze, and describe each of their business processes. The processes that form the focus of these efforts are depending heavily on the company's field of business.

Taking for example in the chemical industry the anticipated changes in products and the resulting resegmentation of the industry, it is apparent that all four segments place different requirements on business processes.

Commodity producers, who are required to supply products reliably at the lowest possible price, must in particular focus on production, quality, warehouse, and delivery processes, while R&D, sales, and marketing processes take more of a back seat. The exact opposite is true for product innovators. As the future developers of new specialist products, they must focus on processes related to research and development as well as sales and marketing of new products. Production and quality management and the distribution of goods are of no concern to them, since these tasks fall under the remit of the product specialists. As subcontractors of the product innovators, the product specialists also have to ensure their planning is as accurate as possible.

The group with the widest range of business processes to manage is that of the portfolio masters. Their core competence lies in the ability to deliver an accurate portfolio management. This is a process that places requirements on both research and development and sales and marketing. Moreover, they must be in a position to produce and ship their product portfolios, which means that over and above production, warehouse, and delivery processes, they must also pay close attention to planning processes.

The pharmaceutical industry too, must focus on a diverse range of different business processes. Research pharmaceutical companies will have to intensify their efforts to ensure their products are on the market for as long as possible before patents expire. This means shortening drug development cycles, which cannot be achieved without closely examining R&D processes. Conversely, generic drug manufacturers in particular must pay greater attention to their production, sales, and delivery processes.

To help chemical and pharmaceutical companies analyze their business processes, SAP Consulting has developed business process maps (BPM), which can be used as a starting point to classify a company's process areas. The company's value chain is examined on the basis of its process areas. In the chemical industry, the process areas are:

- Research and development
- Planning
- Procurement
- Production
- Quality assurance
- Sales and marketing
- Storage and delivery.

The company's process areas are then examined at the next level, namely as process groups. At this point, the first industry-specific play a role. Examples include trading businesses in procurement, batch production and packaging in production, or the management of dangerous goods in storage and delivery. Furthermore, every company has a number of supporting processes that cannot be assigned to a particular process area but that concern the entire value chain. These include industry-specific compliance requirements and financial accounting processes, for example. Figure 1.33 shows the SAP business process map for the chemical industry.

At a first glance, at process area level, the pharmaceutical industry appears to match the chemical industry, the only slight difference being that the production area accounts for the fact that production processes are regulated (Fig. 1.34). However, a look at the process groups soon reveals considerable differences. For instance, the research and development process in pharmaceutical companies is unique, which means the process groups in this area cannot be compared with any other industry. Similarly, the process groups of "active ingredient production", "indirect sales", and "supply chain security" are very particular to the industry.

Nevertheless a certain amount of overlapping with the chemical industry can be identified. The planning process groups are identical, for instance. Both industries

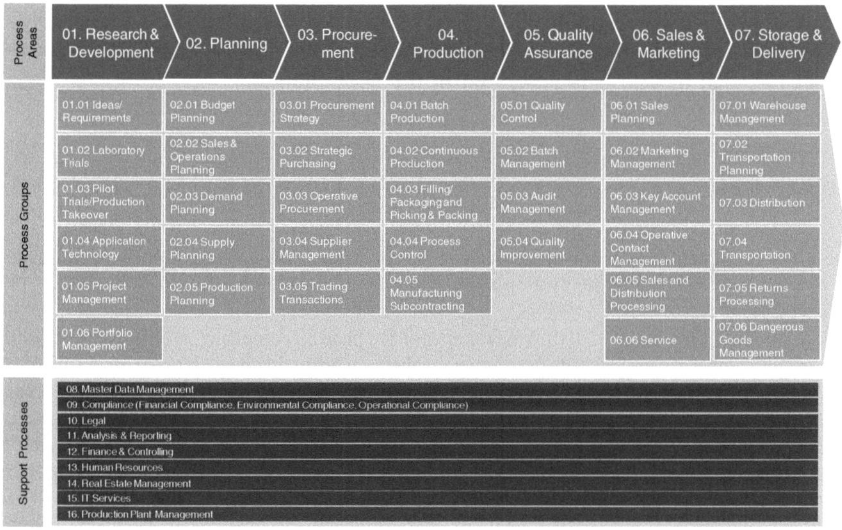

Fig. 1.33 Process areas, process groups and supporting processes in the chemical industry

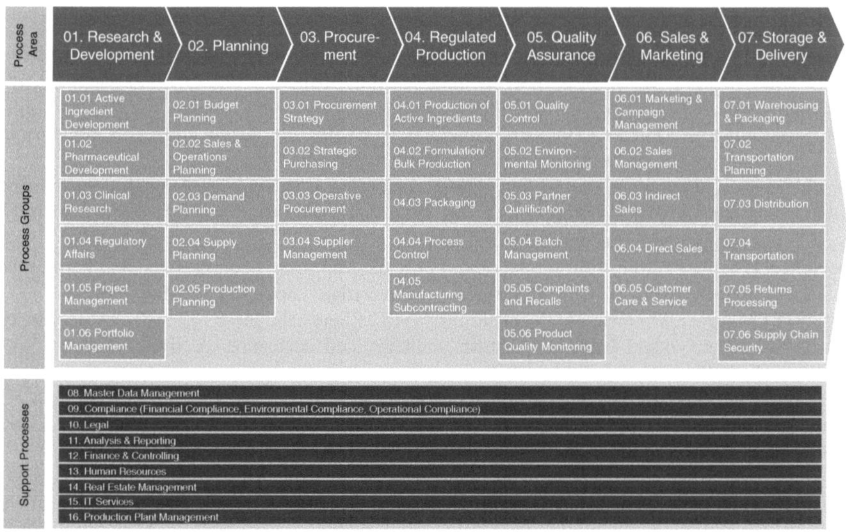

Fig. 1.34 Process areas, process groups and supporting processes in the pharmaceutical industry

also feature manufacturing subcontracting, transportation planning, distribution, and transportation itself. In addition, both industries rely on the same supporting processes. It is important to note, however, that differences may occur in these processes under closer inspection. The compliance process provides one such example. In the pharmaceutical industry, compliance is dictated by validation requirements, while in the chemical industry, REACH is applicable.

Based on the resulting customer-specific business process map, concrete business process management measures can now be taken. The underlying process model for such measures is described in the next chapter.

References

Abele C (2010) Innovation mit chinesischem Antlitz. https://www.gtai.de/DE/Content/Online-news/2010/06/medien/b2-innovation-mit-chinesischem-antlitz,https=1.html. Accessed 30 Aug 2011

Achema World Wide News (2010) A new hot spot for pharma companies. The current situation of China's pharmaceutical industry, process achema world wide news Nr. 851 on 11.03.2010 PG 14. http://presse.achema.de/dechema_media/Downloads/Presse/AWN1_2010.pdf. Accessed 29 Mar 2012

American Chemistry Council (ACC) (2009) 2009 guide to the business of chemistry. http://store.americanchemistry.com. Accessed 15 June 2010

American Chemistry Council (ACC) (2010) 2010 guide to the business of chemistry

American Chemistry Council (ACC) (2011) 2011 guide to the business of chemistry. http://store.americanchemistry.com/detail.aspx?ID=273. Accessed 29 Aug 2011

Asher M (2010) The global economic crisis: an opportunity for strengthening Asia's social protection systems? Asian development bank institute (ADBI) Working Paper 198. http://www.adbi.org/working-paper/2010/02/23/3556.gec.asia.social.protection.systems/. Accessed 30 Aug 2011

Banomyong R (2010) Supply chain dynamics in Asia. Asian development bank institute (ADBI) working paper 184. http://www.adbi.org/working-paper/2010/01/07/3427.supply.chain.dynamics.asia/. Accessed 30 Aug 2011

Biopharmaceuticals Hoover's industry snapshots (2010) http://www.hoovers.com/industry/biopharmaceuticals-biotherapeutics/1495-1.html. Accessed 14 June 2010

Börsch-Supan A, Ludwig A (2009) Old Europe ages. Can it still prosper? Asian development bank institute (ADBI) Working Paper 168. http://www.adbi.org/working-paper/2009/11/25/3387.old.europe.ages/. Accessed 30 Aug 2011

Cacciotti J, Clinton P (2011) 12th annual pharm exec 50. http://www.pharmexec.com/pharmexec/article/articleDetail.jsp?id=719596&pageID=1&sk=&date. Accessed 11 May 2012

Cassidy D, Gotpagar J, Morawietz M, Verity R (2011) 2012 Chemicals industry perspektive. Booz&Co. http://www.booz.com/global/home/what_we_think/featured_content/perspectives_12/chemicals_2012. Accessed 23 May 2012

Challenger C (2008) Global chemical industry R&D is well despite declining research intensity. http://www.icis.com/Articles/2008/10/13/9162812/global-chemical-industry-r.html. Accessed 30 Aug 2011

Chang J (2010) Is the financing introduction: After the turmoil of the financial and economic crisis of 2008–2009, what's next for the chemical market? ICIS chemical business. http://www.allbusiness.com/banking-finance/financial-markets-investing-funds/14140532-1.html. Accessed 30 Aug 2011

CHEMIE.DE Information Service (2010) Chemische industrie sucht nach der Erfolgsformel. http://www.chemie.de/news/115157/chemische-industrie-sucht-nach-der-erfolgsformel.html. Accessed 30 Aug 2011

China Petroleum and Chemical Industry Federation (CPCIF) (2009) China petroleum & chemical information. Vol 1 No 1 10th August 2009. www.cpcia.org.cn/english. Accessed 16 June 2010

China Petroleum and Chemical Industry Federation (CPCIF) (2011) CPCIF annual report 2010. http://www.cpcia.org.cn/English/view.asp?id=87467. Accessed 30 Aug 2011

Deloitte (2010) The decade ahead: preparing for an unpredictable future in the global chemical industry. www.deloitte.com/multifiledownload?solutionName=deloitte.com&fileIds_bfb6d7a964695210VgnVCM200000bb42f00aSTFL. Accessed 30 Aug 2011

Deutsche Bank Research (2008) World chemicals market: Asia gaining ground. http://www.dbresearch.de/PROD/DBR_INTERNET_DE-PROD/PROD0000000000228520/World+chemicals+market%3A+Asia+gaining+ground.PDF. 29 Aug 2011

Dvorocsik A (2010) An uneven introduction: as the chemical industry looks to 2010 for better times, demand will vary significantly by end market and geographic region. ICIS chemical business. http://www.allbusiness.com/economy-economic-indicators/economic-conditions-decline/13687704-1.html. Accessed 30 Aug 2011

Eisberg N (2010) From science to innovation. http://www.soci.org/Chemistry-and-Industry/CnI-Data/2010/5/From-science-to-innovation. Accessed 30 Aug 2011

European Biopharmaceutical Enterprises (EBE) (2008) Annual highlights 2007/2008. http://www.ebe-biopharma.org/index.php?option=com_news&task=view&id=149&Itemid=67. Accessed 29 Mar 2012

European Chemical Industry Council (CEFIC) (2004) Horizon 2015: perspectives for the European chemical industry—executive summary of 'chemical industry 2015: roads to the future' a study by the CEFIC. http://www.cefic.org/Documents/PolicyCentre/Horizon_2015_perspectives_for_European_chemical_industry.pdf. Accessed 29 Aug

European Chemical Industry Council (CEFIC) (2009a) Facts and figures 2009: the European chemical industry in a worldwide perspective. http://www.cefic.org/Documents/FactsAndFigures/FF%20Reports%20per%20Sections/FF_Chemical_Industry_Profie_Section.pdf. Accessed 1 June 2010

European Chemical Industry Council (CEFIC) (2009b) EU chemical industry expected to show gradual improvement in 2010. http://cefic.org/files/NewsReleases/PPT-Economic-Outlook-May2009.pdf. Accessed 21 June 2010

European Chemical Industry Council (CEFIC) (2009c) Graphs for EU chemical industry expected to show gradual improvement in 2010. http://cefic.org/files/NewsReleases/PPT-Economic-Outlook-May2009-Graphs.pdf. Accessed 21 June 2010

European Chemical Industry Council (CEFIC) (2010) Facts and figures 2010: the European chemical industry in a worldwide perspective. http://www.cefic.org/Documents/FactsAndFigures/FF%20Reports%20per%20Sections/FF_Chemical_Industry_Profie_Section.pdf. Accessed 16 June 2010

European Chemical Industry Council (CEFIC) (2011) Facts and figures 2011: the European chemical industry in a worldwide perspective. http://www.cefic.org/Global/Facts-and-figures-images/Graphs%202011/FF2011-chapters-PDF/Cefic_FF%20Rapport%202011.pdf. Accessed 07 Feb 2012

German Pharmaceutical Industry Association (BPI) (2009) Pharma-data 2009. http://www.bpi.de/fileadmin/media/bpi/Downloads/Internet/Publikationen/Pharma-Daten/Pharmadaten_2009_EN.pdf. Accessed 29 Mar 2011

German Pharmaceutical Industry Association (BPI) (2010) Pharma-data 2010. http://www.bpi.de/fileadmin/media/bpi/Downloads/Internet/Publikationen/Pharma-Daten/Pharmadaten_2010_EN.pdf. Accessed 29 Mar 2011

German Pharmaceutical Industry Association (BPI) (2011) Pharma-data 2011. http://www.bpi.de/fileadmin/media/bpi/Downloads/Internet/Publikationen/Pharma-Daten/Pharmadaten%202011%20EN.pdf. Accessed 29 Mar 2011

Goodall (2005) Contract research and manufacturing services provide boost for Indian pharma. World markets analysis

Greaney TM, Li Y (2009) Assessing foreign direct investment relationships between Japan, the People's Republic of China, and the United States. ADBI Working Paper Series No 161. http://www.adbi.org/working-paper/2009/11/09/3363.foreign.direct.investment.japan.prc.us/. Accessed 30 Aug 2011

Illert G (2009) Big pharma im Umbruch. Schritt für Schritt aus der Krise. Pharmind 71 No 12 2021–2026

Kerney AT, Inc (2010) Controlling complexity in the chemical industry. http://www.atkearney.de/content/veroeffentlichungen/whitepaper_detail.php/id/50667/practice/energy. Accessed 30 Aug 2011

Lord P, Jacobson S, Scott F (2010) Findings: risk caused by complexity emerges as top concern for chemical manufacturers. AMR Research. http://www.gartner.com/technology/supply-chain-professionals.jsp?N=4294967228+4294967150&Ns=P_PubDate%257C1&sortBy=0. Accesed July 2010

Morawietz M, Bäumler M, Thiedig C (2009) The future of chemicals: an overview. Booz and company inc. http://www.booz.com/media/uploads/The_Future_of_Chemicals.pdf. Accessed 30 Aug 2011

Population Reference Bureau (PRB) (2011) http://www.prb.org/Educators/TeachersGuides/HumanPopulation/PopulationGrowth.aspx. Accessed 30 Aug 2011

Preschitschek N, Bresser D (2010) Research section nanotechnology patenting in China and Germany—a comparison of patent landscapes by bibliographic analyses. J Bus Chem 7(1):3–13

PricewaterhouseCoopers (PWC) (2007) Pharma 2020: the vision. Which path will you take? http://www.pharmamanufacturing.com/Media/MediaManager/pharma2020final.pdf. Accessed 29 Mar 2012

PricewaterhouseCoopers (PWC) (2008a) Politik-Check Pharmastandort Deutschland: Potenziale erkennen—Chancen nutzen. http://www.hwwi.org/fileadmin/hwwi/Publikationen/Policy/HWWI_Policy_Report_Nr._7.pdf. Accessed 29 Mar 2012

PricewaterhouseCoopers (PWC) (2008) Pharma 2020: virtual R&D. Which path will you take? http://www.biovalley.ch/files/documents/p2020_virtual-rd.pdf. Accessed 30 Aug 2011

PricewaterhouseCoopers (PWC) (2009) Biotech. Lifting Big Pharma's prospects with biologics. http://www.pwc.com.ar/es/publicaciones-por-industria/assets/biotech-final.pdf. Accessed 30 Aug 2011

RNCOS Industry Research Solutions (2010) New product launches led US pharma market to grow strongly in 2009. http://www.rncos.com/Blog/report_list.php?year=http://www.rncos.com/Blog/blog_report.php&month=05&blog_pagename=New-Product-Launches-Led-US-Pharma-Market-to-Grow-Strongly-in-2009. Accessed 08 May 2012

Siu JA (1999) Mergers and acquisitions in the global chemical industry. http://www.allbusiness.com/buying-exiting-businesses/mergers-acquisitions/322134-1.html. Accessed 30 Aug 2011

Standard & Poor's (S&P) (2010) S&P current environment report: Pharmaceuticals. www.standardandpoors.com. Accessed 11 June 2010

The European Federation of Pharmaceutical Industries and Associations (EFPIA) (2006) The pharmaceutical industry in figures. http://www.efpia.eu/content/default.asp?PageID=559&DocID=7023. Accessed 29 Mar 2012

The European Federation of Pharmaceutical Industries and Associations (EFPIA) (2009) The state of pharmaceutical innovation in Europe. http://www.efpia.eu/Content/Default.asp?PageID=559&DocID=5441. Accessed 29 Mar 2011

The European Federation of Pharmaceutical Industries and Associations (EFPIA) (2010) The pharmaceutical industry in figures. http://www.efpia.eu/content/default.asp?PageID=559&DocID=9158. Accessed 29 Mar 2012

The European Federation of Pharmaceutical Industries and Associations (EFPIA) (2011) The pharmaceutical industry in figures. http://www.efpia.eu/Content/Default.asp?PageID=559&DocID=11586. Accessed 29 Mar 2012

United Nations (2010) World population ageing 2009. http://www.un.org/esa/population/publications/WPA2009/WPA2009-report.pdf. Accessed 29 Mar 2012

Verband der chemischen Industrie (VCI) (2010) EU-Strategie: 'Europa 2020: daten und Fakten. http://www.vci-nord.de/fileadmin/VCI_Nord/news/Europa_2020__Daten_und_Fakten.pdf. Accessed 29 Aug 2011

World Economic Forum (2011) The global competitiveness report 2011-2012. www3.weforum.org/docs/WEF_GlobalCompetitivenessReport_2010-11.pdf. Accessed 30 Aug 2011

World Trade Organization (WTO) (2011) International trade statistics 2011. http://www.wto.org/english/res_e/statis_e/its2011_e/its2011_e.pdf. Accessed 29 Mar 2012

Chapter 2
Business Process Management

Volker Kluy

Process Management is not a new phenomenon in microeconomics or corporate planning and controlling. Since decades the organization and management of enterprise processes was studied and analyzed by interested bodies from university and business practice. Initiated by Hammer and Champy Business Process Management became a new management concept in the nineties of last century (Hammer and Champy 1993).

As the market leader of enterprise application software, SAP possesses a long experience in methods and procedures of business process management. Related know how on industry and topic specific reference and best practice processes was more and more developed in recent years (Rosenberg et al. 2010).

Before discussing the SAP Business Process Management approach in detail, a brief look regarding different meaning of processes and the context of process management in business practice shall be provided in next chapter.

2.1 Business Process Management in the Context of Business Practice

The term 'Business Process Management' is indeed widely used, but often with different meanings, because until now a common accepted definition is missing. On the one hand process management is understood as a management discipline which deals with re-engineering, optimization and standardization of in-plant activities. Corresponding economic methods focus on collection, modeling, documentation and especially optimization of business processes independent from related IT support. On the other hand process management embraces tools including software products which are used in IT organization for modeling, implementation and execution of processes. From an IT point of view the objective of process management was for a long time mainly the implementation of

G. Grüne et al., *Business Process Management within Chemical and Pharmaceutical Industries*, DOI: 10.1007/978-3-642-11717-6_2,

enterprise resource planning (ERP) systems, the automation of workflows and the integration of IT landscapes by so-called enterprise application integration (EAI) tools (Keller and Teufel 1998).

The isolated co-existence of both process management disciplines was proven as inefficient in business practice and led again and again to frustration and doubled project efforts in business and IT organizations. For example, processes modeled before by business could not be implemented in a software package because the process descriptions were often not detailed enough. Or essential business requirements were not considered during implementation of IT systems especially by usage of standard software (Scheer 2002).

Nowadays a holistic view on process management has become accepted cross industries. Business and IT organizations recognize that the cost reduction potential by usage of enterprise application software can only put into effect, if the complete software configuration flexibility to support business processes will be used. Whenever possible and appropriate, standardized processes shall be selected. Business critical processes providing competitive advantage however, must not lose their differentiating characteristics by usage of standard software packages.

One important factor for this necessary holistic view on processes is to incorporate a unique process management approach on enterprise level. Thus a framework or governance structure will be set. There are global, regional and local responsibilities defined, modeling and documentation tools established as well as process design and roll-out procedures clearly specified.

In numerous companies process management projects are promoted and pushed by business and IT organizations together. Beside a standardized process modeling and optimization approach, the process understanding within a company is one factor for project success.

Based on SAP's extensive project experience a comprehensive process meaning is across industries one key pre-requisite for a collective process optimization by business and IT organizations.

2.2 Process Management in Process Industries

2.2.1 Business Process Management Practice

Nowadays, business processes must be both globally oriented and in a position to meet the needs of every group that uses them, be employees, management, business partners, or customers. This balancing act, coupled with the complexity and changeability of the business world, requires, among other factors, ongoing consolidation, subdivision, and data provision across all locations and levels so that everyone can access the business information they need, when and where they need it. On top of this come legal requirements, changes to corporate strategies, the ongoing search for ways to stand out from the competition, and much more besides.

Due to the necessity to take care of the particular needs of each individual company while identifying ideas for measures to help the company gain a competitive edge, every BPM project kicks off with an analysis of the current topics and trends affecting the industry or field in question.

Companies in process industries must now adhere to various compliance requirements, be environmental protection laws, the European legislation on chemicals (REACH), or the validation of manufacturing processes and systems as required by the US Food and Drug Administration (FDA) and the European Union.

Not all BPM projects have a strict industry focus, however. Many projects aim to optimize cross functions within a company. In this respect, the topics and trends of these supporting functions (finance, real estate management, human resources, purchasing, risk management, etc.) are also of interest. Taking human resources as an example, the spread of globalization both demands and encourages the harmonization of personnel data and processes. Traditional personnel tasks such as payroll and administration take a back seat as the spotlight is turned to strategic personnel topics such as finding, retaining and developing staff. Similar trends can be observed in the area of purchasing, where the department's contribution to the overall success of the company is no longer based solely on operational purchasing topics. Instead, strategic purchasing topics such as contract management and evaluation of suppliers are gaining importance. Since the traditional supporting functions are often regarded as a necessary evil, BPM projects also look at options for outsourcing these business processes.

Process Management plays an important role in different project and program types. On the one hand process management is part of huge business transformation programs. Such programs focus to a lesser extent on a detailed process optimization rather than a process harmonization across the whole enterprise. Usually so-called template programs are accompanied by implementation of enterprise application software for business process support.

Next to huge business transformation programs the business process management approach is of course also a vital part of every smaller process optimization project. Independent from project scope and type there is no fundamental difference in use of a business process management methodology.

2.2.2 SAP's Business Process Management Approach

2.2.2.1 BPM Process Model

The reasons mentioned above help to explain why companies have become so intensely concerned with business processes in general and are applying methods and tools to manage their business processes. The individual reasons are always strongly dependent on the situation, industry, and environment of each company. Therefore SAP Consulting's generic BPM approach to identify and address specific action areas for process improvement and optimization shall be presented.

Based on their extensive project experience SAP Consulting had developed a cross industry process model, including specific methodology and procedures. Processes corresponding to this model are typically described using following dimensions:

1. process flow, i.e. the sequence of single process steps containing relevant process parameters and key performance indicators for process outcome measurement,
2. organizational view, i.e. the persons and organizational units involved and
3. IT system view, i.e. the process support by IT applications especially data processing and process automation.

The process model provides a framework of four mandatory modeling elements, each representing a specific process hierarchy level. Following a top-down approach the first level modeling elements are used to describe the value chain and supportive process areas. Every process area, e.g. Sales and Marketing will then be broken down into several process groups, like Sales Planning, Key Account Management and Service. The matrix of first and second process hierarchy levels results in a Business Process Map, which offers a holistic view of a company's processes. A company's value chain, its process areas as well as its process groups and supporting processes are mapped in a standardized and compact form. In contrast to SAP Solution Maps, which are based on SAP's solution portfolio, the business process map is based on the customer's business processes. This holistic view is useful when deciding how to structure and prioritize necessary changes best.

For a detailed process description further refinement is required. Therefore additional modeling levels are used to achieve the required degree of detail. In the chosen approach, the process groups itself contain business processes at level three which itself are divided into process steps (level four). Business processes comprise the activities and actions carried out in the company. Process steps are the smallest business-related element of a process and do not possess any further subordinate elements.

Depending on circumstances in a particular project environment the above mentioned mandatory process modeling elements can be enhanced by additional elements like process variants and sub processes (Table 2.1).

Table 2.1 Modeling levels

Modeling levels		
Level	Mandatory	Optional
1	Main process (process area)	
2	Process group	
		Process variant
3	Business process	
		Sub-process
4	Process step	

2.2.2.2 BPM Predefined Content

For efficiency reasons, i.e. to decrease project duration and implementation costs SAP Consulting provides business process related industry-specific predefined content beside the generic process model with its modeling convention.

SAP Consulting's BPM methodology contains as basic parts so-called industry and topic fact books which provide up-to-date information on each of the industry and topic areas covered. For process industries SAP's industry and process experts compile fact books for companies of chemical and pharmaceutical segments.

All fact books have following common structure (Fig. 2.1):

- Summary
- Market environment analysis (PEST)
- Competitive forces (Porter's five forces)
- Holistic process view (Business Process Map).

The analysis of the market environment is based on the PEST structure (political, economic, social, and technological), which offers a framework for analyzing factors in a market's macro environment. This means that the industry's political environment, economic situation, socio demographic circumstances, and technological possibilities are examined and charted.

The competitive forces at work are examined using Michael E. Porter's five force's model, which looks at a market's micro environment (Porter 1980). The

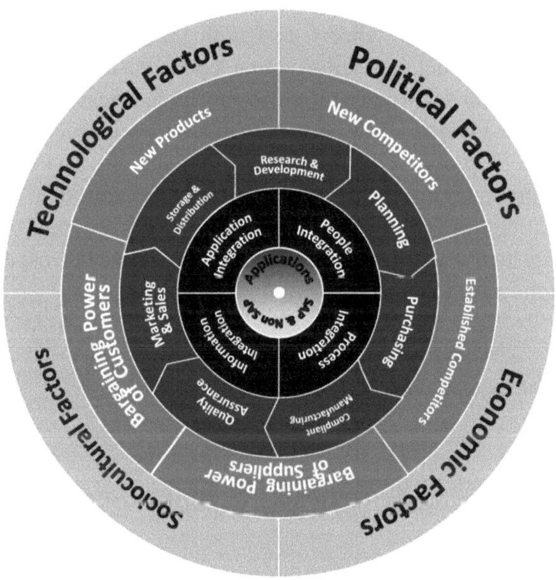

Fig. 2.1 Analytical structure used in industry fact books

model determines the competitive intensity and therefore attractiveness of a market. On the one hand, it considers the risks of horizontal competition caused by the threat of substitute products, the threat of established competitors, and the threat of new entrants. On the other hand, it examines the risks of vertical competition caused by the bargaining power of suppliers and the bargaining power of customers.

This holistic view on each industry offers a complete overview about relevant trends and changes. Presented as fact book, the information can be used to support discussions with management about potential improvements within a company. Once a broad consensus has been reached on the areas in which action is potentially needed to align the corporate strategy or to adopt processes further steps shall be started. At this point, corresponding business process map can be a valuable asset in providing a basis for discussions between the company's management team and process owners about relevant process changes.

Another industry specific content document is related to process group level. The details of those process groups are set out in process descriptions known as process fact sheets (PFS). The process fact sheets offer some insights of the process groups being described, how it fits into the business process map, and an explanation of the business processes involved. A process fact sheet exists for every process group in a business process map.

The process fact sheet is a structured text document containing a description of the business context of the process group, all key information required to describe the process and a short description of the associated business processes and any process variants and sub processes these may have.

The already described predefined content documents (fact book, business process map, and process fact sheet) deal with the BPM topic from a general perspective and provide detailed information up to business process level only. Since a further layer of detail is required to model business processes, important processes were selected by SAP Consulting's industry and process experts in order to provide complete process descriptions as predefined content, too. Process descriptions are preconfigured, process-specific forms presented in tables. Their purpose is to facilitate the tasks of analyzing as-is processes and describing to-be processes. Taken together, the following 10 fundamental aspects provide a complete description of a business process:

- Aim and purpose

  Why is the process executed?

- Objects

  What objects are used, modified, and produced?

- Technology

  What technology enables the process to be executed?

- Medium

  What media are used to interact with the process?
- Process flow

  Which processes come first and which follow?
- Organizational units

  Which organizational units are responsible for executing the process?
- Roles

  Which roles are needed to execute the process?
- Process owner

  Who has main responsibility for the process?
- KPIs (key performance indicators)

  How are the process and its results measured?
- Business rules

  What business rules apply?

A short description with examples of these 10 aspects can be found in the following Fig. 2.2.

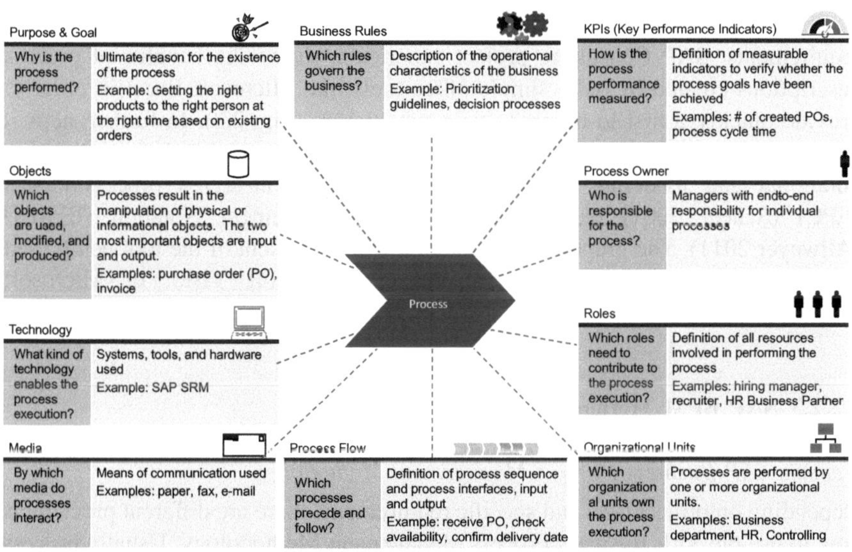

Fig. 2.2 Aspects of business process description

Each process description consists of two work areas. The first provides key organizational information about the process as well as an overview of the business process in the particular context. In conclusion, selected process characteristics are set out clearly (for example, aim and purpose, KPIs, and business rules) along with additional background information to support the analysis (for example, typical issues, SAP Consulting experience, and implementation options using SAP).

In the second work area, each process is analyzed and described step by step. Each process step is mapped to the IT solution and corresponding roles are allocated in accordance with the RACI method (Smith et al. 2005). RACI is an abbreviation for responsible (R), accountable (A), consulted (C), and informed (I).

The RACI method is used to describe which role is responsible for which activity and which other roles are involved. This produces a clear description of responsibilities at process level. The benefits of the RACI method are that it is straightforward, adaptable, and can be used at all organizational levels.

A RACI analysis typically involves the following steps:

- Break down the process into the individual steps.
- Enter the person(s) or groups at the top of the RACI segment on the work sheet.
- Identify and define the roles and responsibilities (enter the corresponding letter, that is, R, A, C, and I).
- Analyze the matrix for weak spots in respect of roles and responsibilities.
- Devise a target matrix depicting the ideal scenario.
- Derive a job description and document any required organizational changes/ adjustments.
- Reach a consensus on the target model and detailed implementation.

The RACI process description shape may vary depending on project requirements. SAP Consulting project experience shows the benefits of process descriptions created by quite simple office tools like Microsoft Excel in order to provide quickly a first to-be process documentation (Fig. 2.3). In further steps it might be helpful to transform selected processes in graphical form using a notational and modeling convention, usually as event-driven process chains (EPC) (Scheer 2001) or Business Process Management Notation (BPMN) (Allweyer 2011). The graphical presentation is independent of the tool being used (for example, ARIS for SAP NetWeaver, Microsoft Visio, or Microsoft Powerpoint).

2.2.2.3 SAP BPM Methodology

Generic SAP Business Process Management Methodolgy

Depending on project type and specific requirements there are different procedures how to use the SAP Business Process Management Methodology. Usually process

Processing			Involved Roles				
Input	Processing	Output	Responsible Audit - Team	Lead Auditor	Audit Team Assistant	Approver	Auditee
Audit Decision							
Next audit plan need to be planned	Select suitable suppliers	List of suppliers	R				
List of suppliers with calculated risk factor	Generate audit records and audit plan	Audit plan generated (or enhanced) audit records assigned to audit plan	R				
Audit plan created (or enhanced) audit records assigned to audit plan	Select suitable audit records	List of selected audit records	R				
List of selected audit records	Generate GxP relevant audit plan document	Audit plan document	R				
Audit plan document	Initiate approval process	Approved audit plan document	R			C	
Approved audit plan document	Check-in audit plan document in DMS	Approved audit plan document in DMS	R				
Detailed Audit Planning & Scheduling							
Approved audit plan	Select suitable audit records	List of selected audit records	R				
List of selected audit records	Assign lead auditor per audit record	Lead auditor assigned per audit record	R	C			
Lead auditor assigned per audit record	Group audits by region/country and optimize planned audit schedule	Audits scheduled (planned)		R			
Audits scheduled (planned)	Check planned dates with auditee	Audit schedule checked		R			C
Audit record checked	Confirm audit schedule	Audit schedule confirmed			R		
Audit schedule confirmed	Update audit record	Audit record updated			R		
Audit record updated	Perform travel arrangements	Travel arrangements booked		I	R		I

Fig. 2.3 Process description example according RACI

optimization projects following the generic SAP BPM methodology can be split into following four phases: calibration, as-is analysis, to-be process design, and solution transformation (Snabe et al. 2008). These phases are integrated into the overall SAP implementation method ASAP 7.0. Result of those phases is a Business Blueprint. This generic procedure is typically used in such projects, when neither a corporate process governance nor a process understanding is available (Fig. 2.4).

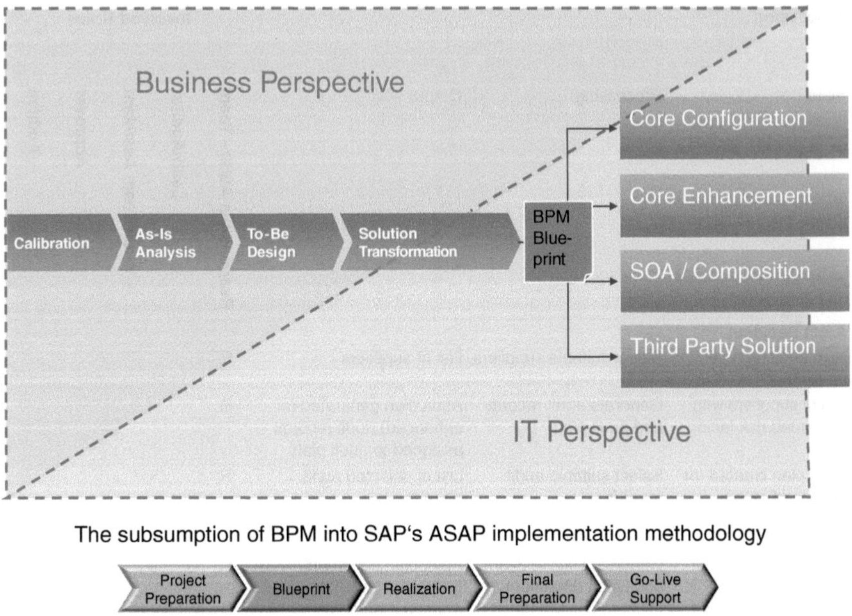

Fig. 2.4 Generic SAP business process methodology

The phases in detail:

1. The purpose of the calibration phase is to identify the business processes that are to be examined in detail. It features a comprehensive overview of the company's process landscape and the business success factors derived from the corporate strategy. On the basis of this information, criteria for evaluating business processes are defined and each process is assessed. The outcome of this phase is a prioritization of the processes to be analyzed.
2. The overall goal of the as-is analysis is to understand business reality and its weaknesses, and develop solution ideas in order to finally define optimized to-be processes. Understanding the business reality is a precondition for the later process optimization. The first step of the as-is analysis is to record relevant processes. Interviews and workshops are held to identify process steps and corresponding key performance indicators and process parameters. In a second steps process related weaknesses need to be determined and documented. Afterwards these areas should be analyzed more closely in order to identify root-causes and interdependencies. Based on identical causes the weaknesses shall be clustered and prioritized according to their potential for process improvement. This results in a list of most promising processes for to-be process design.

3. In the to-be process design phase initially concepts to eliminate the weakness cluster of the previous phase shall be developed and documented. Then appropriate to-be processes must be defined in order to realize the benefits from previous elaborated concepts. A precise description of all relevant process parameters is crucial. Defining to-be processes is an iterative procedure and the optimization potential shall be evaluated during this procedure by comparison of as-is and to-be processes. Usually such process changes also incorporate organizational adjustments. Therefore this phase results beside optimally defined and documented to-be processes in accompanying organizational changes.
4. The last phase, the solution transformation, deals with the construction of to-be processes within the IT infrastructure. IT systems, applications and services required to implement the to-be design shall be identified in the existing or a planned solution landscape. In an SAP environment the to-be processes will be mapped against corresponding standard software packages which results in following categories of SAP coverage:

- Processes supported by core configuration,
- processes supported by core enhancements (e.g. user exists),
- processes supported by composite applications/enterprise services and
- processes supported by non SAP solutions.

Finally a detailed target architecture is planned, and the required implementation, development, and integration steps are defined. In an SAP environment, the outcome corresponds to a SAP blueprint.

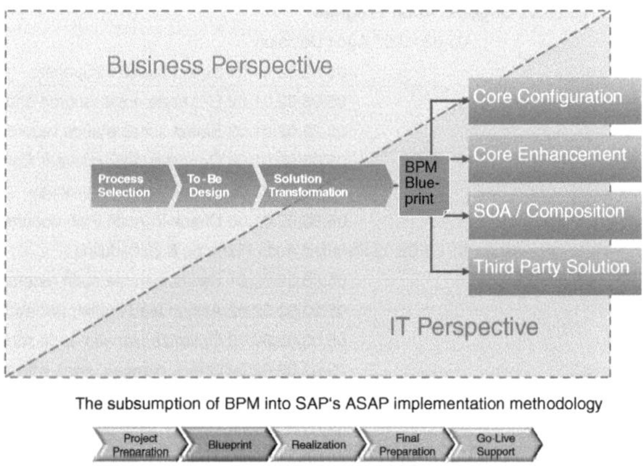

Fig. 2.5 Accelerated SAP business process management methodology

Accelerated SAP Business Process Management Methodology

Due to already mentioned efficiency reasons, i.e. to decrease project duration and implementation costs SAP Consulting provides an accelerated procedure of the BPM methodology (Fig. 2.5). This procedure utilizes 'Business Best Practices' related to business processes, i.e. industry-specific predefined process descriptions provided by SAP Consulting. Therefore the usually time consuming as-is analysis can be reduced in most instances.

The procedure for business process optimization is structured in the following three phases: process selection, to-be process design and solution transformation. Due to SAP's overall approach to reduce implementation costs and time the accelerated procedure will be presented in more detail.

Process Selection

Similar like in the calibration phase of the generic procedure it must be determined which process areas shall be in the focus of the process optimization project. For this SAP Consulting provides predefined industry and process specific lists with typical process weaknesses. These typical weaknesses will then be checked in workshops for their relevance in the particular situation. The process areas with quite high optimization potential will then be in focus of the next phase.

Business Process Catalog - Life Sciences (Pharmaceuticals)

Process Area (Level 1)	Process Group (Level 2)	Business Process (Level 3)	Subprocess (Level 4)	Process Step (Level 5)
05. Quality Assurance				
	05.03 Partner Qualification			
		05.03.02 Ongoing Audit Program		
			05.03.02.01 Audit Decision	
				05.03.02.01.01 Select suitable suppliers
				05.03.02.01.02 Generate audit records and audit program
				05.03.02.01.03 Select suitable audit records
				05.03.02.01.04 Generate GxP relevant Audit Plan document
				05.03.02.01.05 Initiate approval process
				05.03.02.01.06 Check-in Audit Plan document in DMS
			05.03.02.02 Detailed Audit Planning & Scheduling	
				05.03.02.02.01 Select suitable audit records
				05.03.02.02.02 Assign lead auditor per audit record
				05.03.02.02.03 Optimize planned audit schedule
				05.03.02.02.04 Check planned dates with auditee
				05.03.02.02.05 Confirm audit schedule
				05.03.02.02.06 Update audit record(s)
				05.03.02.02.07 Perform travel arangements
			05.03.02.03 Audit Execution	

Fig. 2.6 Process catalog example (excerpt)

To-be Process Design

At the beginning of the to-be process design SAP Consulting provides a reference process catalog with typical processes for chemical or pharmaceutical companies (Fig. 2.6). This process catalog will be discussed with the business and the IT organization and if applicable adopted according to the specific enterprise situation. Purpose is here to establish a common understanding of the initial situation and project scope as well as a common language for further project activities.

One result of the reference process catalog comparison is an enterprise specific business process map. Due to the intensive discussions during the workshops all information is available that are required as an input for the individual to-be processes. Based on the specific business process map corresponding processes must be described in detail and compiled in a final version. Of course all to-be processes shall be documented using the three dimensions process flow, organizational and IT system view. During the creation of the process descriptions relevant key performance indicators and process parameters must be captured. The organizational view will be described by the involved roles and units as well as their responsibilities according to RACI.

Solution Transformation

In this phase the support of the to-be processes by means of IT resources will be designed. This procedure is identical with the generic one. Per process step relevant SAP components and functions are described. If applicable, a list of functional gaps and required enhancements will be assigned, too.

2.2.3 Summary

All methods, tools and elements used by SAP's Business Process Management approach to describe and illustrate the processes that occur in an industry, industry segment, or company area have been presented. With these tools and SAP Consulting's experience, which is documented in reusable form, potential process innovations can rapidly be identified and then transformed into a target concept (Fig. 2.7).

In a huge number of business transformation and process optimization projects the SAP Business Process Management approach contributes valuably by supporting companies in optimization of their processes towards Business Best Practices. The resulting to-be process documentation forms in addition the basis for the further transformation of these processes into an implementable realization within the SAP Business Process Platform.

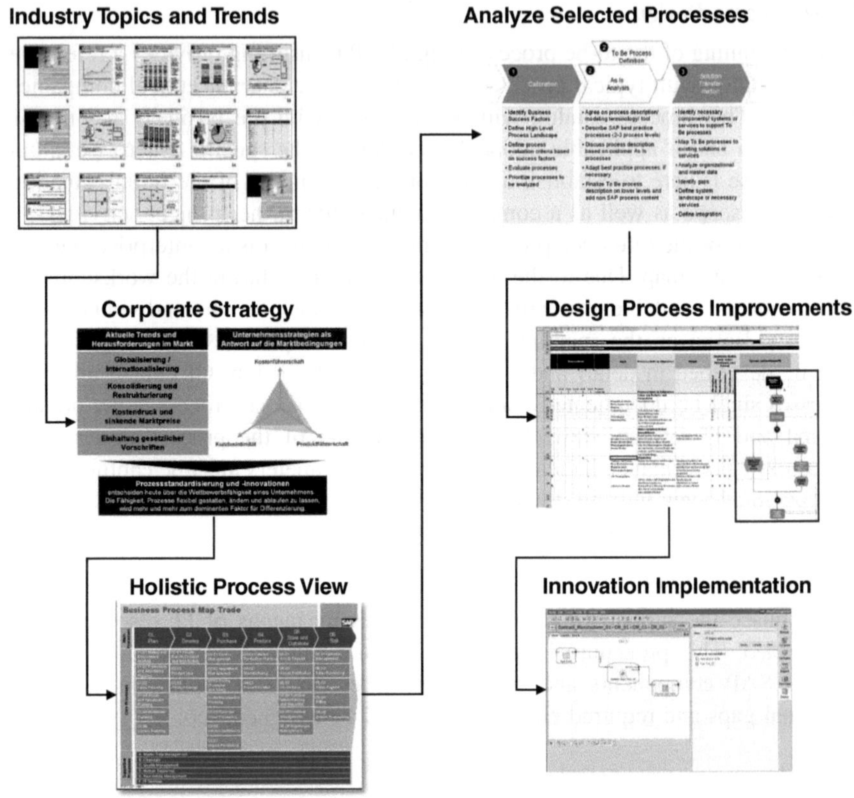

Fig. 2.7 From the generic point of view to the specific process solution by sap business process management

References

Allweyer Th (2011) BPMN 2.0: introduction to the standard for business process modeling, Norderstedt

Hammer M, Champy J (1993) Reengineering the cooperation. New York

Keller G, Teufel T (1998) SAP R-3 process-oriented implementation: iterative process prototyping (transl. by Weinland A), 1st print, reprint. Harlow, England

Porter ME (1980) Competitive strategy: techniques for analyzing industries and competitors, New York

Rosenberg A, Chase G, Omar R, Rosing MV, Taylor J (2010) Applying real-world BPM in an SAP environment, 1st edn. New York

Scheer A-W (2002) ARIS. Vom Geschäftsprozeß zum Anwendungssystem, 4th edn. Berlin

Scheer A-W (2001) ARIS-Modellierungs-Methoden, Metamodelle, Anwendungen, 4th edn. Berlin

Smith ML, Erwin J, Diaferio S (2005) Role and responsibility charting (RACI). http://www.pmforum.org/library/tips/pdf_files/RACI_R_Web3_1.pdf Accessed 2005

Snabe JH, Rosenberg A, Møller C, Scavillo M (2008) Business Process Management—the SAP roadmap, 1st edn. New York

Chapter 3
Mapping Business Processes in the Process Industry: Selected Examples

As illustrated in Chap. 1, it is vital for companies in the chemical and pharmaceutical industries to continuously review their own business processes to meet the varying and formidable challenges of a global world.

In Chap. 2, we presented SAP Consulting's BPM methodology, which offers process manufacturing companies an efficient and standardized way to describe processes and identify potential for improvements based on best practices.

In this chapter, we use selected industry processes to demonstrate how SAP Consulting's BPM methodology can be applied in real-life scenarios. From the total of six process areas for each industry, we have opted to explore the following process areas and corresponding process groups:

- Research and development in the chemical industry.
- Planning in the chemical and pharmaceutical industry.
- Sales and marketing in the pharmaceutical industry.

This will allow us to highlight one process for each industry that will undoubtedly be at the center of process innovation and therefore also of business process management in that industry. By looking at planning, we are able to examine a process area that is of equal importance in both industries and also displays comparable characteristics up to BPM level four.

G. Grüne et al., *Business Process Management within Chemical and Pharmaceutical Industries*, DOI: 10.1007/978-3-642-11717-6_3,

3.1 Research and Development in the Chemical Industry

Ornulf Rexin

3.1.1 Positioning the Process Area of Research and Development in the Value Chain of Chemical Companies

The process area of research and development belongs to the overall business value chain process, which makes it an integral part of the business processes of companies in the chemical industry. It comprises all the process groups and process steps required to research and develop new and innovative products, from the initial idea all the way to production takeover and market launch. This process area has a key impact on the company's competitiveness in strategic future markets. It lays the foundation for all other process areas and is therefore the first process area in the chemical industry value chain.

The process area can be divided into six process groups (Fig. 3.1), which are ideas and requirements, laboratory trials, pilot trials and production takeover, application technology, project management, and portfolio management. While the first four process groups run more or less in chronological order, the degree of overlap is increasing as the traditional sequential approach is replaced by a parallel

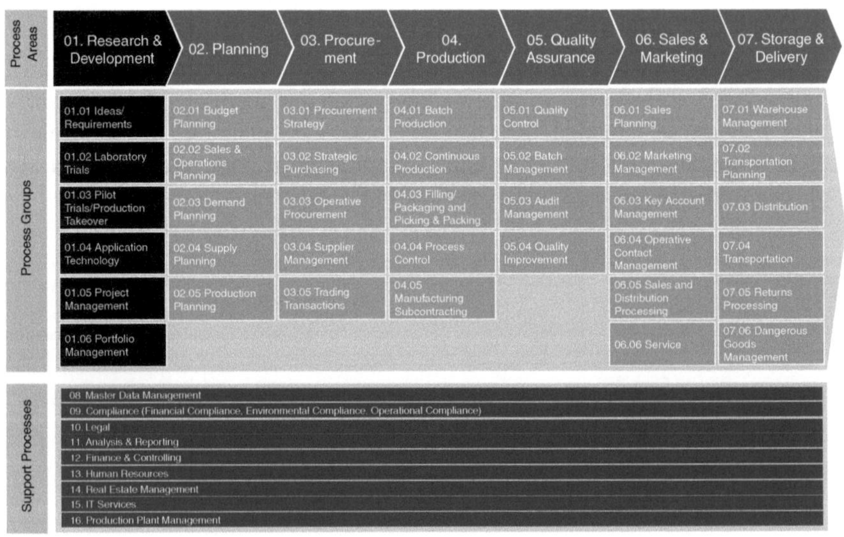

Fig. 3.1 Positioning of the process area of "Research and Development" in the business process map for the chemical industry

approach. The process groups of project management (01.05) and portfolio management (01.06) support the process area for its entire duration. Portfolio management addresses the challenges of bringing new products to market.

Due to functional integration, the process area is characterized by a number of functional interfaces to other process areas. The process group of pilot trials and production takeover overlaps with the process area of production (04) and the process group of portfolio management overlaps with the process area of sales and marketing (06). This process area also provides important information about customer requirements and competitor products for the process groups of ideas and requirements (01.01) and application technology (01.04). The process group of strategic purchasing (03.02) is also closely related to the process group of ideas and requirements (01.01) with regard to new and innovative raw materials.

In addition to process area integration within the company, there is a clear trend toward integration with external development partners, customers, suppliers, research institutes, and so on in terms of research or development cooperations.

In practice, the process area of research and development can vary much in its degree of application orientation. Therefore, a distinction is made between fundamental research and applied product/process development depending on where the emphasis lies. While the boundaries are fluid, fundamental research is more commonly conducted within the scope of research cooperations with external research institutes, whereas applied product and process development aims at producing a financial return and is carried out within the company. Cooperations have become much more significant in the last 20 years in light of the multiple benefits they bring, for instance cost reduction, greater research potential, and access to expert knowledge.

The process area is supported by the secondary value chain processes 8–16. For instance, the compliance process (09) comprises the processes of the REACH regulation on chemicals, and the legal process (10) covers all the processes used to protect, manage, and utilize a company's intellectual property. In the chemical industry, relevant legal provisions include industrial property rights, in particular patents and utility models, and the nondisclosure of company secrets. The value chain process of analysis and evaluations (11) covers the examination, interpretation and archiving of the trial results from laboratories, pilot plants, production, and application technology of the process groups 01.02–01.04.

The success of the process area of research and development is determined primarily by three strategic success factors, namely time, quality, and cost. Crucial factors for achieving a competitive advantage are a company's ability to reduce time-to-market and launch products as early as possible, make full use of patent terms and opportunities for market exploitation, and rapidly and flexibly respond to customer requirements with marketable products (Wildemann 1990). From a total quality management (TQM) perspective, quality as a success factor also involves the process area of research and development and leads to increased customer value and greater quality of the product or process being developed. A company can minimize the time of amortization of development costs and reach the break-even point by reducing time-to-profit. This increases the profitability of the development process and limits investment costs. Minimized production costs are also an important product policy factor, since they help a company achieve a competitive advantage in product costing.

Functional integration, mentioned previously, is an important success factor in the innovation and R&D process. Products should not be developed as part of an isolated process in the research and development department; instead, all relevant departments of a company must be involved in the process as early on as possible. This link to other process areas such as production, marketing, and purchasing ensures that all relevant influencing factors, requirements, and constraints associated with the development process can be identified early on and taken into account.

3.1.2 *Ideas and Requirements*

3.1.2.1 Process Overview and Characteristics

The basis of every successful innovation is a good idea. Innovation management is responsible for identifying potential internal and external sources of ideas, making use of these sources, and ensuring that ideas are exploited. This represents a major challenge for research-based companies, since less than 1 % of all ideas result in a successful product.

The process group of ideas and requirements comprises the business processes in the chemical industry that generate new ideas on the basis of particular requirements. The most promising ideas must be selected from all the ideas to emerge. The new idea triggers a new development project and the development of a new product. At some point in the course of its life cycle, every product passes into a phase of saturation in which margins begin to be eroded. This means that it is crucial to the success of the company to continuously add new, fast-growing and high-margin products to its product portfolio. Only in this way can the company retain a long-term competitive edge.

The main variants of the process group are principally product innovation and process innovation. Other variants include organizational innovation and social innovation (Fig. 3.2).

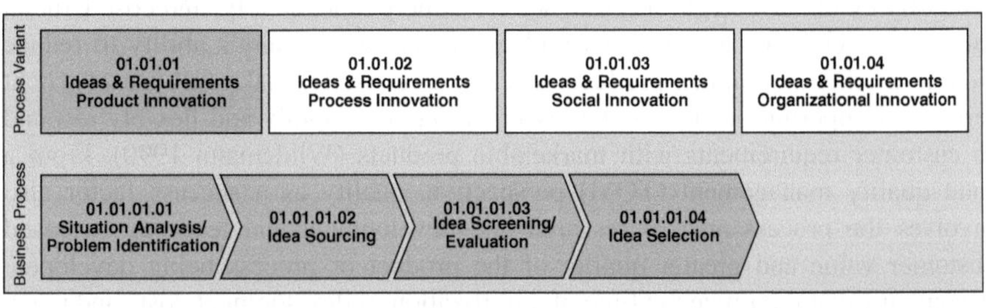

Fig. 3.2 Process variants and business processes of the process group "Ideas and Requirements"

This process group mainly concerns a company's research and development department, whereas in the innovation process, other internal departments as well as external suppliers, customers, and development partners may already be involved in this initial product development phase. A large number of process stakeholders and promoters (Witte 1973) can result in an extremely complex project structure.

The business processes of the process variants are divided into four phases based on the established phase models of the innovation process as defined by Geschka (1993), Thom (1980) and Witt (1996). Innovations can be initiated by both external and internal triggers. External triggers are the requirements of the market (market pull), which lead to an economical solution that meets customer requirements. In this problem-based search for innovation, the company generally has to compete directly with competitors, which exerts considerable time pressure on product development. Alternatively, new ideas can be generated technology-driven by internal triggers (technology push). Market pressure is not an issue in this case and time can be taken to develop the product carefully and prepare the market launch. However, there is a risk of ignoring market requirements and customer demands, which is why internally generated ideas should always be aligned with actual market requirements (Corsten et al. 2006).

The process group begins with a systematic analysis of the situation and the problem. The initial situation should be described and assessed as accurately as possible. By analyzing the difference between the as-is and target status, the company can gain valuable knowledge of the problem and derive possible solutions.

The analysis of a company's current product development situation is guided by strategic goals (for example, corporate strategy, product strategy, and marketing strategy), financial goals (for example, target revenue, returns, and markets), development-specific requirements (for example, properties of existing products, operational knowledge, industrial property rights, and technical infrastructure), and other requirements (capacity utilization, willingness to invest, personnel capacities).

Based on market and product related needs for actions, resulting out of analysis of problems, ideas can be generated in the following business process.

The business process of ideas sourcing comprises all methods and process steps required to identify potential internal and external sources of ideas, make use of these sources, and ensure that ideas are exploited. Fundamental significance lies in implementing a systematic and company-specific procedure for sourcing ideas because this is a crucial success factor for a company's innovativeness.

When sourcing new ideas, a distinction can always be made between gathering and generating ideas. When ideas are being gathered, all available information can be analyzed and evaluated, for example, market studies, information from suppliers and customers, publications, industrial property rights, and knowledge and experience within the company.

The process of generating ideas entails developing new ideas from scratch and demands a high level of creativity. Techniques and methods used to support this process include brainstorming, brainwriting, morphological analysis, synectics, and mind mapping, which are usually carried out in a process involving three phases (Macharzina 1995).

In practice, the lead user approach (Hippel 1986) has proven effective. With this approach, a company cooperates with a customer to jointly develop new product ideas. Ideas are gathered market-driven with the advantage that the product exactly meets customer demands and can be launched on the market by being sold to this customer as soon as development is complete.

In the business process of idea screening and evaluation, all ideas undergo initial screening in the form of a selection process based on search fields to identify potentially successful ideas. Only a manageable number of ideas make it into the subsequent evaluation phase. These ideas often take into account the limited personnel, financial and material resources available in research and development. In the evaluation phase, the product idea is assessed in terms of its technical feasibility, for example, by engaging experts from the relevant specialist departments, and in terms of its commercial viability and cost effectiveness using scenario techniques. The aim of the evaluation is to ensure that innovations are as successful as possible in order to minimize the risk of failure. A wide range of criteria and methods are used in the evaluation (Pleschak and Sabisch 1996; Schlicksupp 1988), all of which must be adapted to suit the particular situation of the company.

In the final business process, idea selection, only the most promising ideas of all those evaluated are selected to be pursued in the following process groups within the process area of research and development and finally launched on the market.

3.1.2.2 Opportunities and Optimization Potential

Compared with routine processes, innovation processes are always associated with a high degree of uncertainty due to the newness of the products. This often makes it impossible to calculate anything more than the probability of success. Decisions on innovations are extremely complex and are made in multiple stages. Unforeseen problems make it difficult to predict the course and outcome of processes, and this leads to delays and budget overruns.

Changing requirements placed on the product being developed (for example, legal, quality, and chemical property requirements) and the resulting uncertainty of the innovation objectives present major hurdles when planning the innovation process.

It takes a high degree of creativity to come up with fundamentally new ideas that are not based on a variation of a known product. One of the greatest challenges in idea generation is to find a systematic and goal-based approach to initiating and realizing creativity; a factor that has proven difficult to manage.

Evaluating and subsequently selecting ideas often proves difficult in practice, since factors such as technical feasibility, particularly in chemical innovations, cannot be forecasted with certainty. This can result in incorrect evaluations and potentially successful ideas being ruled out too soon.

As part of total quality management (TQM), the business processes in the process group of ideas and requirements are also subject to the quality management standards of EN ISO 9000 et seq. In certain cases, industry-specific standards must also be met.

3.1.2.3 Success Factors and Key Performance Indicators

The process group comprises the following success factors:

- Organization

  Manageable hierarchy levels, communication and cooperation between departments that promote innovation

- Planning

  Full problem analysis, clear innovation strategy, systematic approach to generating/realizing ideas, well-timed market launch

- Personnel

  Willingness and ability to innovate, clear communication processes, high availability of knowledge within the company

- Efficient use of evaluation procedures
- Accurate appraisal of the market and customer demands

The key performance indicators are related to the problem analysis (for example, quality, completeness, granularity), ideas sourcing (for example, number of ideas per year or assignment of tasks), idea evaluation and selection (for example, quality of ideas, number of development projects resulting from ideas per year). There are also numerous indicators that describe the success of the innovation process as a whole. These are discussed in more detail in Sects. 3.1.6 and 3.1.7.

The process group of ideas and requirements primarily requires personnel resources in the area of R&D. Given the high degree of interdependence between R&D and production, sales and marketing, patenting, and strategic purchasing, the personnel resources in these departments must also be taken into account. Moreover, costs may arise for externally commissioned market research or consulting services.

3.1.3 Laboratory Trials

3.1.3.1 Process Overview and Characteristics

The process group of laboratory trials covers the processes required to conduct and evaluate trials. A scientific method is applied when conducting laboratory trials to achieve reliable causal information (cause and effect relationships). This approach gradually brings us to the problem we are seeking to solve from Sect. 3.1.2 so that we eventually find a solution in the form of a recipe or process parameters that meet all or at least as many as possible of the requirements set out in the specification.

In regards to its field of application, the process group of laboratory trials can be divided into four process variants. Focuses of them are (fundamental) research, technology development, preliminary development, and product and process development. The business processes in product and process development are described in our example (Fig. 3.3).

First, the idea and underlying problem are taken as the basis for generating suitable laboratory trials. Either a rational deductive approach is applied to existing knowledge, or experiences from previous trials designed to handle similar problems are drawn upon. Alternatively, in the case of extremely complex structure-effect relationships, very often statistical or iterative processes are applied to solve the problem (design of experiments, Taguchi methods) (Montgomery 2001).

The second business process involves planning the trials. Figure 3.4 depicts the RACI matrix with all process steps. The capacity and working times of individual employees and specific facilities and equipment must be taken into account. Depending on the properties and condition of the test facility, additional time must be added to the actual duration of the trial, for example to allow for cleaning, heating up, handling, and changeovers. For technically complex test facilities in particular, adequate time for repairs and maintenance should be factored in. In addition, it is essential that the required raw materials are available in sufficient quantities and quality. Otherwise they have to be supplied from internal stocks or ordered from external suppliers, in which case the ordinance on hazardous substances and occupational health and safety regulations must be adhered to as agreed with the department for EH&S (environment, health, and safety). This is especially relevant for new raw materials or processes that have not been used previously in the company (Fig. 3.4).

Ideally, the trial should run according to plan. The trial is conducted, documented, observed, and supervised by laboratory staff. Once it has been carried out successfully, the resulting trial product is usually finished off in a separate step (for example, drying, cleaning). Figure 3.5 provides a detailed breakdown of the business process into the process steps.

Next, the product is sent for analysis to verify whether the requirements defined in the specification have been met. These analytical examinations are usually undertaken by internal analytics or materials testing departments. Since these

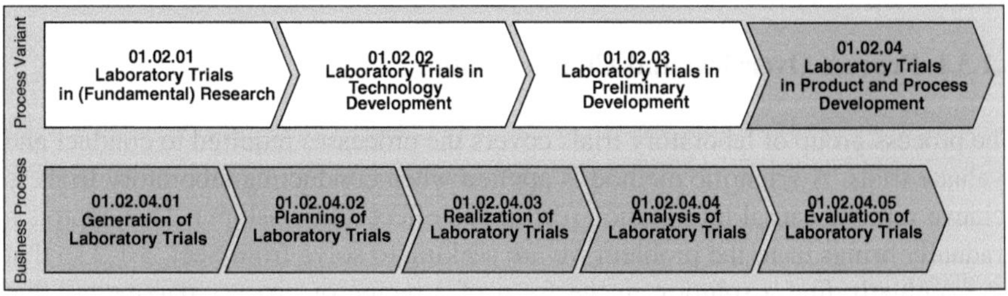

Fig. 3.3 Process variants and business processes of the process group "Laboratory Trials"

Business Processes
(Process flows, i.e. selecting & sequencing business processes from the Business Building Blocks of the Process Catalog)

L	Process ID	Process Area (Level 1)	Process Group (Level 2)	Process Variant (Level 3)	Business Process (Level 4)	Process Step (Level 5)	Input	Output	R&D Manager	Lab Manager / Project Lead	Lab Assistant	Strategic Purchaser	Analytics Clerk (internal or external)	EHS Clerk	Warehouse Clerk
							IPO Processing		Roles & Responsibilities						
L1	1	Product Development													
L2	1.2		Laboratory Trials												
L3	1.2.4			Laboratory Trials in Product & Process Development											
L4	1.2.4.1				Generation of Laboratory Trials										
L4	1.2.4.2				Planning of Laboratory Trials										
L5	1.2.4.2.1					Plan lab trials on trial facility	Process instructions, recipe	Planned lab trials		E	D				
L5	1.2.4.2.2					Order raw materials (internal, external)	Recipe, specification	Raw materials avalable	E	D	I				
L5	1.2.4.2.3					Organize lab equipment and auxiliaries	Process instructions	Lab equipment and auxiliaries available		E	D				B
L5	1.2.4.2.4					Create new raw materials (material number, informations about health & safety, product safety)	Recipe	Raw materials created	E	D	I	B		C	
L5	1.2.4.2.5					Plan preparation of new raw materials (e. g. destillation of solvents, dry of equipment)	Raw material, process instructions	Preparation of raw materials and equipment		E	D				
L5	1.2.4.2.6					Plan laboratory staff	Recipe, process instructions	Laboratory staff planned	E	D	I				
L5	1.2.4.2.7					Plan safety precautions	Recipe, material safety data sheet	Safety precautions ensured	E	D	D			B	
L5	1.2.4.2.8					Plan analysis / testing in analytics dept. or material testing	Recipe, specification	Internal tests scheduled	E	D	I		I B		
L5	1.2.4.2.9					Plan external analysis/testing	Recipe, specification	External tests ordered and scheduled	E	D	I		I B		

Fig. 3.4 Process steps of the "Planning of Laboratory Trials" business process

Business Processes
(Process flows, i.e. selecting & sequencing business processes from the Business Building Blocks of the Process Catalog)

IPO Processing | **Roles & Responsibilities**

L	Process ID	Process Area (Level 1)	Process Group (Level 2)	Process Variant (Level 3)	Business Process (Level 4)	Process Step (Level 5)	Input	Output	R&D Manager	Lab Manager / Project Lead	Lab Assistant	Strategic Purchaser	Analytics Clerk (internal or external)	EHS Clerk	Warehouse Clerk
L1	1	Product Development													
L2	1.2		Laboratory Trials												
L3	1.2.4			Laboratory Trials in Product & Process Development											
L4	1.2.4.1				Generation of Laboratory Trials										
L4	1.2.4.2				Planning of Laboratory Trials										
L4	1.2.4.3				Realization of Laboratory Trials										
L5	1.2.4.3.1					Transfer raw materials internally to lab	Raw material in warehouse	Raw materials in lab		E	D			C	D
L5	1.2.4.3.2					Discuss trial with lab assistants (schedule, preparation, specifics, safety, etc.)	Recipe, specification, process instructions	Lab assistants instructed		E D	D			C	
L5	1.2.4.3.3					Prepare raw materials and lab equipment (e.g. destillation of solvents, drying of equipment)	Recipe, process instructions	Raw materials and equipment prepared		E	D				
L5	1.2.4.3.4					Prepare trials (Educts, auxiliary material, trial / measurement / safety equipment, etc.)	Recipe, specification, process instructions	Prerequities for trial realization fulfilled		E	D				
L5	1.2.4.3.5					Perform trial	Recipe, specification, process instructions	Trial product, samples, measurement results		E	D			C	
L5	1.2.4.3.6					Draw samples	Lab trial	Samples		E	D				
L5	1.2.4.3.7					Label samples	Samples	Samples labelled		E	D				
L5	1.2.4.3.8					Transfer samples to analytics dept., quality control, material testing	Samples	Samples handed over to analytics		E	D		I		
L5	1.2.4.3.9					Comply with safety instructions	Process instructions, MSDS	Compliant with safety instructions	E	D	D			C	
L5	1.2.4.3.10					Finalize trial (stop trial, disassemble and clean equipment, Versuch beenden)	Running trial	Finished trial		E	D				
L5	1.2.4.3.11					Transfer raw materials internally to stock	Raw materials in lab	Raw materials stocked		E	D				I
L5	1.2.4.3.12					Document lab trials in lab journal	Observations, measurement results	Lab trials and results documented		E D	D				

Fig. 3.5 Process steps in the "Realization of Laboratory Trials" business process

departments often carry out analysis orders for other areas of the company, it is important to schedule those orders accordingly. In addition to these examinations, it is also common for trial parameters to be measured during the trial (for example, temperature and pressure).

In the final business process, the completed analyses and process parameter measurements are evaluated. The recipes and/or process parameters that satisfy the requirements profile are selected on the basis of these findings. It is often necessary to repeat the process group several times to finally achieve the optimum recipe.

The process group of laboratory trials is supported by the specifications and recipe management process, which is used to manage the developed and deployed recipes together with all relevant information (Fig. 3.6). Recipes are used at different levels of the company. They lay the foundation for company-wide decisions on investment as well as location-specific long-term planning and the implementation of manufacturing processes in the plant. Recipes are taken as the basis for product costing, which, in turn, provides important information about the positioning of products in the portfolio (see also Sect. 3.1.6).

All data on materials (pure substances, formulations, compounds, and residual substances), products, exposures, packaging, and waste is defined in the specification. This data also includes information pertaining to identification, material assignment, composition, listings, and properties. For example, if a new raw material is ordered for a trial, all of its characteristic physical and chemical data and any safety information, such as risk and safety phrases, are recorded in a specification. The data in the specification can be used to create product data sheets or safety data sheets so that this information can be made accessible to all areas that work with the material (including warehouse and laboratory staff).

Next, the recipe for manufacturing a product is created. This recipe contains the input substances for the reaction or compound, the relevant quantities, which are often calculated on the basis of a molar amount ratio or percentage ratio using the supplied formulas, and the product yield. The recipe also includes process steps, for instance phases for heating up and reaction times, which, depending on the type of reaction and plant, may be extremely complex. Finally, the specification defines what equipment is to be used to conduct the trial (for example, experimental facilities, reactor vessels, and processing machinery). In the course of product development, numerous trials are conducted on different recipes, meaning that recipes are developed and optimized in several steps.

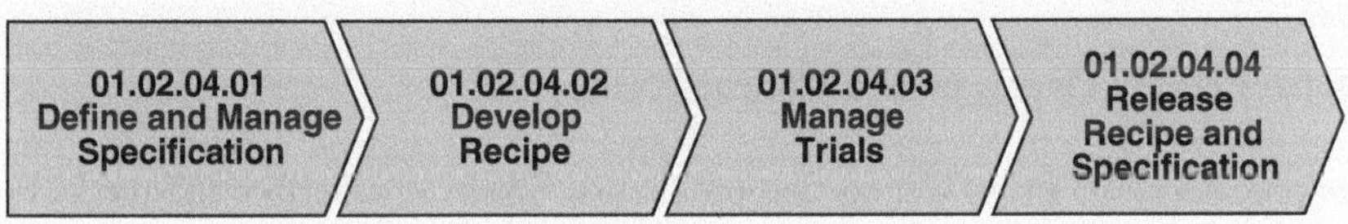

Fig. 3.6 Parallel business processes of the process group "Laboratory trials"

3.1.3.2 Opportunities and Optimization Potential

When creating laboratory trials, there is always an effort to keep the number of trials, and thereby costs, to a minimum. Statistical methods for conducting trials have therefore become very important when dealing with extremely complex problems with a large number of target factors in particular.

Optimizing planning times has a direct impact on the duration of product development and time-to-market. A particular challenge is to make the best possible use of all required capacities. There is a real risk of planning delays and capacity bottlenecks, especially if the frequency of trials fluctuates greatly and if unforeseen events should arise, for instance equipment failure.

3.1.3.3 Success Factors and Key Performance Indicators

Success factors for the process group of laboratory trials are the required time and costs associated with the entire process (time-to-market) and each of the business processes, for example, from scheduling the trial to obtaining the results of analyses, the time between scheduling and conducting a trial, or the time required to conduct a trial and carry out analyses. The overall costs of developing a suitable recipe within a project are also relevant, including the transfer to the production scale. Indicators that describe the productivity and efficiency of research and development, such as the average number of trials required to develop a general recipe, also provide insight.

Quantity structures cover tangible assets (such as technical changeovers of machinery and plants), consumable goods (such as raw materials), staff capacities in research and development and other departments (analytics, materials testing), investments in new plants or equipment, and special analyses commissioned externally.

The process group is conducted mainly in the research and development department. It also has an influence on other departments, however, whose recipes serve as a basis for calculations, for instance production, purchasing, controlling, and EH&S.

3.1.4 Pilot Trials and Production Takeover

3.1.4.1 Process Overview and Characteristics

The process group of pilot trials and production takeover describes the process of transferring a product or its recipe and manufacturing methods from the laboratory to the production scale. While the laboratory tests provide a first direction on how production should be executed, it is necessary to first develop the skills needed to operate the plants and facilities and build up knowledge of the manufacturing processes. The duration of the process group should be as short as possible to minimize time-to-market and thereby stay ahead of the competition. After successful production takeover, the product can be produced in salable quantities and quality. Samples can be issued and the product can be sold to customers. Some of the business processes of this process group are derived from the process area of "production".

The process group of pilot trials and production takeover is divided into three process variants: pilot trials in pilot plants, pilot trials in production, and production takeover (Fig. 1.19). In turn, each of these process variants can be divided into a number of business processes. The five business processes of the first process variant, "pilot trials in pilot plants", are presented here as an example (Fig. 3.7).

In the first business process, suitable pilot trials are generated by scaling up the recipe and process parameters from the laboratory scale to the pilot plant scale and then to the production scale. The recipe and in particular the process parameters that proved optimal in the laboratory often have to be adjusted when they are scaled up to consider the proportions of the new scale, for example, in a reactor vessel.

Next, the pilot trials are scheduled in the pilot plant. Whereas the pilot plant represents a separate department with independent planning procedures, trials in production must be planned using the normal production planning procedures just like any other standard production order. In both cases, any special preparatory measures must be taken into account, for example, plant changeover activities or the use of special raw materials. Unforeseen events should also be accounted for by including time buffers in the schedule. In most cases, a series of several trials is planned, each with varying process parameters.

The trials in the pilot plant are conducted by specially trained pilot plant operators who have expert knowledge of the technical aspects and challenges of pilot runs and are able to act accordingly. During a trial, all key process parameters are recorded and samples are drawn. Either during or after the trial, these samples are examined in an analytical laboratory or by the materials testing department. In the case of non-standard examinations, it may be necessary to commission analyses at external laboratories. Unforeseeable events such as longer mixing or

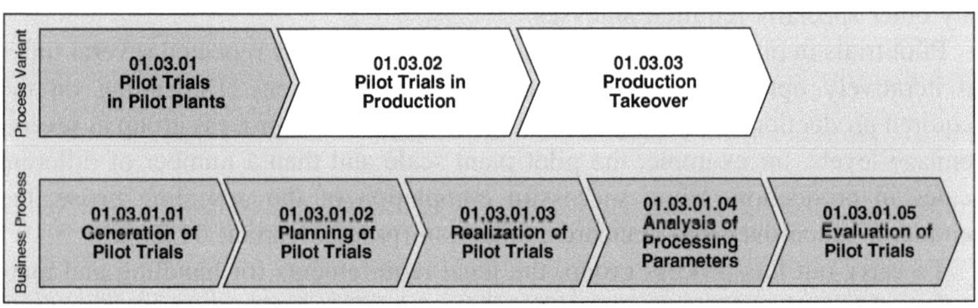

Fig. 3.7 Process variants and business processes of the process group "Pilot Trials and Production Takeover"

heating times can delay or compromise the pilot trial and require a certain degree of flexibility.

In the final business process, the pilot trial is evaluated on the basis of the results of the analysis to help identify measures to optimize the trial parameters and conditions.

As an output of the pilot trials, sample quantities of the product can be approved for initial customer samples. These product batches are usually marked with special (pilot) product names so that the customer can identify them as preliminary pilot material whose quality does not yet match that of the end product. This information for the customer is usually provided by quality management, for example, by including a relevant note on the product data sheet or certificate.

After the trial product in process variant 01.03.01 has been successfully transferred to the trial plant scale, regular production trials are scheduled (process variant 01.03.02). Unlike regular production planning, trials are scheduled not on the basis of customer demand or warehouse capacities, but by the project manager in the research and development department in consultation with the production planning department. When carrying out planning, available capacity must be found during regular production runs, for example, between two production orders, so that delivery deadlines are not affected.

Due to the newness of the product, its recipe, and its process parameters, it is in contrast to standard production often necessary to schedule unusual processes in good time, for example, to account for the use of raw materials in unusual containers, plant changeovers, or special reprocessing procedures. Additional staff from the company's technical service departments, for example, plant engineering, may be needed to help alter or adapt the technical infrastructure.

The pilot trials are conducted in production in accordance with standard production processes. In certain circumstances, however, more staff may be needed than on a standard shift to ensure the production trial is supported in every way possible. Product developers and process engineers support production personnel in an advisory role.

After production has been completed successfully, the product is usually analyzed by the quality assurance department within the scope of standard quality inspections to gather statistical process control data as soon as possible. The company's analytics department can be assigned the task of manually performing any other specially required analyses.

Pilot trials in pilot plants and in production are generally repeated several times to iteratively optimize process parameters and conditions. Depending on the required production scale, the product is piloted within the process group at several tonnage levels, for example, the pilot plant scale and then a number of different scales in production. Upon successful completion of the upscaling phase, the product is taken over into standard production (process variant 01.03.03).

To carry out this process group, the legal requirements for handling and marketing chemical substances must be observed. Chemicals must be registered (REACH regulation on chemicals) and industrial health and safety standards must be met. Depending on the segment of industry and product category, additional regulations must be followed, for example, the ordinance on hazardous substances and the chemicals prohibition ordinance.

The process group of pilot trials and production takeover is also supported by the specifications and recipe management process. The transfer of the recipe and specification between the different process scales, for example, from the pilot scale to the production scale, is supported and controlled by release processes to ensure the transition takes place as smoothly as possible. All relevant company departments must agree to the release. This primarily concerns research and development, production, quality management, application technology, controlling, purchasing, sales and marketing, and EH&S. Recipes are also often released in stages for different countries or regions, for example, a recipe is first launched in the company's development location and, if it achieves market success, is then released for other locations in a second phase.

This is followed by the release of the general recipe used by production to manufacture the salable product. The specification is also released and issued to the customer upon delivery as part of quality management activities. The company has a major responsibility toward the customer when the product is first marketed, which is why quality management must carefully check all of the data in the specification.

3.1.4.2 Opportunities and Optimization Potential

The production introduction stage is always accompanied by a unique and completely new set of challenges. The pilot phase for a new product is therefore highly likely to differ from standard production processes, and this necessitates a certain level of flexibility so that standardized processes can be adapted accordingly. Time buffers should be included at the planning stage because unforeseen events during the trial can cause time delays and hamper regular production operations. Before the pilot trial begins, the planned process steps should be agreed upon with all persons and departments involved so that problems can be identified and dealt with swiftly. The availability of personnel is also a key success factor when conducting trials. All knowledge carriers from R&D, process development, and production should be present or on-call during the trial. This requires a certain amount of coordination in advance, especially if trials are to take place over long overnight periods or across shifts. Standard production activities must be halted while pilot trials are conducted on production plants. This requires sufficient available capacity to prevent bottlenecks from affecting the production of standard products.

3.1.4.3 Success Factors and Key Performance Indicators

Success factors for the process group of pilot trials and production takeover are the required time and cost associated with the entire process (time-to-market) and each of the business processes, for example, from scheduling the trial to obtaining the results of analyses, the time between scheduling and conducting a trial, or the time required to conduct a pilot trial and carry out analyses. In addition, the number of pilot trials and costs associated with introducing a product into production are also relevant factors.

Quantity structures cover tangible assets (such as technical changeovers of machinery and plants), consumable goods (such as raw materials), staff capacities (primarily in the research and development, pilot plant, and production departments), and secondary technical service personnel (in the metalworking, electrical, and plant engineering departments). The company may also have to invest in new plants or equipment or commission special external analyses.

The process group is carried out mainly in the pilot plant and production departments and managed to a significant extent by the research and development and process engineering teams.

3.1.5 Application Technology

3.1.5.1 Process Overview and Characteristics

The process group of application technology describes the task of assigning and optimizing a product for a specific customer application. The product may be a standard product or a new development aimed at replacing another existing product that the customer uses. The first step in the process is to define the customer requirements and transform them into a requirement specification. The product is then tailored to the customer application by producing samples and performing measurements and tests. These application technology tests can be carried out either directly on-site at the customer or in the manufacturer's application technology plant. In the latter case, the equipment used must match the production conditions at the customer site as closely as possible, such as reactor vessels or processing machinery.

The process is extremely consultative in nature, since the producer—who possesses considerable technical expertise and experience—is able to offer advice and recommendations to help the customer introduce the new product. Application technology represents the interface between the product and technology on the one hand, and the market or customer on the other, which means it plays a key part in new product or process launches.

In the case of newly developed products in particular, application technology provides valuable indications as to the potential of different customer applications as well as any difficulties that may be encountered.

The process group of application technology consists of a process variant that can be divided into four business processes (Fig. 3.8).

In the first business process, the customer requirements are compiled and recorded in a requirement specifications document. This requirement specification describes the immediate requirements of the customer in respect of the ordered product. Within the framework of a statement of work and the corresponding

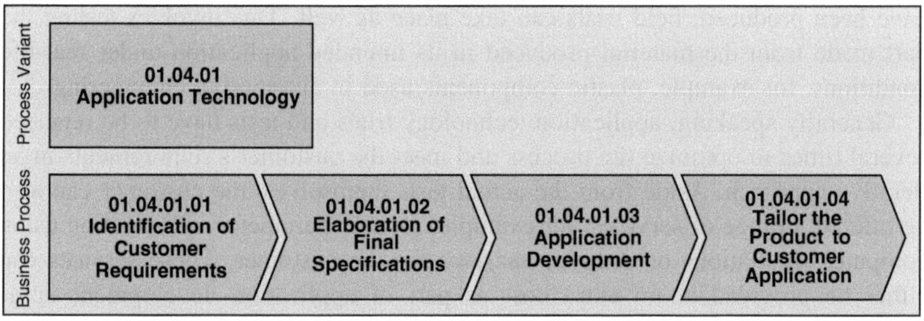

Fig. 3.8 Process variant and business processes of the process group “Application Technology”

formal acceptance process, requirement specifications provide details of the verifiable goods and services. Requirement specifications typically include details of the initial situation and objectives, product deployment, functional requirements (for example, chemical, physical, and mechanical properties), non-functional requirements (for example, price, efficiency, and lifespan), scope of supply, and acceptance criteria. Requirement specifications are compiled on the basis of intensive dialogues between the product manufacturer and the customer. The customer is required to describe the respective application in as much detail as possible with regard to the process, parameters, special technical features, and any problems to be anticipated. In many cases, the application is not completely new, but the customer’s aim is to optimize an existing application with a different product, for example, by reducing costs or improving the technical characteristics.

In the second business process, the requirements defined in the specifications are assigned to one or more services detailed in the technical specifications. The technical specifications contain the realization plans derived from the customer requirements. In practice, a number of different terms are used synonymously to describe “requirement specifications” and “technical specifications”, which can lead to misunderstandings.

In the third business process, application technology trials, examinations, and tests are carried out to optimize the product for the required application from a procedural point of view. To this end, samples are produced in a test run, for example, a compound with a new additive or a component part made from plastic. These samples must possess the properties defined in the specifications. If it is not possible to produce a sample for a particular material used in the process, certain characteristic process parameters are measured. In the first instance, the tests are carried out in the manufacturer’s application technology laboratory or plant under conditions that reflect those of the customer as closely as possible. For example, plants of similar dimensions featuring comparable technology are employed and the same raw materials and process parameters are used.

If these trials have positive outcomes, they are repeated in the fourth business process, this time on the customer’s equipment. If the customer process is technically too complex or too unique to be simulated at the manufacturer’s site, these trials can also be conducted in the very first step. If samples of component parts have been produced, field trials can take place as well. This involves testing the part made from the material produced in its intended application under real-life conditions, for example, plastic components used in automotive engineering.

Generally speaking, application technology trials and tests have to be repeated several times to optimize the process and meet the customer's requirements in an iterative approach. Aside from the actual tests themselves, the customer can also be offered a range of services, for example, process parameter optimization using computer simulations or contract analyses for the customer. These services can either be provided at no extra cost as part of application development or as additional services subject to a charge.

Application technology trials and tests provide valuable information for the product manufacturer; this information pertains to possible opportunities for new application areas as well technical limitations. This knowledge should be passed on to the research and development department to enable the product to be further optimized in the next development cycle or to generate ideas for new products. This feedback process is a cornerstone of a market-driven, customer-oriented product development and innovation process. During the process group of application technology, however, only small changes if any at all should be made to the product itself. Otherwise, the result is additional, unplanned development work, which has a negative impact on the development costs and time-to-profit of the product under development. Any extra adjustments should be carefully managed by the product manager and the head of research and development.

After application development has taken place, the customer application can be supported and optimized as part of ongoing customer service.

3.1.5.2 Opportunities and Optimization Potential

The structure and content of requirement specifications may differ greatly depending on the field of application and the industry. Even in practice, a number of different terms are used synonymously to describe "requirement specifications" and "technical specifications". The fact that these terms are used so loosely and that there is a lack of separation between technical information and operational intentions often results in misunderstandings. Aside from the quality of application development, ensuring that all customer requirements are recorded accurately and fully in the requirement specifications has a key bearing on customer satisfaction.

Furthermore, the capacity of both manufacturer and customer equipment and machinery required to conduct application development trials is limited. Test runs must be planned in advance, particularly when they involve the customer's production equipment.

The number of trials or tests should be kept to a minimum to prevent soaring costs for the manufacturer and the customer.

Manufacturers often come up against competitor products. This means they must position themselves as quickly and clearly as possible and differentiate themselves from their competitors' products to close the contract.

3.1.5.3 Success Factors and Key Performance Indicators

Success factors for the process group of application technology are the associated time and cost of performing the process to successfully optimize a product for a customer application. Customer satisfaction is an important indicator of the quality of application development.

Quantity structures in the process group of application technology cover tangible assets (such as technical changeovers of machinery and plants), consumable goods (such as produced products, raw materials, and processing aids), staff capacities (primarily in the application technology department but also in the analytics, materials testing, R&D, and pilot plant departments), and equipment capacities in the application technology plant.

The process group is performed mainly in the application technology department and is supported by product development and sales and marketing.

3.1.6 Project Management

3.1.6.1 Process Overview and Characteristics

Project management in the process area of research and development is the process used to execute projects aimed at developing new products. It comprises all the methods and processes needed to achieve this goal. Project management is defined in a number of ways. The German Institute for Standardization (DIN 1987) and the Project Management Institute (PMI 2004) define the term as all managerial functions, organizational procedures, techniques, and resources connected with the successful completion of a project (DIN 69901).

The general principles of project management are also applied in the area of product development in the chemical industry. However, there are certain features that are specific to the process and the industry. Depending on the degree of the product and process change being sought, projects are categorized as further developments, next generation developments, and radical innovations (Specht et al. 2002).

Development projects are often executed within cooperations or knowledge networks established between the manufacturer and research institutes, universities, and other partners. The process must consider a high degree of communication and synchronization between stakeholders.

The process group of project management can be split into seven process variants. In practice, however, the boundaries between these variants are often blurred. In turn, the variants can be divided into five business processes (Fig. 3.9).

In the first business process, project definition, the development project is analyzed in respect of its goals, problems, and potential, and is approved by the project sponsor and any other parties involved. All of the requirements of a product to be developed are described by the client in requirement specifications.

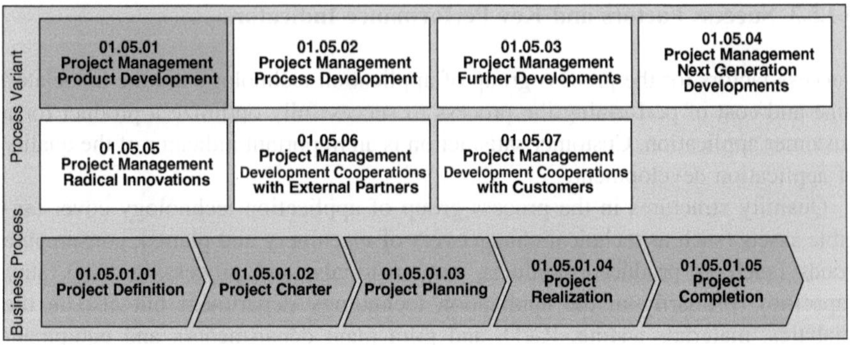

Fig. 3.9 Process variants and business processes of the process group "Project Management"

These are then converted into technical specifications, which describe the deliverables that the contractor must achieve to meet the requirements, for example, certain chemical or physical properties of the product being developed. Creating requirements and technical specifications can involve a significant workload because the process of defining and assessing product requirements often necessitates preliminary work such as feasibility studies, pretesting, and patent research on prior art. This work can be carried out as a separate preliminary project before the development project itself begins. The general organizational framework of the project is defined on the basis of the achievements and deliverables detailed in the specifications. It covers aspects such as expected personnel time and effort, project cost, business plans and business cases to investigate cost-effectiveness, assessment of opportunities and risks, constraints, project-specific assumptions, distinction from other projects, time frames, target project completion date, that is, market launch of the product, and key performance indicators. The project objective consists of a defined achievement, that is, requirements of the product being developed that compete with the required time, resources, and cost for the project. These three parameters form what is known as the "magic triangle", in which each change to a parameter made within the scope of change management must be assessed in terms of its impact on the other parameters. Since they focus more on fundamental exploratory work or application-oriented technological research, the objectives of research projects are not as clearly defined as those of development projects. The creativity of employees and the generation of new ideas cannot be planned accurately in advance, which raises the degree of uncertainty of project progress and objectives and increases the associated risk (Burghardt 2001).

Next, the project is recorded formally in a project charter. This involves entering the content from the project definition in a certain form. The project charter is then signed off using a workflow; this is done across all participating departments by all persons involved in or responsible for the product development process. This marks the approval and commencement of the project, whereupon the controlling department transfers the agreed budget to the development project manager.

In the next business process, project planning, the project management plan is created. It consists of the detailed project scope, schedule, planned costs, resource planning, quality planning, and project risks. Based on the technical specifications, the development project is structured from a technical (product structure), task-related (project structure), and business-based (account structure) point of view. Task packages are derived from the work breakdown structure and converted into work packages within work scheduling. Planning methods such as network plans support this process. Interim goals (referred to as milestones or quality gates) are defined in schedule planning so that the progress of the project can be assessed and managed. Typical milestones in the product development process include the successful development of the product in the laboratory, the takeover of the product to production, and the beginning of the go-to-market phase (Fig. 3.1, process groups 01.02, 01.03, and 01.06). Resource planning ensures the best possible use of personnel (laboratory assistants and technicians) and materials (laboratory and equipment capacity).

The following business process describes the realization of the project, which denotes the actual execution and monitoring of the development project. This phase focuses on the content defined in the project management plan and is characterized by two aspects: First, the project is executed according to the plan by coordinating employees and other resources and assigning them to the activities and processes defined in the project plan; second, the project is monitored. Comparisons between plan and actual are used to identify any deviations from the project plan early on so that any necessary actions to safeguard project objectives and overall progress can be taken. For this reason, project-related quality management is of great importance. Quality management is responsible for defining quality objectives and performing reviews and audits to ensure that the planned quality level of the project result is achieved. If no suitable measures can be identified, the project plan or other parameters must be adjusted as part of change management in response to events that have a bearing on the project. The main aspects that are monitored are deadlines, spending and costs, product development progress, and product quality.

The last business process, project completion, ensures that the project is completed properly. The developed product is accepted, which involves conducting an inspection to check whether the product meets all of the requirements set out in the requirements specifications. The results are presented and documented in a final report. A review is held to discuss all project phases and identify the lessons learned. As part of knowledge management activities, knowledge obtained in the course of the project is recorded in a central database for use in future projects. The final project analysis aims to identify the causes and possible solutions for deviations from deadlines, budgets, service standards, and quality characteristics. The final process step is project closure, which ends the project charter or contract, formally discharges the project manager, and concludes the project administratively.

Projects require a high degree of communication and information exchange between the individual project members with regard to goals, schedules, risks, and so on. Communication management is a parallel process that helps project members to create, gather, distribute, store, access, and use project information on time and in the right way. The parallel process has four business processes, namely communication planning, information management, reporting, and actual communication management between project members.

3.1.6.2 Opportunities and Optimization Potential

Project management errors can severely compromise the success of a project. Time and budget requirements may be underestimated and uncontrolled extensions to the project scope that are not covered by the change management process present the risk of budget and schedule overruns.

Long-running development projects in particular are susceptible to changing market demands, which can cause delays or even cast doubt over the entire project. This risk can be mitigated by consciously opting for a long preliminary project phase and keeping the main project phase as short as possible.

In product development in the chemical industry, there is always a risk that the requirements can be achieved only in part or not at all for reasons of technical feasibility.

From a personnel perspective, there is a risk of losing key knowledge carriers, who then have to be replaced as quickly as possible.

In contrast to the traditional approach of sequential processes, by introducing a degree of overlap and executing processes in parallel, the development time and therefore time-to-market of a new product can be reduced, the need for changes during the project can be prevented, and the coordination of each business process, for example, during the transition from development to production, can be improved (Cooper 1994).

Patent protection risks must also be taken into account in development projects. Competitors can raise objections to patents that have been submitted and thereby impede patent registration. If there is a lack of clarity over the patent situation at the outset of the project, it may emerge that the product can no longer be patented or has already been patented by a competitor and may no longer be marketed.

3.1.6.3 Success Factors and Key Performance Indicators

Key figures fulfill a number of purposes during projects. They are used as basic data to estimate work during project planning, as analysis and comparison data for project monitoring during realization, and as key values for final analysis upon project completion. They can be split into success factors and key performance indicators that relate to the product (for example, product properties to be met), development (for example, completeness of the requirement specifications, changes to the development process), the project (for example, project duration, budget, productivity, deviations from the plan, revenue losses as a result of deadline postponement, time-to-market, time-to-profit, and time-to-volume), and personnel (for example, employee turnover rates).

Similar to the product portfolio analysis described in Sect. 3.1.7, project portfolios can be analyzed in respect of cost-effectiveness and the probability of success. This makes it possible to prioritize promising projects and manage innovation.

Projects require a high degree of communication and information exchange between the individual project members with regard to goals, schedules, risks, and so on. Shortcomings can make it difficult to reach agreement, which, in turn, can cause delays and even result in projects being suspended.

Quantity structures in the process group of project management cover financial resources (project budget) and personnel capacity in research and development and a number of other departments (analytics, materials testing, pilot plant, and so on).

3.1.7 Portfolio Management

3.1.7.1 Process Overview and Characteristics

The process group of portfolio management describes all the processes for managing a company's product portfolio that involve selecting, further developing, and marketing products or groups of products. Portfolio management is important for companies since it can help them to safeguard or increase their sales in a changing world that consists primarily of customers, suppliers, and competitors.

Every product innovation passes through a product life cycle that describes the ideal–typical growth pattern, from development and market launch to market withdrawal. The life cycle is divided into four to six phases: development and launch, growth, maturity/saturation, and negative growth/degeneration. Each phase is characterized by specific effects on profit and cash flow (Nischlag et al. 1994). In practice, the negative growth/degeneration stage in particular is rarely reached, since the product is either withdrawn from the market beforehand or replaced by a new product with a stronger growth rate.

The established method for presenting a product portfolio based on the life cycle concept is the Boston Consulting Group's portfolio matrix (BCG Matrix), which can be used for both portfolio analysis and strategy determination (BCG 2008). Using this matrix, it is possible to evaluate strategically relevant business units on the basis of probability of profit (market growth) and current competitive position (relative market share). Similar models include McKinsey's Nine-Field Matrix and Arthur D. Little's ADL Matrix. Numerous other instruments, such as the ABC analysis (Hopfenbeck 2000), are also used to analyze the product portfolio.

The process group of portfolio management covers two process variants focusing on project portfolios and product portfolios, the latter of which forms the subject of this section. The process variants can be divided into four business processes: analysis, planning, strategic alignment, and controlling of the product portfolio (Fig. 3.10).

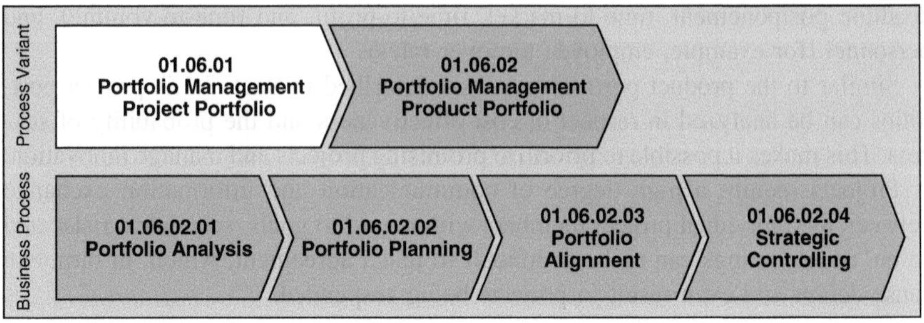

Fig. 3.10 Process variants and business processes of the process group "Portfolio Management"

First, the product portfolio is analyzed using methods such as the portfolio matrix. For the purpose of analysis, relevant factors with a bearing on the success of a strategic business unit are reduced to main variables. These factors relate to an internal value (such as relative market share) and an external value (such as market growth). The products are assigned to the different sections (question marks, stars, cash cows and dogs) and weighted in terms of their importance, for example, expressed in sales or profit contribution figures. After all products have been positioned, the result is a two-dimensional as-is portfolio of the company assessed according to strategic factors. The same approach can be taken to analyze the portfolio of all development projects, which may then be transformed into the product portfolio in the future (Zimmermann et al. 2003). This product portfolio provides information about the distribution of market and technology risks and the attractiveness of innovative products, technologies, and new markets for a company.

In the next business process, portfolio planning, recommendations for action are derived from the analysis in the form of generic strategies. Depending on the company's strategic alignment and market position (competitive strategy), it will aim to achieve a certain product portfolio weighting (Porter 1983). The classic tools of product policy are used for this purpose, namely innovation, variation, differentiation, diversification, and elimination of products. For example, a chemical company offering research-intensive products must continuously launch new, high-margin growth products to achieve lasting success and maintain a high share of stars and cash cows in the future. The company must take into account competitive strategies of competitors in its own strategic planning, since its competitors' market share has an impact on its own share.

In the next business process, portfolio alignment, the planned changes to the product portfolio are implemented operationally, that is, measures to attain the target portfolio are initiated. These measures are largely dictated by the specific situation of the company. However, they are often aimed at increasing the number of products developed and accelerating time-to-profit, that is, converting question marks into stars. Newly developed products should contribute to revenue as soon as possible and pass the break-even point.

Possible strategies for the individual quadrants include expanding products with high market growth and market share (stars) in the product portfolio to safeguard or boost the company's competitive edge in the long term. The cash cow achieved in this way must be reinvested and a willingness to make additional investments is required.

In the case of products with high market growth but a low market share (question marks), the market share must be improved by pursuing an aggressive investment policy funded by the cash cows. At the same time, if there is a predominance of question marks, the most promising products with the greatest chance of success should be selected.

In the case of products with slowed market growth and a high market share (cash cows), the position should maintained and strengthened, meaning that the market saturation phase in the product life cycle is extended, for example, through marketing campaigns. The surpluses made can be used to finance newer products (question marks and stars).

Products with low market growth and market share are retained as long as they continue to make a positive profit contribution. Otherwise, they should be withdrawn in the long term.

The alignment of the portfolio generally covers long-term developments and activities that extend over a long period. In addition, the strategy must be continuously adjusted and monitored in light of changes caused by internal and external company influences. This takes place in the final process step, strategic controlling, which encompasses both traditional feedback monitoring (for example, budget control) and strategic control at management level. The main task here is to initiate measures to adapt and correct upstream business processes (Hopfenbeck 2000). Implementation of strategic planning is also actively promoted (Schreyögg and Steinmann 1985). There are three different monitoring tasks: The accuracy of strategic key factors (assumptions) is monitored, planned progress is monitored, and strategic monitoring takes place at a general level to compensate for any aspects overlooked by the other two types of monitoring activities.

3.1.7.2 Opportunities and Optimization Potential

The portfolio management process group is extremely important for strategic planning considerations. However, it is important to remember that a single method of analysis, such as the portfolio matrix, only ever represents a simplified view of a complex situation. Therefore, all resulting information and measures should always be assessed in conjunction with other planning, analysis, and forecasting instruments.

A significant part of the analysis, such as the choice of influencing factors, tends to be subjective. Products are positioned differently depending on which strategic business unit is analyzed, which leads to a different set of measures. The chosen boundaries must be continuously reviewed and adapted to suit market conditions, especially when business areas undergo restructuring.

Due to technical advances on the manufacturer side and changing requirements on the customer side, the product portfolio is subject to considerable and unforeseeable fluctuation. Strategic controlling therefore has the important task of identifying these changing market conditions and managing the upstream business processes accordingly. Otherwise, the product portfolio would very quickly fail to meet the needs of the market.

3.1.7.3 Success Factors and Key Performance Indicators

The portfolio analysis is the starting point for the process group, making the quality of the product portfolio analysis (for example, selecting the right success factors) extremely important for subsequent business processes (Andrew et al. 2007).

Forecasting future market requirements and estimating the likely success of future products on the market often proves extremely difficult to achieve in practice, which is why the product portfolio has to be continuously adjusted and realigned in response to changing market conditions. As a result, crucial key performance indicators are the accuracy of forecasting future market conditions and the average time required to respond to market changes, that is, how long it takes to achieve the target portfolio after market changes have been identified. Other indicators include the planning accuracy and speed with which the individual business processes are executed.

The purpose of evaluation and controlling in the innovation process is to ensure that both technical and business goals are achieved. Measuring, managing, and assessing the success of innovations can be considered the main objectives of the evaluation process. The available controlling instruments range from traditional cost element, cost object, and cost center accounting and the use of value benefit analyses and budgeting methods to the newer techniques of target costing, activity-based costing, and life cycle costing (Vahs and Burmester 2005; Hauschild 2004).

Life cycle performance charts the success of the product life cycle. A typical key figure for the profitability of the product portfolio would be sales of products developed and launched in the last 5 years. The quality of the project portfolio is essential for assessing the success of development projects. It can be measured, for example, by the number of projects that achieve the planned objectives (projected vs. actual performance).

The size and structure of a company determines where portfolio management is positioned organizationally. For example, it can be incorporated as a staff position, in the line, within a matrix organization, or in different functional areas such as purchasing, production, and marketing.

3.2 Planning Processes as the Basis for Managing Companies

Carola Feind-Just and Klaus Schölzel

3.2.1 Positioning of the Process Area Planning in the Value Chain of Process Manufacturing Companies

The process area 'Planning' impacts all phases of a company's value chain and offers them the opportunity to shape their activities in a forward-looking way. The associated process groups provide a set of tools to interlink operational and strategic planning can be closely. In addition, the horizontal, value-added processes such as product development, procurement, production, and sales can be linked to each other as part of planning.

Thanks to advanced IT support, powerful tools are available today that allow planning to be perfectly aligned with both the strategies of the company and the objectives and constraints of the functional units,[1] and any perceptible deviations to be identified in real time.

In this respect, the process groups discussed in the following sections are central building blocks of an integrated company planning process that also provides a reliable information basis for supporting decision making at strategic, tactical and operational level.

Process industries benefit considerably when operations are both reliably planned and optimized with regard to corporate goals and technical constraints, since considerable savings potential exists in the aspects that often have to be addressed in these industries. Typical examples include the need to create campaigns, implement cost-intensive changeovers and cleanup procedures, and consider joint production. The basis for exploiting this potential lies in modeling individual planning processes along with their integrative relationships, target values, and constraints, as realistically as possible.

First of all, this requires a careful design of the planning processes to make sure that they are synchronized with the company's goals and constraints. A methodical approach like the one described in this book helps to accomplish this often complex task more efficiently.

The following sections use examples of process groups for budget planning, sales and operations planning (S&OP), demand planning, supply planning, and production planning to explain how such processes can be structured and organized.

---

[1] For example, sales, financial, and inventory objectives, and resource bottlenecks.

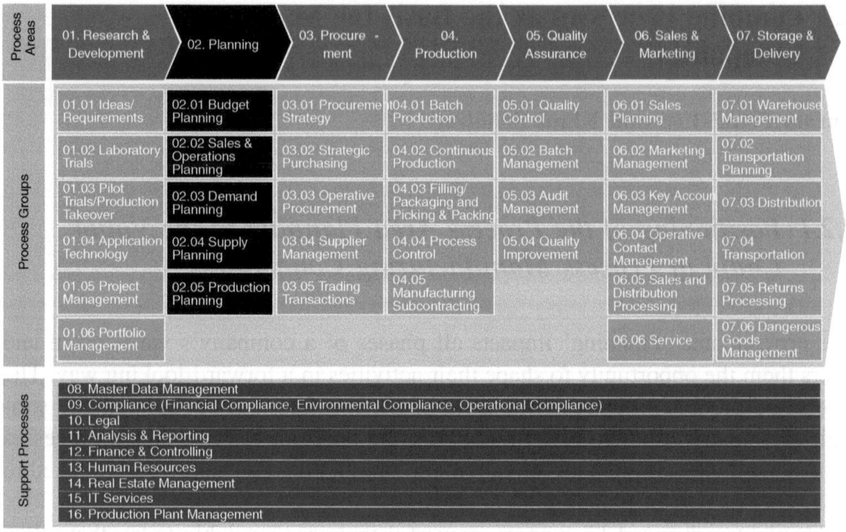

Fig. 3.11 positioning of the process group "Planning" in the business process map for the chemical industry

The Fig. 3.11 depicts how the process group 'Planning' fits into the business process map and how the process group is divided into individual business processes.

3.2.2 Budget Planning

3.2.2.1 Process Overview and Characteristics

Position in the Process Model

The process of budget planning is part of the process area of planning in the business process map for the chemical industry (Fig. 3.12). Budget planning consists of the following processes that are described in more detail below:

- Prepare budget planning.
- Plan sales volume.
- Plan production volume.
- Plan purchasing and transportation volume.
- Implement the results of budget planning.

Definition of Budget Planning

Budgeting can be seen as a process that comprises all the activities involved in creating, approving, implementing, and adjusting the budget. The starting point for

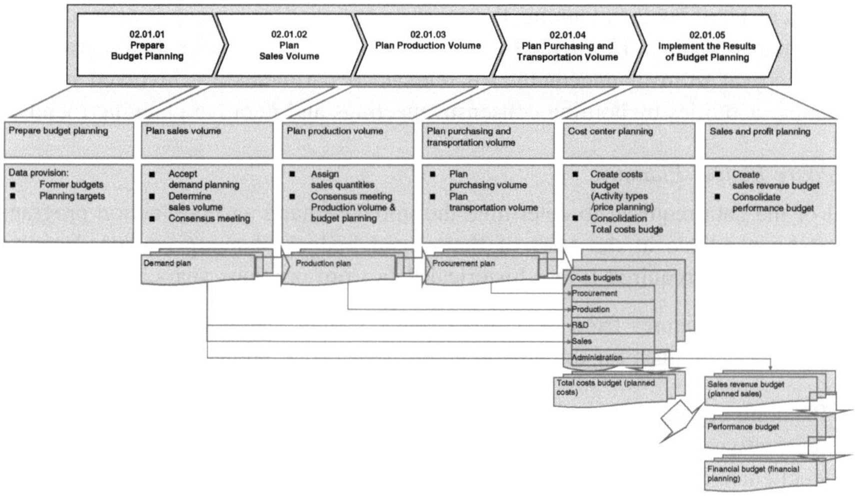

Fig. 3.12 Process flow for "Budget Planning"

annual budget planning is strategic business planning. It contains the goals and measures being pursued that have to be incorporated into the budget as financial values (such as costs, revenues, and financial requirements). Only if planning documents of this type are not available budgetary requirements have to be developed to define the broad framework for individual budgets.

Budget planning is an annual, medium-term planning activity for defining the budgetary requirements of the next planning period in the company. Cost budgets and sales revenue budgets are drawn up for all operational processes. The costs and demand planned for the company are consolidated in the performance budget.

Budget planning is part of the annual company planning round and usually takes place between 2 and 5 months before the new financial year begins. Responsibility for this process is assumed, to a large extent, by the controlling department, which involves all the areas and departments relevant to the process.

Objective of Budget Planning

The main objective of budget planning is to integrate strategic business planning (sales, profits, investments) and operational logistical planning, which takes place during the year. The result is a plan that harmonizes annual sales forecasts with strategic business planning. Budget planning is based on a continuous planning approach within the organization and is used to define future business objectives.

- Integration of the long-term planning view between quantities and costs.
- Agreed planning between sales (sales figures) and management.
- Basis for calculating internal cost rates and manufacturing costs.
- Evaluation standard for key figures in the following year.
- Controlling of parts of the company.

As a result of budget planning, the subsequent period's planning is defined in the performance budget. The agreed planning result is reached after final agreement and approval from management. All relevant departments are involved in joint planning activities by holding consensus meetings and iterative planning rounds.

Prepare Budget Planning

All of the data required to determine the initial demand and production program must be available at the start of the annual budget planning rounds. Version management is required to use historical data from previous years, such as:

- Comparison figures from the current year's budget planning.
- Existing guidelines for the new planning year (price targets, sales targets).

Planning objectives can also be specified as percentage changes compared with the current year. It is essential that master data is adjusted to account for planned product changes or new products to be included in plans. All datasets required for the process have to be checked for consistency and quality before being released.

Plan Sales Volume

Demand planning incorporates both sales and marketing planning and involves defining target annual sales quantities and promotions. The basis for budget planning is the demand plan, which defines the quantities to be sold on the market during the planning period. The demand plan is usually created by the sales department, which then passes the results to the production department so that it can plan capacities and activities in line with the planned sales quantities.

Historical data is uploaded to a demand planning system. For the most part, data from the previous year is used. The data can be propagated to future periods with seasonal fluctuations. The demand plan can be calculated using mathematical methods based on this data. Target sales must be calculated for each calendar month of the planning year. This allows the budget quantity to be used as a benchmark for sales quantities achieved in the past. The target annual sales figure must be broken down to the individual months of the budget year.

The objective is to draw up a demand plan that will be approved by management as a basis for further planning steps. Sales and marketing must be carefully coordinated to arrive at a final, unlimited demand plan that can be used to plan the production volume. Sales volumes from other areas of the company may prove useful here.

Plan Production Volume

The production plan is drawn up on the basis of the demand plan and specifies the quantities of raw, auxiliary, and operating materials required. The activity requirements determined in the production plan are communicated to the cost centers, which must then make these activity quantities available. The managers of these cost centers plan the costs that will be incurred on the basis of planned capacities and activities.

To define the production plan, the agreed sales volume must be distributed across different production processes and sources of supply. The purpose of supply network planning is to define where and when the sales quantities will be produced or sourced. The sales volumes must be assigned proportionally to the distribution and production plants because the demand plan only contains target quantities. As in operational planning, the sales quantities defined for the planning year are assigned to the respective locations. Next, material requirements planning is carried out for the production volume, which includes calculating capacity requirements in the supply network. All of the requirements in the supply network are determined for the planning year by planning the staging of materials. The process is similar to the operational process of supply network planning, but in this case the results are merely simulated.

A consensus meeting for the calculated production volume is necessary to reach an agreement among all plants regarding how capacities are to be divided for the planning year. Any overabsorption or underabsorption of the sales volume is calculated and the demand plan is harmonized with the production plan. In the event of capacity overload or underload, the planned production quantities have to be redistributed in the supply network and the requirements adjusted according to available capacities. Measures to adjust capacities also have to be taken if an overload or underload situation cannot be rectified by means of internal distribution. Final sales and production plans are agreed at the consensus meeting on budget planning. Integration between demand planning and production planning is at the heart of this agreement. Management then has to decide if there is a conflict of objectives.

After financial budgeting and cost planning have been approved, the machine hour rates are calculated for the budget planning year on the basis of the planned production volumes.

Plan Purchasing and Transportation Volume

Planning the purchasing volume provides the annual requirement quantities for raw materials as a basis for negotiating contracts with suppliers. Supply network planning for procurement planning is based on a number of different sources of supply.

The objective is to define a binding procurement plan for the planning year, which is usually limited, however, to strategic raw materials with long procurement lead times or delivery times. The procurement quantities and the demand plan are the basis for determining transportation requirements. Transportation and procurement plans lay the foundation for budgeting in these areas of the company.

In the course of production volume planning, the requirements for all third party procured materials are also calculated. The same applies to services to be performed by subcontractors. This information provides an important basis for contract negotiations between purchasing and the suppliers. The calculated stock transfer requirements between company locations as well as deliveries to customers form the basis upon which the transport logistics department calculates the transportation volume. The transportation volume is required for negotiating with forwarding agents. Transport logistics evaluates the calculated transportation requirement quantities according to a range of criteria:

- Evaluation of the resulting stock transfer requirements and delivery requirements according to forwarding agents.
- Transportations in a certain region or transportation zone.
- Evaluation of the resulting stock transfer requirements and delivery requirements according to transportation deadlines.
- Transfer of evaluations to the transport logistics and purchasing departments.

Implement the Results of Budget Planning

The aim of this process is to manage the final handover of the performance budget determined for the planning year to all downstream planning processes. It is divided into the sub-processes of "cost center planning" and "sales and profit planning".

The purpose of cost center planning is to calculate planned costs, that is, define the planned figures for costs, activities, prices, and statistical key figures at cost center level for the planning period. Deviations from the plan can be identified by comparing actual events with planned events. Cost center planning is a prerequisite of standard costing. The key characteristic of standard costing is that it is used to plan values and quantities for certain time periods, independently of the actual values from previous periods. During cost center planning, the budget for each cost center is defined. First, all primary and secondary costs incurred by the cost centers are calculated. Primary costs are costs incurred through the use of goods and services sourced externally (from the procurement market). Secondary costs are cost types that represent the value of activities defined internally and partial activities performed within the scope of the flow of services within the company. Cost center planning consists of the following areas:

- Planning of activity quantities and/or prices.
- Planning of likely costs.
- Planning of statistical key figures that serve as a basis for calculating costs.
- Cost planning to calculate prices.

Cost center planning is mainly an iterative process that comes at the end of annual budget planning. Guidelines are sent to cost center managers, who devise the budget in several planning rounds. The financial and controlling department has overall responsibility within the company. After planning iteration and the consensus meeting, the final budgets are agreed upon with management and approved. These final budgets are the company's targets and plans for the forthcoming period. Together with demand planning, cost center planning is the basis for sales and profit planning. Cost center planning aggregates all the individual budgets into one total costs budget that consolidates all planned operating costs for the planning period.

Sales revenue planning involves creating a sales revenue budget. Sales revenue planning is a prerequisite of the company's financial planning. The planned company activities are consolidated in the sales revenue plan. All planned sales revenues from operational processes are totaled for the planning period. The final agreed demand plan is taken as the basis. All profit centers in the company are included in sales revenue planning and create the final sales revenue plan after a series of iterative planning rounds, as in cost center planning. This plan contains the value-based, planned annual sales revenue for each profit center. Top-down planning enables the sales revenue targets defined in demand planning and the planned sales prices to be used here. After budgets have been planned, the calculated volumes are multiplied by the planned prices. The cost budgets for each functional area are compared with the sales revenue budget and condensed into the profitability plan (performance budget). Revenues can be calculated on the basis of planned sales quantities and prices. Planned contribution margins can then be derived by comparing revenues with planned costs. The performance budget provides input for the following processes:

- Financial budgeting and liquidity planning in the company.
- Rolling demand planning.
- Rolling sales and operations planning.

3.2.2.2 Opportunities and Optimization Potential

Here we take a detailed look at opportunities and optimization potential within budget planning.

As more effective the budget planning process is as more the company quickly has the latest planned values at its disposal and can respond immediately with any necessary operational adjustments. Communication problems and drawn-out consultation rounds can be avoided and costs minimized by establishing a clearly structured process with well-defined responsibilities. Since integrating different areas of the company is a core element of budget planning, it is crucial that a workflow is in place for agreeing the final budget. Otherwise, risks may arise with regard to cost development and process efficiency, for example, as in the following cases:

- Budget is approved too late, which prevents the company from reacting to changes of plan.
- Final plans that have not been agreed upon by all parties give rise to conflicts, constant planning adjustments, all of which result in imprecise planning.
- Increased controlling costs (lack of efficiency).
- Increased follow-up costs due to corrective actions (personnel costs in the event of production changes).
- Increased prevention costs to safeguard the company against risks (cost of holding safety stock).

Planning accuracy describes the extent to which the actual values achieved differ from the original plans. The best time to assess the accuracy of annual budget planning is during the mid-year control period. The control period involves performing a target/actual comparison and a variance analysis of the individual budgets and the overall budget. All the required figures from operational business activities are obtained, documented, and compared with the planned figures. The variance analysis examines not only the target/actual variance but also the effect this has on overall performance. Causes of the variance and suggested corrective actions are also analyzed. If plans are shown to be extremely inaccurate, corrective actions must be taken during the control period to align developments with planned targets. Experience shows that the work associated with corrective actions is greater than the work required to define more accurate plans. Examples of costly corrective actions include changes in production (supply network planning) or sales volume (substitution of product groups). Improvements in planning accuracy can eliminate the need for buffers and safety stocks created to protect the company against the risk of planning errors.

Data must be complete, consistent, and reliable to ensure successful budget planning. An integrated system solution is the only way to manage a budget system that meets all requirements. All company areas implicated in the budget planning process must also be interconnected through the data basis. If datasets are not available at the same logical level, they are not comparable and therefore only of limited use for the process. A lack of data integration between company areas or poor version management complicate the process of budget planning, since additional process steps must be taken to create a solid raw data basis. If this cannot be achieved, the poor quality or shortage of raw data leads to an inaccurate final plan, which, in turn, results in countless changes with the drawbacks outlined here.

In relation to the company as a whole, budgeting represents a central coordination function since the individual plans have to be harmonized with each other within the budgeting process. This function has to be performed centrally to ensure effective planning and allow progress to be monitored within the company. By specifying precise target values (sales, costs, revenue, and so on) to be achieved within the next planning period, the individual budgets serve as benchmarks for measuring performance. In this sense, they perform a control function. Given that target budgets automatically attach certain expectations to the behavior of those affected by the budget, the budgeting process is also a means for managing behavior, for example, by binding decision makers to certain cost targets and sending them a clear signal as to the course of action. The starting point for the control period is usually the subsequent comparison between the budgeted target values and the actual values achieved.

3.2.2.3 Success Factors and Key Performance Indicators

There is no single calculative assessment basis for budget planning because the process incorporates several company areas and medium-term annual planning takes place at a rough level. The key figures considered here can be broken down into the following categories:

- Assessing the effectiveness of budget planning, since this process has to be completed within a one-year time frame.
- Assessing the accuracy of planned figures compared with actual results; in other words, the different final plans are compared with the actual quantities and values achieved (control period).
- Key performance indicators for the budget figures (planned costs) in Controlling. The budgets can also be assessed against other budgets or as part of the target/actual comparison using the respective key figure.
- Key performance indicators for planned logistics figures. The plans can also be assessed against other planned figures or as part of the target/actual comparison using the respective key figure.

Key Performance Indicators: Process

- Process costs—budgeting
  (Number of parties involved, length of meetings, reports).
- Process duration compared with previous year
  How quickly and effectively is the plan created?
- Number of parties involved.
- Number of planning iterations.
- Number of analyses and reports to be created.
- Number of open parties subject to approval.

Key Performance Indicators: Planning Accuracy

- Benchmark that is created to establish the accuracy of forecasts. The difference between the forecast amount and the actual amount that represents consumption in a certain period.
- Demand planning/sales revenue planning deviations
  Sales variance.
  Planned sales values in relation to actual sales values (for sales revenue in volume and value).
- Production plan deviations
  Planned values in relation to actual production values.
- Procurement plan deviations
  Planned values in relation to actual procurement values.
- Budget plan deviations
  Cost variance.
  Planned costs in relation to actual costs of individual budgets and aggregated at the level of the overall budget.

Key Performance Indicators of Controlling for the Plan Comparison or Target/Actual Comparison

- Contribution margin
  The contribution margin in cost and activity accounting is the difference between the revenues achieved (sales) and the variable costs. It is therefore the amount available to cover fixed costs.
- EVA (earned value analysis)
  Value of the services performed in a project.
- Result
  Operating profits (sales revenue—costs).
  Revenue from the standard business activities of the company minus costs and expenses.

Key Performance Indicators of Logistics for the Plan Comparison or Target/Actual Comparison

- Demand plan
  Definition of sales quantities for future periods.
- Comparison of different demand plans for different regions, similar product groups, and different times.
- Variance of the sales price per product or product group.
- Production plan
  Production target quantities for materials or product groups.
- Procurement plan
  Procurement target quantities for materials or product groups.
- Projected stock
  Forecast inventory in quantity and value.
- Target inventory level
  Inventory level that should be achieved through planning to facilitate smooth production and cover sporadic requirements.
- Capacity utilization
  Utilization with regard to production lines or plants (capacity overload and underload).
- Days of inventory.
- Defines how long the available stock will last in days assuming coverage of an average/estimated daily requirement.

3.2.3 Sales and Operations Planning

3.2.3.1 Process Overview and Characteristics

Current Situation and Objectives

Today, many companies still use *sales and operations planning* (S&OP) mainly for the purpose of assessing and ensuring the "feasibility" of their sales forecasts by matching resource requirements resulting from demand with their availability.

Although important conclusions about managing the company can be gained from this approach, focusing on this aspect only does not provide companies with answers to questions such as: Can sales and profitability targets be achieved with the current plans? How to identify appropriate options to solve known conflict situations and to assess them against the company strategy and other given targets or restrictions? Can the plan be executed within the defined budget?

In addition to the functions offered by traditional sales and operations planning, one of the main targets of the process group S&OP, as it is defined here, is to help answer questions like these. In this respect, it bridges the gap between the strategic and tactical or operational planning levels.

After providing a definition of S&OP, we will look at the opportunities and optimization potential that this process group is able to unlock and describe how it differs from other processes in the area of supply chain planning.

We will then focus on how S&OP sub-processes are structured (these sub-processes belong to the business process level of the process hierarchy defined in this book). When doing so, we will examine the following aspects in more detail:

- Integration of the S&OP business processes in the surrounding process landscape.
- The relevant roles and other organizational aspects of the processes.
- The process steps of each business process.
- Key figures and key performance indicators to quantify the quality of the results and the performance of the process.

Definition and Scope

According to Tom F. Wallace a concise definition of the S&OP process that addresses the key characteristics of the process can be made as follows:

Sales and operations planning is
a decision-making process
to balance demand and supply (at the volume level) and
to integrate financial and operating plans (Wallace 2005).

In practice S&OP often represents a rolling, multistage decision making process that helps companies create and define a feasible,[2] cross-functionally agreed,[3] unique[4] demand and supply plan.

The primary objective is to consolidate planned and expected demand and to ensure that demand can be supplied by manufactured or externally procured products in the medium-term to long-term planning horizon at *volume level.*[5]

A common trait of the different decision processes that take place within the scope of S&OP is the inclusion of the goals agreed in marketing, sales, and logistics as well as the aspiration to achieve the company's profitability targets.

In this sense, the process helps to harmonize the entire supply chain within the company's business units and facilitates a (not always particularly established) link between the strategic level and processes at execution level.

In the chemical and pharmaceutical industries as well as the consumer goods industry, the S&OP is a particularly effective tool for helping to identify critical situations and risks that may jeopardize company goals and for proposing appropriate options to respond to them at an early stage.

S&OP, as we define it in this book, explicitly excludes "neighboring" business processes such as financial planning, budget planning, annual planning, sales and marketing planning, demand planning, and production planning.

However, we do look at how S&OP interacts with these processes and how it uses their results to anticipate success as well as identifies opportunities and risks, thereby helping the company make necessary decisions.

Conversely, at the end of each S&OP cycle, the final result is integrated in the aforementioned processes with the aim of achieving a consistent planning view agreed upon by all areas of the company.

3.2.3.2 Opportunities and Optimization Potential

> Sales and Operations Planning has helped many companies give better customer service, lower their inventories, shorten customer lead times, stabilize production rates, work better with suppliers, give Top Management a real handle on the business, and build teamwork between Sales, Operations, Finance, and Product Development (Wallace 2005, p. 3).

The following is a list of typical success factors associated with implementing S&OP:

---

[2] A plan that is technically feasible using the resources of the company (which may be yet to be provided).

[3] Agreed upon between the functional areas like sales, marketing, product development, supply chain coordination, production, and business planning.

[4] All areas of the company refer to a *single* plan. The key concept is "*one set of numbers*".

[5] *Volume level* denotes an appropriate aggregated planning level that supports the aims of S&OP (examples include hierarchy elements like "product family" or "product group"). By contrast, there is the *mix level*, which represents the finished products at sales or stock keeping level. In most cases, it is not appropriate to carry out S&OP at mix level (Wallace 2005).

- There is *one* business plan. All sub-plans relate to this one business plan to give a *consistent* view of the different aspects of events within the company.
- Improved company-wide transparency and acceptance of plans.
- S&OP opens the window to enable looking at a company's medium-term and longer-term visions. A key characteristic of S&OP is its potential to cut down the number of "surprises" in a company by recognizing the warning signs early on.
- Specifically, this relates to foreseeing future capacity issues (such as over-utilization but also under-utilization of critical resources). This helps to significantly reduce the number of problems, which otherwise would occur in detailed planning and thus, could make this process a cumbersome exercise.
- Options for action can be assessed by visualizing relevant key performance indicators.
- Active involvement of management is routinely sought in the final step of the process for decisions that have to be taken from an overall company perspective.
- Improved cooperation between the operational units in the company.

In the following sections, we want to demonstrate how S&OP can be designed to help companies tap into the numerous potentials, this process provides.

3.2.3.3 Overview of S&OP Process Steps

S&OP is divided into the following business processes (Fig. 3.13):

The Demand Review

The objective of the demand review *business process* is to create a complete, consolidated view of the expected demand situation in the medium-term to long-term planning horizon. The result also accounts for actions driven by sales and marketing intended to shape demand helping to ensure sales and profit targets are met. The figures have already been harmonized with the targets set out in the business plan and financial plan.

The Supply Review

The main objective of the supply review *business process* is to compare the demand plan approved in the demand review with the capabilities of production, logistics, and procurement.

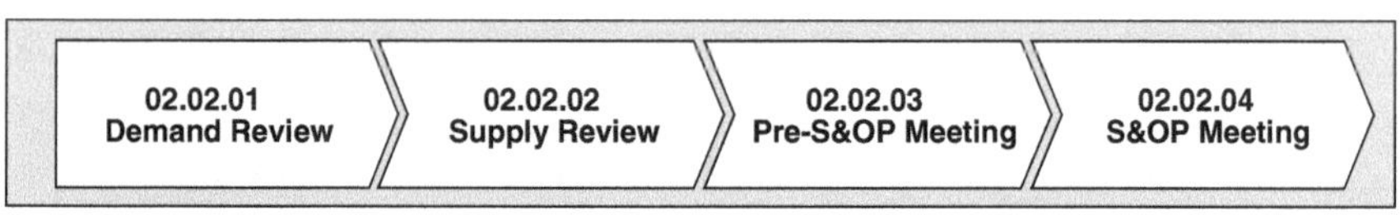

Fig. 3.13 Overview of S&OP business processes

The Pre-S&OP Meeting

The objective of the *pre-S&OP meeting* is the attempt to resolve any conflicts between demand and supply that were identified but could not be settled in the previous process steps. The meeting also clarifies any remaining open points to be decided in the S&OP meeting.

The S&OP Meeting

The S&OP meeting is the final decision-making meeting in the monthly S&OP cycle at senior management level. The main objective of the meeting is to assess the options that emerged from the previous process step from the perspective of the company as a whole[6] and then to reach final decisions.

3.2.3.4 The *Business* Processes of S&OP in Detail

In this section, we describe the S&OP process group in more detail and consider the following aspects in particular:

- Granularity of planning.
- Organizational aspects (roles, meeting organization).
- Process steps inside each of the business processes.
- Key Performance Indicators.

The business processes described in this section only include those, which fall under the specific scope of the S&OP process group in the narrower sense. We therefore do not examine here the up- and downstream processes or supporting processes in further detail.

Examples of this kind of neighboring business processes include financial planning, key account planning, demand planning, production and (rough-cut) capacity planning, etc. Details of these business processes can be found in other parts of this book or in the relevant literature.

S&OP Planning Levels

The efficiency and performance of the S&OP process group is strongly influenced by the choice of a suitable aggregation level at which planning takes place and how it is being visualized. In most cases, S&OP can be performed without compromising quality at this kind of chosen aggregation level (volume level). In addition, it is easier to focus on key aspects in the S&OP context on the basis of suitably aggregated planning data than at the detailed level (mix level) (Wallace 2005).

---

[6] In larger companies decisions are reached at the level of the business unit or responsible division.

The volume level recommended for the S&OP process group is usually represented by planning levels such as "product family", "product sub-family", and "product group". Here, product family is used as a generic term representing the actual aggregation levels at which S&OP is performed.

In general, sales-oriented product structures differ from production-oriented product structures. Therefore both types of planning hierarchies are relevant to S&OP depending on the focus of the respective business processes within the S&OP process group.

- Sales-Oriented Product Families

  The demand plan is usually created in S&OP on the basis of sales-oriented product families (PF), which structure the product portfolio according to sales and marketing considerations. Additional hierarchy levels usually appear above and below this level for visualization purposes.

- Production-Oriented Product Families

  For the purpose of rough-cut capacity planning (also referred to here as *rough-cut planning* for short), the "production product family" (PPF) is used. PPFs usually are defined in sync with the structure of critical resources being needed to make the product.
  As a result, when the aggregated demand plan is transferred to rough-cut planning, each PF has to be converted into one or more PPFs.
  This process step is required because the PF and PPF views rarely match in practice. A detailed explanation of this topic can be found in (Wallace 2005).
  The term "aggregated" in the context of master data primarily means "simplified"; in other words, structurally simplified product, routing, and resource master data can be used.[7] These structures can be simplified to such an extent that the demand and supply comparison process can be applied to *critical resources* without diminishing the value of conclusions on feasibility. As an example, such a *simplified* routing within a recipe would contain only those resources, which are regarded as being critical from an S&OP perspective.

- Exceptions

  It is worth noting that in certain production environments, particularly in the chemical industry, planning at aggregated product level does not always deliver a sufficiently precise picture as to the technical feasibility of the plan and the relevant financial key figures.[8] In such instances, it is necessary to support S&OP at *mix level* using more complex planning models, which, in light of the

---

[7] And should also be used to simplify the process.

[8] This proves difficult, for example, when production capacity utilization and operational efficiency depend to a major extent on the product mix (which may involve manufacturing co-products) and the sequence of the dispatched orders.

longer-term approach required for S&OP, is often associated with increased complexity.[9] The challenge here is to strike a balance.

In the section below we describe in more detail the business processes within the process group S&OP (see Sect. 3.2.3.3). For each of the business processes we will look at following aspects: purpose and objectives, organizational aspects, key information needed, process flow, key results of the business process.

Demand Review

The objective of the demand review process is to agree upon a complete, consolidated view of the expected demand situation in the medium-term to long-term planning horizon.[10] The result also accounts for actions driven by sales and marketing intended to shape demand to ensure the sales and profit targets are met.[11] The aim here is to harmonize the demand plan with the targets set out in the business plan and financial plan.

In this phase, the demand plan is still unconstrained. Possible constraints on implementing the demand plan may arise, for example, due to capacity bottlenecks or limited availability of a raw material or other resources in short supply.

- Roles

  The demand review process should involve every person who is in charge of assessing or influencing the different factors that have an impact on demand (see input information).
  The group of people involved usually covers a role from the list below:

  - Key account manager.
  - Sales manager.
  - Marketing manager.
  - Product manager.
  - Product portfolio coordinator.
  - Forecast analyst.
  - Financial planner/manager.
  - Supply chain manager.
  - S&OP process owner.

---

[9] Increased complexity may, for instance, result from the fact that master data for new product developments is not yet sufficiently complete to be used in a more detailed planning model. It is also often difficult to generate a reasonably reliable long-term sales forecast for these products at a detailed level.

[10] Depending on the planning scenario, the horizon is between 12 and 36 months.

[11] Engl.: *shaping of demand.*

- Input Information

  The updated demand plan constitutes the key input for S&OP. It is vital for making S&OP an effective tool if the final demand plan reflects the *total* anticipated demand in the entire S&OP horizon.
  Therefore, when preparing for the demand review meeting it is important to ensure that all information required to paint a *complete* picture of the demand situation is provided for each product family. Of particular importance is information about strategically significant market players, the go-to-market strategy of the company (or of the *division* or *business unit*), and historical sales figures along with identified trends in future demand. Specifically, this is data and information about customers, competitors, sales history, trends, pricing strategies, and sales forecasts for new product developments and products at the end of their life cycle.
  Information that is often not taken into consideration in operational demand planning is also required for the demand review within the S&OP process,[12] for example

  - Introduction of new products in the more distant future, even if operational master data do not yet exist for these products.
  - Development of potential new customers or market segments if this constitutes a long-term strategic goal.

  Possible market changes that are not yet tangible but that can be simulated within the scope of S&OP.[13] This allows companies to take proactive steps to prepare themselves for different possible developments.
  At this point, one might reasonably question how the aforementioned list of people could conceivably handle this huge number of tasks every month. After all, the range of tasks described generally involves extensive activities usually taking several weeks in the course of annual planning (budget creation).
  Upon closer inspection, however, the workload is lighter than it first appears. Since S&OP is a rolling process, an updated version can be created by incorporating just those events which are new or have changed since the last planning cycle.[14]
  The considerably more extensive process of rebuilding the entire plan from scratch, taking into account *all* relevant influencing factors and generally also new strategic targets, is conducted less frequently, usually once a year within the scope of annual planning and budget planning. In return, the rolling S&OP process carried out on a monthly basis helps making the annual planning process less time consuming and a much more efficient exercise.

---

[12] Due to the different horizon and often also for reasons of complexity.

[13] This will not, of course, feature in every monthly planning cycle, but S&OP is the right instrument for making simulations of this nature.

[14] This type of process can also be described as "*event-driven*".

- Process Flow

  The following section provides certain details of the process steps of the demand review business process. The process is broken down as follows (Fig. 3.14).

  After the changes from the previous month have been gathered together and checked for completeness, the data and information is being reviewed and consolidated. Based on the resulting collection of data, simulations and analyses of different scenarios[15] are carried out in preparation for the demand review meeting to describe how different business developments would impact demand and affect sales and budget figures. Finally, the different scenarios are evaluated in a face-to-face meeting, the demand review meeting, and the final demand plan is signed off and handed over to the next business process (the supply review process).

- Result

  The demand review business process delivers the following results:

– A demand plan providing a comprehensive, consolidated view across functional areas of the expected, unconstrained demand situation in the medium-term to long-term planning horizon.
– Simulations of different demand scenarios (for example, optimistic and pessimistic estimation of the forecast).
– Creation and assessment of associated company key figures and key performance indicators for each scenario.

Supply Review

The main objective of the supply review *business process* is to match the new version of the demand plan approved in the demand review with the capabilities of production, logistics, and procurement.

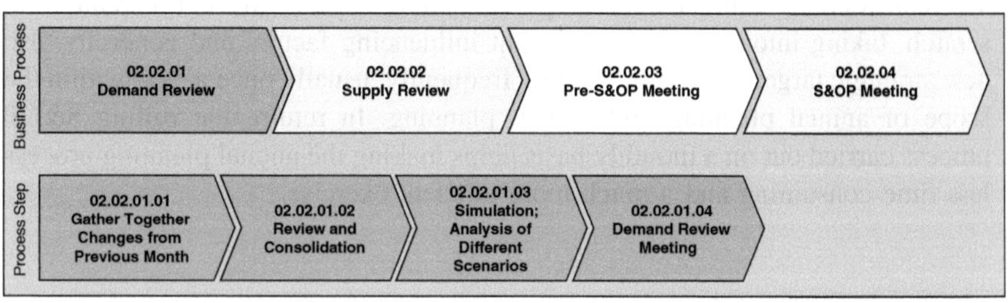

Fig. 3.14 Process steps of the demand review process

[15] For example, simulations of optimistic and pessimistic scenarios.

The challenge, therefore, lies in identifying issues when building a technically feasible supply plan and finding solutions that take into account the company's financial targets.

One example would be a situation in which the anticipated demand for products or services could not be covered by the available company resources or, conversely, demand would not adequately utilize available resources.

Issues and decisions that cannot be settled within the responsibility of the production and supply chain planners are passed on to the next process step.

As with demand planning, it is important to select the right aggregation level to ensure that the supply review is an efficient process.

- Roles

  The supply review process should involve every person who is in charge of building and assessing the supply plan.
  The group of people involved usually covers the following roles:

  - S&OP process owner.
  - Plant manager.
  - Production manager.
  - Production planner.
  - Product manager.
  - Engineering representative.
  - Supply chain manager.

- Input Information

  The updated approved demand plan constitutes the key input information for the supply review process.
  In addition to that a couple of master data and transactional data is required, ideally in an simplified version to streamline the process.
  This includes information about sales- and production-product families, recipes, routings or capacity requirements profiles, resources, capacity profiles and inventory information.

- Process Flow

  The following section provides some more details of the process steps of the supply review business process (Fig. 3.15).
  The first step is to convert the updated demand plan, which still follows a sales-oriented product family structure, into a demand plan, following a production-oriented product family structure (PPF).[16]
  For this demand plan a *rough-cut capacity planning* process is carried out. The underlying idea is that in the medium-term and long-term horizon, it is usually sufficient to demonstrate technical feasibility on the basis of aggregated master data and transactional data and restricted to critical resources.

[16] Details of PFs and PPFs can be found in Sect. 3.2.3.3, "S&OP Planning Levels".

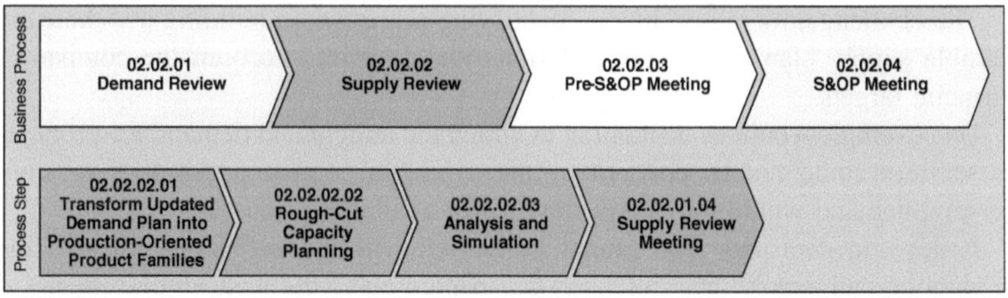

Fig. 3.15 Process steps of the supply review process

This process focuses on

- The evolution of inventory (in a make-to-stock scenario) or the order backlog (in a make-to-order scenario) as a measure of the attainable service level.
- The degree to which critical resources are utilized.
- Strategically important suppliers' abilities to deliver critical raw materials or components.

To evaluate the feasibility of the supply plan created based on the updated demand plan, it is adequate to examine the resources identified as critical since the technical feasibility of the plan in respect of these resources allows conclusions to be drawn on the feasibility of other resources not being regarded as critical.

Scenarios that cannot be simplified as described or whose rough-cut capacity planning would not be sufficiently precise have to be planned in detail, as is usual in operational production planning.

During the supply planning process as well, different scenarios and conflict resolution strategies are frequently executed in *simulation runs* (for example, in the event of capacity bottlenecks) to obtain a range of options for subsequent decision-making processes.

Supply plan simulations are typically used to answer the following types of question:

- What technically feasible alternatives can be identified to balance demand and supply?
- How do alternatives affect stock targets and service levels?
- How would alternatives affect the contribution margin?

To evaluate the different scenarios, the relevant key performance indicators are also determined for each specific scenario.

The business process concludes with the *supply review meeting*, in which solution approaches and identified alternatives are discussed and assessed from a technical and logistical perspective.

The following are examples of problem solving scenarios that are permissible in the supply review:

- Capacity leveling activities.
- Stocking/destocking within agreed limits.
- Capacity increases/reductions within agreed boundaries.

Usually, the following types of decisions are not permitted in a supply review meeting:

- Allowing supply shortages, deciding on the products for which shortages are acceptable.
- Stocking/destocking outside agreed limits.
- Capacity increases/reductions outside agreed limits.

Decisions that may not be made within the supply review meeting are handed over to the pre-S&OP meeting.

- Result

  The supply review process produces the following results:

  - A selection of alternative solutions for a technically feasible supply plan at aggregated level (preferably) or detailed level satisfying the demand plan.
  - A list of open issues (ideally accompanied by proposed solutions) that are in conflict with a feasible supply plan. These are usually decisions that have to be made at senior management level within the company or the respective business area.

Pre-S&OP Meeting

The objective of the *pre-S&OP meeting* is to attempt to resolve remaining conflicts between demand and supply that were identified but could not be settled in the previous process steps. The meeting also prepares any remaining open issue, which needs to be addressed to the S&OP meeting.

To ensure necessary decisions can be made at the pre-S&OP meeting, the right participants must be present. The range of responsibilities represented in this meeting needs to be sufficient so that every relevant topic possible in the context of S&OP can be addressed to an appropriate person who is in charge of this topic.

Furthermore, they must have the authority to make necessary decisions—even on cross-departmental matters—provided these do not require senior management approval.

- Roles

  The pre-S&OP meeting should be attended by representatives of middle management and experts from the areas of finance, sales, purchasing, production, product development, and logistics.

- Input Information

  The demand and supply plans developed in the previous processes, together with the relevant simulation scenarios and key figure evaluations, constitute the key input information for the pre-S&OP meeting.

The work packages are compiled based on the open points from the supply review meeting. The preceding processes are responsible for clearly formulating these work packages and handing them over to the pre-S&OP meeting together with all relevant contextual information. The quality of this information has a major bearing on the efficiency of further steps.

- Process Flow

  The following tasks and types of issues are typically put on the agenda of the pre-S&OP meeting (Fig. 3.16):

  – *Review* of results and solution options being developed in the supply review process from a cross functional perspective.
  – Balance demand and supply in situations that require a decision on priorities, e.g. whether or not the service levels of certain products may fall below agreed targets.
  – Respond to anticipated under or over utilization of critical resources.
  – Include financial aspects into decision making.
  – In cases where no agreement can be reached on proposed solution options, the team has to come up with additional alternatives to resolve the issue and create a decision paper that highlights the characteristics of each alternative to facilitate decisions by senior management in the final S&OP meeting.
  – Analysis of the possible implications of proposed measures for the strategy and success of the company (for example, in the form of a simulative forecast of contribution margins or profit and loss).

The *pre-S&OP meeting* has three recurring agenda points:

– Adopt the solutions identified and decisions reached within the meeting.
– Adopt the decision papers to be presented to the S&OP meeting.
– Adopt the agenda for the S&OP meeting.

This is the last opportunity to reach a cross-departmental agreement before the S&OP executive meeting. All meeting participants ask themselves, "What would I do if I was responsible for the entire company or business unit?". The quality of the results put together in *preparation for the S&OP meeting* is a critical success factor of the entire S&OP process.

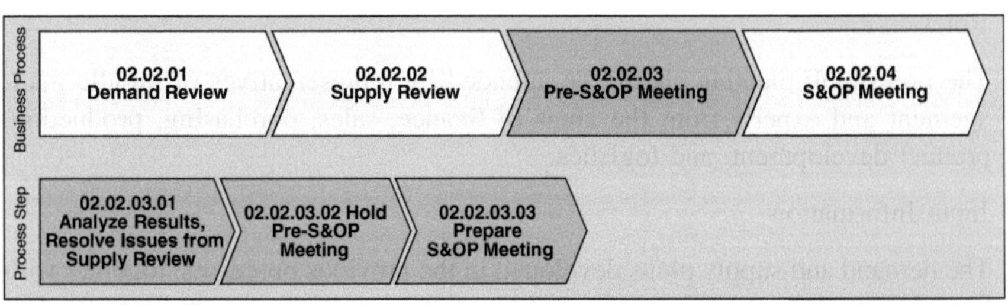

Fig. 3.16 Process steps of the "Pre-S&OP Meeting" process

- Result

  The following are examples of results that are typically handed over to the S&OP meeting:

  - An updated financial forecast based on the current versions of the demand and supply plans.
  - Recommendations for each product family, for example, remain on course (no change), increase/decrease demand plan, increase/decrease supply plan.
  - Recommendations concerning greater capacity increases/decreases that appear necessary.
  - List of remaining issues and conflicts over which no consensus could be reached.
  - Decision papers for pending decisions which require senior management involvement.
  - Agenda for the S&OP meeting.

S&OP Meeting (also S&OP Executive Meeting)

The S&OP meeting is the final decision-making meeting in the monthly S&OP cycle at senior management level. The main objective of the meeting is to assess the options that were evaluated and put together in the previous process step from an overall company perspective and convert these into appropriate decisions (Fig. 3.17).

In this respect, the meeting represents the culmination and conclusion of the monthly S&OP cycle. The active involvement of management in the S&OP meeting must be viewed as essential to the overall success of the S&OP process.

For this reason, the meeting must be well prepared and kept to a strict schedule.[17] Decision papers and the underlying figures must be suitably prepared for consideration by management. In particular, the impact of the various proposed options to be decided should be presented from both a financial and overall company perspective. This is usually done with the help of key performance indicators that are relevant from a management point of view.

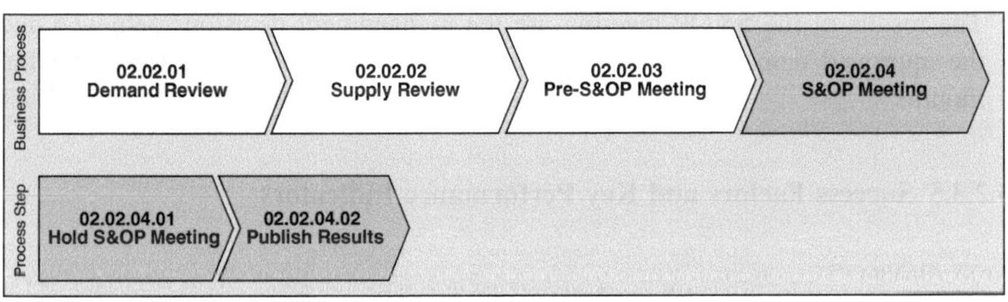

Fig. 3.17 Process steps of the "S&OP Executive Meeting" process

[17] The meeting must not usually last longer than one and one-half to two hours.

The demand and supply plans approved in the S&OP meeting are binding for the business units concerned and must subsequently be implemented in operations.

- Roles

  The following participants (roles) should be present at the meeting:

  - Manager of the business unit or division (chief operating officer, general manager).
  - Managers (vice presidents) of the areas of sales, marketing, production, product management, finance, logistics, and HR.
  - The S&OP process owner.

- Organization

  A fixed agenda structure is recommended for the S&OP meeting (Wallace 2005). The following agenda can be used as an example:

  - Strategy review.
  - Customer service performance review.
  - New products.
  - For each product family: Review and decisions.
  - Production: Changes to available capacity.
  - Impact on the business plan.
  - Recap of decisions made.
  - Review of meeting.

- Input Information

  The S&OP meeting is based on the decision papers and accompanying information prepared in the pre-S&OP meeting. For full details, see the "Pre-S&OP Meeting" section earlier in this chapter.

- Process Flow

  The process is guided by the agenda described above.

- Result

  The results of the S&OP meeting are the management decisions achieved and the approved demand and supply plans, which are binding for the following month.

3.2.3.5 Success Factors and Key Performance Indicators

Keys to Success

Three elements are crucial to the success of S&OP:

- **People**

  The process requires (and promotes) teamwork including people from sales, logistics, finance, and product development to achieve a consensus on decisions concerning the demand and supply plans. The active involvement of senior management is crucial to the success of the S&OP process in the company (see "S&OP Meeting").

- **Information**

  The decision-making process requires an appropriate information basis so that participants can identify and understand open points and deviations from targets.

- **Tools**

  To do so effectively, participants need tools to help them extract and understand these open points and deviations from the information basis. In an IT system, this could be done using predefined warning messages, key performance indicators, or suitable graphical illustrations.

In addition to decisions at an operational or tactical level, the S&OP process often calls for decisions of strategic significance. This is the case, for example, when the sales department requirements can no longer be met with the planned production and purchasing resources alone, or when a decision has to be made between two options that have a significant impact on the goals of different departments or the company's overall objectives. Therefore, the active involvement of senior management in the S&OP process must be considered a key success factor.

In addition to that, management involvement demands for excellent preparation of the four decision meetings in the course of the S&OP process to ensure the meetings can be conducted effectively in a short space of time. This is a crucial prerequisite to ensure that the participants—in particular management—accept routine involvement in the S&OP process.

High data quality is equally important to provide a reliable basis on which decisions can be made. In particular, full and complete data is required from the areas of marketing, sales, production, and finance.

Key Performance Indicators

Key figures or *key performance indicators (KPIs)* help companies measure success or performance in a very general sense and monitor changes over time. These indicators are always measured against predefined targets, which provides information about any shortcomings and highlight any need for action in the areas affected (the company as a whole, a department, production line, process, and so on).

The use of standardized KPIs also enables cross-company performance benchmarking.

- Selection Process

  When selecting the KPIs for measuring success, it is not particularly useful to define a whole catalog of (undoubtedly thoroughly reliable) key figures and then implement them.

  A more meaningful approach to defining or revising the KPI system is to begin where "corporate success" is defined. In most cases, this can be found in the details of the corporate strategy and the catalog of corporate sub-goals derived from it. When a goal is achieved, success is, by definition, recorded in the area being measured.[18]

  The list of S&OP-relevant KPIs below provides, in the sense described above, a catalog from which a suitable sub-set of KPIs that seem appropriate for measuring the success of specific corporate goals and process targets have to be selected.

- List of S&OP-Relevant KPIs

  The following is a list of common KPIs that can be significant in the context of the S&OP process. This is a slightly abridged version of the list published in (Augenstein and Alexander 2007b) "… the most important KPIs for the S&OP process".

  Each KPI should be verified against corporate goals and process aims to establish its relevance. As a rule, a small number of suitable KPIs is more useful than a large number of KPIs unrelated to the goals pursued.

  The KPIs have been arranged in categories for classification purposes. A detailed explanation is not provided for each one. More information can be found in the extensive literature that exists on the subject. A number of references to sources of further information are provided in the next section.

  - **Strategic KPIs**—These include customer satisfaction (survey), on time in full, perfect orders, new account openings, distribution, penetration, market share, brand investment as % of revenue, price levels, % margin, overall margin, budget vs. projected sales forecast, overhead costs as % of revenue, supply chain costs as % of revenue, EBITDA/EVA, working capital utilization, and sales revenue.
  - **Inventory-oriented**—These include total inventory value (in USD), inventory turns (in USD and units), days' supply (DOI), and slow moving/obsolete inventory as % of total inventory.
  - **Production-oriented/receipts-oriented**—These include production to schedule, delivery to schedule (procurement), delivery to schedule (customer), and capacity utilization.

[18] Achieving goals does not necessarily imply that the company has also achieved success in the market. To be able to draw this conclusion, the "right" goals have to be set, which itself presents a difficult challenge.

- **Process**—These include forecast error (MAPE), forecast bias (PE), statistical forecast vs. consensus forecast tracking, production schedule adherence (average weekly), production plan adherence (monthly volume), and demonstrated capacity as % of planned capacity.
- **Efficiency of meetings**—These include decisions in time, decisions deferred, people availability, availability of information, action items from previous cycle not completed, quality of information, and external S&OP process assessment score.

3.2.3.6 Further Reading

To gain a deeper understanding of S&OP, we recommend the following sources of further information.

A thorough discussion of the significance and delimitation of the process groups "Demand Planning" and S&OP can be found in (Augenstein and Alexander 2007a) "…Where does Forecasting Fit in the S&OP Process?".

Further information about the S&OP process and related challenges and pitfalls can be found in Sheldon (2006), in Higdon (2005), a video session documenting experiences of S&OP implementations with an approximate running time of 25 min, and in (Augenstein and Alexander 2007c) "The S&OP Process Rollercoaster?".

SCOR (2008) contains an extensive collection of KPIs described in terms of their business significance and calculation methods.

3.2.4 Demand Planning

3.2.4.1 Business Process Overview and Characteristics

The Importance of Demand Planning

The ability to forecast customer requirements—referred to as demand planning—is extremely important in supply chain management. Customers are at the heart of supply chain activities and their requirements are the starting point for designing and planning all processes along the entire supply chain. Production, packing, distribution, transportation, and storage activities are all planned in advance on the basis of the customer requirements that are forecast and set out in demand plans. Demand planning is used to define production and purchasing quantities as well as the inventory level and ranges of coverage at every stage in the value chain. Both production resources and financial resources are determined based on the results of demand planning. This makes demand planning one of the vital core processes in supply chain management for all companies and an indispensable instrument for company-wide planning.

In the process industry in particular, great importance is attached to demand planning. Chemical industry customers are usually companies with just-in-time delivery requirements and often supplies at short notice are required. While there is a need to be able to supply customers rapidly, process manufacturing is often subject to conditions that require production and procurement to be carried out on the basis of planned figures. These include:

- Ingredients with long procurement lead times.
- Consideration of capacities and downtimes for maintenance and cleaning in the case of continuous production.
- Diminished ability to respond to requirements at short notice during joint production, since several products need to be included in the planning process.

Avoiding the Inability to Deliver

One of the primary aims of the chemical industry is to avoid situations in which requirements cannot be met due to an inability to deliver. Of equal importance is avoiding the buildup of unnecessary stocks.

If forecast sales quantities are lower than customer demand, stock produced up to that point is used up and safety stock also has to be used to meet demand. If this delta exceeds stocks, the company suffers an inability to deliver, loss of sales and market share, and damage to the profitability of products with high margins.

If the demand plan is greater than actual customer demand, this can lead to excess stocks that have to be recycled, destroyed, or written off as the circumstances dictate. This results in a poorer margin and lower profitability.

Finally, safety stock is also dependent on the quality of the forecast. If actual consumption values deviate significantly from the forecast, safety stock levels fluctuate.

Key levers to avoid situations in which it becomes impossible to deliver are

- Increased demand plan accuracy.
- The ability to respond flexibly to requirements that are unplanned and that occur at short notice.

Increased Demand Plan Accuracy

The quality of demand planning has a bearing on all supply chain processes. The impact that inaccurate demand planning has on the various areas of the company are outlined here:

- Production
  - When more is produced than is actually needed, this results in increased unnecessary resource utilization and therefore reduced availability of resources that could potentially be required to complete other orders.
  - When shortfall quantities have to be produced separately, this results in reduced flexibility and disrupts production.

  - When overproduction causes increased capacity requirements, this results in increased capital lockup.
  - The upshot is that production cycles take longer to complete as a result of capacity overload and the constant need to manage exceptions to make up for quantity shortfall orders.

- Procurement
  - Suppliers' reliability suffers when production processes are constantly interrupted by rush orders.
  - Procurement costs go up because the increased production costs faced by the supplier (due to rush orders) are passed on in the long term.
  - Raw material stocks increase because the produced products are changed due to a lack of demand.

- Distribution and Logistics
  - Supplier performance and reliability (service levels) drop due to shortfalls in warehouse stock.
  - Loss in sales due to failure to deliver and the possibility of the customer switching to a rival for commodity chemicals.
  - Longer sales order cycle times when product unavailability results in production or procurement being triggered only when the sales order is received.
  - Higher capital lockup due to excessive stocks.
  - Higher capital lockup (warehouse resources) due to increased warehouse capacities.
  - Higher destruction rates.

Impact of Demand Plan Quality

The quality of demand plans has a bearing on the company's earnings statement and balance sheet. Customer satisfaction and the suppliers' readiness and ability to deliver have a direct impact on sales and an indirect effect on demand and market share. Cycle times, warehouse resources, destruction, procurement, and labor utilization affect costs. Stocks are recorded as current assets on the balance sheet.

Ability to Respond Flexibly and at Short Notice to Unplanned Demand

Unplanned or short-notice demand is caused by sudden demand peaks that may be the result of promotions or upside demand, for example. If this demand is earmarked as "special requirements" and incorporated into rolling demand planning, the estimated demand data for all downstream planning units is transparent.

Demand Planning: Process Overview

- Analyze market influencing factors.
- Analyze product influences.
- Optimize the demand plan data basis.
- Demand planning organization and responsibility.

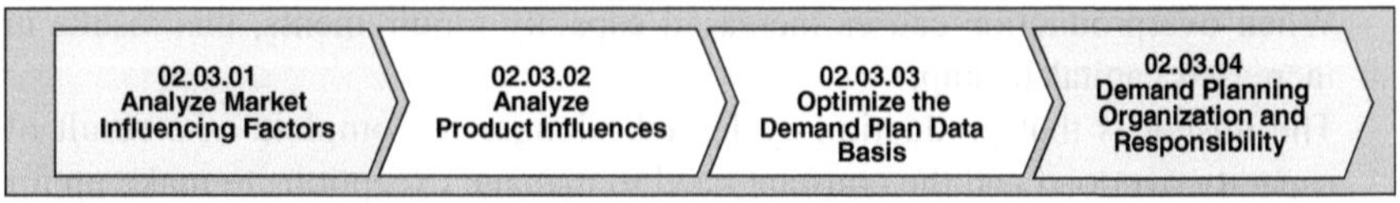

Fig. 3.18 Business processes of "Demand Planning"

The business processes that involve analyzing market influencing factors and analyzing product influences integrate both market and customer orientation in the demand planning process (the starting point for the demand-driven supply chain) and therefore help improve the accuracy of the demand plan (Fig. 3.18). The business process optimizing the demand plan data basis is designed to establish one or more suitable forecast methods and the most appropriate planning horizon, which also increases the quality of the plan. An optimal data basis for the demand plan must also include safety stock data, planning data for any extra demand that may occur but is not scheduled, and demand planning data for tenders and promotions. This data basis helps the company respond flexibly to these types of demand, which are, by their very nature, less certain. The business process demand planning organization and responsibility ensures that demand planning takes place as part of a structured and rolling process, and also contributes toward the two objectives of increasing the quality of the plan and boosting the ability of the company to react to uncertain or unexpected demand.

3.2.4.2 Opportunities and Optimization Potential

We will now take a closer look at the business process of demand planning and highlight opportunities and optimization potential.

Analyze Market Influencing Factors

Demand planning is based on an analysis of the market situation. Market influencing factors such as market dynamics, market type, and competitive situation are included in the analysis. The market characteristics determine:

- Frequency of demand planning.
- Intervals between demand planning and planning horizons.
- Degree of accuracy required for demand planning.
- Market Dynamics.

In a rapidly changing market, demand has to be planned more frequently so that market changes can be incorporated into the forecast as early as possible.

If the products have a short lifespan, forecasts have to be reviewed more regularly and the planning interval is shorter.

It is difficult to plan demand for new and innovative products due to the lack of experience. Therefore, the tolerance limits for deviations from plans are higher.

With this in mind, the demand planning process should account for the position of products in the product life cycle, and the planning horizon and intensity should be adjusted as and when this position changes.

- Market Type

  In strong growth markets with cut-throat competition (buyer's markets), companies should opt for slightly exaggerated forecasts to ensure they do not lose out on sales and market share due to an inability to deliver. This means that demand has to be planned more frequently.
  Another example would be countries with hyperinflationary economies. In this case, companies might deliberately overproduce in order to tie up their capital in stored products as opposed to monetary values. The accuracy of demand planning becomes less important in light of this strategy.
  Demand and competitors are more likely to be transparent in local markets than in global or far-off markets. Generally speaking, demand planning grows less accurate the greater the distance to the market.

- Competitive Situation

  The competitive situation and market dynamics can rapidly alter demand for traditionally stable products. Market influences should therefore be closely monitored and analyzed. A new competitor in the market can have a major impact on demand so it is important to evaluate the influence of competitors. If a new competitive situation arises, it may be necessary to adapt the frequency of demand planning or the planning horizon.

Analyze Product Influences

After the market situation has been analyzed, the spotlight is turned to the influence of products on demand planning. The analysis looks at where products are in the product life cycle and how they are differentiated according to product groups.

- Position in the Product Life Cycle

  The product life cycle covers phase-in, growth, maturity, saturation, and phase-out. During phase-in, demand grows with each period. In the growth phase, demand increases at a greater rate than during phase-in. The same trend is perpetuated in the maturity and saturation phases. If demand planning fails to identify the moment these phases are reached, the demand forecast is too high and stocks begin to build up. Products in the saturation phase have a long demand history and deviations from the demand plan are rare.
  In many areas, product life cycles are becoming shorter and shorter. As a result, products have a high replacement rate.
  When it comes to new products, comparable products with as many similarities as possible can be used as a basis for demand planning. Nevertheless, actual demand can still differ from the forecasted demand. Such situations have to be identified early on and with a high degree of transparency and flexibility.

Demand for a new product can also have an impact on demand for existing products (cannibalization).

- Differentiation According to Product Groups

The strategy of focusing on selected product groups (perhaps on the basis of position in the product life cycle) in demand planning can, for example, be beneficial for premium products with high contribution margins. The method of differentiating according to product groups or product hierarchies can also be used to achieve more accurate forecasts at an aggregated level, since this approach allows demand fluctuations to be balanced more easily and provides a larger data basis. Suitable rules are then used to disaggregate these groupings back to the level of individual products, for example, proportionally or based on demand history.

Optimize the Demand Plan Data Basis

- Highly Accurate Demand Planning Data by Choosing the Right Forecasting Methods

The most important basis for increasing the accuracy of the demand plan and selecting the right forecasting method is actual historical demand data that is usually made available to planners in IT systems. In practice, quantitative statistical forecasting techniques such as trend analysis, time series analysis, indicator forecasting, and exponential smoothing are applied to optimize the forecast and offer as much support as possible to demand planners.

In the first step, IT systems are used to update the demand history based on the time series of the chosen forecasting technique and present expected sales quantities. It is necessary to define how many historical periods are included and how these are weighted.

Demand planning can also be facilitated by arranging products in an ABC-XYZ matrix. Under ABC, articles are classified according to their cumulated revenue value. The XYZ analysis relates to fluctuations in demand for each product in a given period. Demand for X products remains very constant but for Z products is extremely volatile. The ABC-XYZ matrix helps distinguish products that always need to be planned manually with a high degree of accuracy (AZ products) from products that can be planned in fully automated processes (CX products).

To achieve high-quality demand planning, it is usually not enough to update the demand history and employ automated planning support mechanisms; historical data and data calculated automatically must then be analyzed and adjusted in response to current developments and new market knowledge. As more and more relevant and up-to-date information is incorporated into the forecast, the quality of the results improves. For example, the sales department has knowledge of promotions and short-term price reductions resulting from product launches and discontinuations. Marketing has information about pricing and product policies as well as advertising expenditure. Market research can provide relevant data about competitors. All of this information should be combined in a forecasting approach and taken as the basis for the demand review within sales and operations planning (see Sect. 3.2.3.4). This brings considerable benefits to demand planning and significantly improves the quality of forecasts.

• Setting the Right Planning Horizon

  A number of demand planning horizons are common in the chemical industry. In the short-term planning horizon (6–12 months), it should be possible to respond flexibly to customer demands at short notice. Demand planning is adapted monthly (or even weekly within the current month) and is usually carried out on the basis of stock keeping units. Demand planning accuracy is measured in the short term.
  A long-term planning horizon is needed in the chemical industry for two reasons.
  First, some products have long lead times due to the replenishment lead times of critical raw materials and ingredients. The products concerned are planned at product or product group level based on the lead time and the forecast horizon is defined accordingly (usually 1–3 years).
  Second, long planning horizons are required to support investment decisions that are made on the basis of demand planning. Investments in the construction of new chemical facilities, for example, require long lead times in the process manufacturing sector. The planning horizon can be up to 5 years or more.

• Differentiating Demand Plan Data According to Types of Special Requirements

  Companies can meet the challenge of responding flexibly to unplanned requirements and sudden demand by including specific data fields in their demand planning. These can then be used to cover uncertain or unplanned requirements or any demand arising from promotions or tenders. Requirements of this type are entered into planning systems as special requirements so that they are transparent for all downstream planning stages and can be taken into account in all subsequent stages of the value chain. Types of special requirements include:

  – Urgent, previously unplanned requirements.
  – Upside demand to cover potential but not certain or confirmed requirements.
  – Additional safety requirements to cover potential demand peaks.

For each type of special requirement, specific planning and implementation processes can then be set up to ensure that customers' orders can always be met, despite the apparent "absence of plannability".

Demand Planning Organization and Responsibility

The key to achieving high-quality demand planning is the ability to evaluate market and customer requirements as they emerge. Demand planning should be delegated to business units with direct customer contact, usually the marketing and sales departments. These units are best placed to evaluate customer requirements and should be responsible not only for sales revenue planning but also demand planning.

Many companies appoint a forecast manager to act as a link between marketing, sales, and other relevant departments such as production, supply chain management, and finance/controlling. Organizationally, this function is relatively high up. Together with the marketing and sales managers, the forecast manager regularly compares current customer requirements with operational marketing and sales goals. He or she also involves the production and finance/controlling departments in the forecast process, for example, by holding cross-departmental meetings (see Sect. 3.2.3). The forecast manager is responsible for creating, maintaining managing, and monitoring the detailed demand plan centrally.

Within the scope of his or her responsibilities, the forecast manager must also ensure that the rolling demand planning process is strictly observed and maintained. This involves managing the demand planning process, regularly updating demand planning data, and monitoring a fixed schedule for all relevant departments to maintain disciplined planning. The consultation rounds within the sales and operations planning process help ensure that the demand plan and the conditions attached to it are universally understood and upheld. The structured demand planning process ensures that the tasks for each department involved in planning are transparent, which promotes acceptance of the plan throughout the company.

3.2.4.3 Success Factors and Key Performance Indicators

The elements of the demand planning process facilitate market and customer orientation in the supply chain. The demand planning process takes place at the start of the supply chain and lays the foundation for all other process steps. This means the quality and accuracy of demand planning are directly linked to the quality and management of subsequent process steps. The result is a complex planning landscape whose impact on all processes in the supply chain, such as production, procurement, storage, and transportation, is often not overlooked. Seen in this light, the demand planning process is extremely important for sales, revenue, internal resource utilization, and capital lockup due to the inventory level. Increasing the quality of the demand planning process results in a correspondingly high degree of improvement potential.

- Key Performance Indicators

  Tying in with the most important levers for avoiding inability-to-deliver situations (increased accuracy of demand planning and the ability to respond flexibly to unplanned requirements and sudden demand), the main key performance indicators in the demand planning process are

  – Readiness to deliver (end customer)
  – Demand planning accuracy (forecast accuracy)

  - Inventory value at the end of the period

- Readiness to Deliver (End Customer)

  This term refers to the ability to meet a requirement within the agreed time.

$$\textit{Readiness to deliver} = \textit{quantity delivered on time divided by the total quantity of demand}$$

- Demand Planning Accuracy

  The forecast accuracy is the reversal of the percentage forecast error:

$$\textit{Forecast accuracy}\,\% = 1\,\textit{minus forecast errors}$$

  The forecast error total is the sum of the difference between the forecast value and actual value in each period. The error total is always measured in absolute terms so that positive and negative differences do not cancel each other out.

$$\textit{Error total} = \textit{sum}\,(\textit{consumption}_t - \textit{forecast}_t)$$

- Inventory Value in a Period

$$\textit{Inventory value} = \textit{warehouse stock at the end of the period multiplied by the current price}$$

  The average inventory value at the end of the period is used because stocks may have to be used to maintain readiness to deliver during the period. By the end of the period, however, the inventory value should have reached an optimum level.

3.2.5 Supply Planning

3.2.5.1 Business Process Overview and Characteristics

This section explores how global supply planning for a network of production and subcontract manufacturing sites takes place in the chemical industry.

Global supply planning is preceded by rolling demand planning. The mostly stock keeping unit-based data used in demand planning is usually consolidated at product level for supply planning and cleared of existing stocks. The resulting net requirements are taken as the basis for supply planning.

Supply planning is a method of rough-cut planning in the short, medium, and long term to cover estimated sales quantities.

The aim of supply planning is to plan the supply situation in advance to ensure a defined service level at the best possible price. Supply and demand must therefore be harmonized as early as possible and take into account the respective conditions, which are optimized in planning. These include limited production and

Fig. 3.19 Business processes of "Supply Planning"

transportation capacities, delivery times for materials and preliminary products, suppliers' ability to deliver, storage costs, production costs, transportation costs, and penalties for late deliveries or quantity shortfalls.

The result of supply planning is an executable plan at the lowest possible cost for the given service level.

Planning and optimization are carried out throughout the entire value chain and involve procurement (of preliminary products, ingredients, and packaging materials), production, and, if applicable, subcontract manufacturing, filling, packing, distribution, and transportation.

Planning covers all capacities and resources available at internal and external production plants that can be considered for the product.

Supply planning is of particular importance in the chemical industry. Reasons for this include

- The complexity of multistage production, a process in which the procurement, production, and distribution of ingredients and preliminary products have to be preplanned in the medium term.
- The complexity of recursive material flows with joint products and by-products.
- Possible long procurement cycles for preliminary products or ingredients that must be accounted for accordingly in planning.
- Possible make-or-buy decisions, since capacity bottlenecks may make purchasing or subcontract manufacturing the right solution.
- Increased coupling between production stages caused by low buffer capacities and the resulting need to harmonize supply and demand as precisely as possible.

The supply planning process is divided into the following business processes (Fig. 3.19):

- Assign requirements to production plants and check capacity.
- Optimize demand fulfillment.
- Supply planning organization and responsibility.

3.2.5.2 Opportunities and Optimization Potential

In this section, we look at the business processes of supply planning and highlight opportunities and optimization potential.

Assign Requirements to Production Plants and Check Capacity

During planning, all of the options available in the supply chain model to fulfill demand through additional purchases, stock transfers, or production are explored along the entire value chain.

First, the requirements are assigned to the possible options for covering demand. At this stage, it is assumed that all plants have available capacities.

In the chemical industry, where ingredients and preliminary products frequently come from other production plants or are procured externally, the finished product is normally planned in the initial planning round.

In the second step, ingredients and preliminary products can then be planned in accordance with the plan for the finished product. An excerpt of the bill of materials detailing the most important ingredients and preliminary products is taken as a basis for this plan.

Next, an initial capacity check provides an indication of possible resource bottlenecks or utilization below capacity. Taking into account current production and transportation capacities, the use of each production plant is planned.

In the case of dedicated production, there may only be one production option. If production lines are non-dedicated, several can be used.

The medium-term and long-term planning horizon offers an early indication of capacity bottlenecks that cannot be eliminated by switching to alternative or even multiple production plants. This can be used as a basis for making decisions on investments or strategic acquisitions.

This process step results in a requirement being assigned to a production plant under consideration of available capacities.

Optimize Demand Fulfillment

Besides capacity utilization, other optimization criteria can be used in supply planning, in most cases supported by IT systems:

- Product costs or product value.
- ABC product classification.
- Bin locations.
- Transportation options such as air, sea, and rail.
- Type and nature of the production process.

Particular customer requirements can also be given preferential treatment or prioritized in demand fulfillment planning, for example, if the customers have contractually defined service level agreements.

To make further optimizations, companies can

- Calculate optimal lot sizes.
- Calculate optimal safety stocks.
- Allow for production slots for special requirements.
- Carry out planning in a rolling iterative process.
- Optimize according to push and pull planning strategies.

- Calculate Optimal Lot Sizes.

  A conflict of interest over lot sizes exists between logistics, production, and procurement. While the logistics department generally prefers a small lot size to save on storage costs and allow it to respond quickly, the production department needs certain minimum lot sizes to meet its objectives and optimize setup costs and capacity utilization. Lot sizes have an impact on manufacturing costs and lead times.

  The optimal lot size is fundamental to optimizing manufacturing costs, while setup costs are compared with the variable costs of warehousing and capital lockup.

  When it comes to lead times, the challenge is to calculate the lot size such that the total lead time of all orders in production within a given period can be minimized. This is necessary to increase capacity utilization and minimize unit costs. If the lot size is small, setup takes place more frequently and the portion of the lead time spent setting up equipment grows.

The decision over lot size creation also concerns external procurement orders; fixed order costs must be weighed up against warehouse costs.

- Calculate Optimal Safety Stocks

  In supply planning, a certain service level is usually defined by creating safety stock for all intermediates and end products in each location along the entire supply chain. For this purpose, the following two questions must be addressed: On what date should safety stock be replenished and how much safety stock should be created? Overall, calculating the optimal level of safety stock presents a major challenge but it is worthwhile given the considerable potential it offers for cost reductions.

- Allow for Production Slots for Special Requirements

  Supply planning should allow for production slots for special requirements, ideally on the basis of figures in the demand plan for special requirements. Supply planning covers the external procurement of raw materials and ingredients through to transportation. The advantage is a significant increase in flexibility and the ability to respond rapidly to special requirements. Planning can include a cost calculation that sets any additionally incurred production and material costs against the revenue brought in by the special requirements.

- Carry Out Planning in a Rolling Iterative Process

  Further optimization can be achieved through the rolling iterative supply planning process. In the short-term range where the planning cycle is short, supply production and transportation planning are continuously aligned with each other. Supply availability is controlled by detailed production planning. The resulting production availability is subject to operational fluctuations, which are continuously taken into account in supply planning, thereby allowing the production network supply plan to be continuously adjusted. However, since production also requires setup time, for example, "frozen zones" are occasionally used. These are time slots just before the production deadline during which no further changes are taken into consideration.

In the event of bottlenecks, fair share issues that arise can be dealt with in supply planning based on a set of rules.

- Optimize According to Push and Pull Planning Strategies

  Other aspects with potential for optimization in supply planning include the push and pull planning strategies used in the value creation process. Here, companies can endeavor to produce goods in the value chain for as long as possible according to push criteria, and only switch to pull criteria (that is, according to the customer's wishes) to finish off products once production is complete or at the packing stage. The challenge lies in identifying the right point in the value chain to switch from the push to the pull strategy.

  Optimized demand fulfillment results in an executable solution set down in a suitable plan that addresses procurement, production, subcontract manufacturing, warehousing, and transportation. The results of supply planning are usually passed on to production using IT systems. When the supply planning orders enter the production horizon, they are transferred to production planning and detailed scheduling, where they are converted into detailed production orders and purchase requisitions.

  Since supply planning constitutes the interface between demand planning and production planning, the results should be transparent and accessible to all of the departments involved in the value creation process, such as sales, procurement, production, supply chain, warehousing, and transportation.

Supply Planning Organization and Responsibility

Organizationally, supply planning is generally assigned to supply chain management. Supply planning should be a separate unit from sales, marketing, and production because its responsibility lies in harmonizing demand and demand fulfillment throughout the entire value chain according to optimization criteria. This can only be achieved by pursuing independent objectives.

In the event of problems and delays affecting delivery dates and quantities in the short-term and medium-term planning horizon, those responsible for supply planning face the challenge of incorporating these into planning as well as into communication and information chains almost as soon as they are identified. To achieve this, they rely on regular rolling planning runs and transparency in the supply chain in the short-term and medium-term planning horizon.

Companies should demonstrate discipline by genuinely applying the results of supply planning for the short-term horizon in production.

3.2.5.3 Success Factors and Key Performance Indicators

Supply planning can be used as a planning aid to determine the best sources of supply.

The strengths of supply planning are the ability to

- Select the most suitable source of supply based on costs and the given service level.
- Roughly identify the production deadline based on procurement and warehouse costs.
- Plan resources and requirements for ingredients in advance with optimized inventory levels and costs.

The key performance indicators of lead time, delivery service (taking into account readiness to deliver and delivery time), and average inventory costs tie in with these success factors.

Lead Time

The lead time is the sum of processing times, transportation times, control times, and wait times across all stages of procurement and production. Experience has shown that wait times make up the bulk of the lead time in the chemical industry. By reducing wait times, the overall lead time is cut and work-in-progress stocks are also reduced.

Readiness to Deliver

Readiness to deliver refers to the ability to meet a requirement within the agreed time. Readiness to deliver can be measured by the number of quantity units sold using this formula:

$$\begin{aligned}\textit{Readiness to deliver} &= \textit{quantity delivered on time divided}\\ &\quad\textit{by the total quantity of demand}\end{aligned}$$

Delivery Time

The delivery time is the time between the order being placed and the customer receiving the goods. It can be calculated with the following formula:

$$\begin{aligned}\textit{Average actual delivery time} &= \textit{order fulfillment date minus}\\ &\quad\textit{order received date}\end{aligned}$$

$$\begin{aligned}\textit{Average requested delivery time} &= \textit{date requested by customer minus}\\ &\quad\textit{date on which order was received}\end{aligned}$$

Average Inventory Costs

The inventory level and inventory costs in the planning period should be optimized as part of the supply planning process. Therefore, the average inventory value is used as a key performance indicator. The inventory value increases with the processing time because this is where value is actually created. There is considerable optimization potential here that can lead to lower costs and stocks. The average inventory value is calculated by multiplying average warehouse stock by the price according to the position in the value creation process.

3.2.6 Production Planning

3.2.6.1 Process Overview and Characteristics

Production planning helps ensure that the required products are supplied in the right quantity on the requirement date. Production planning therefore has a crucial bearing on service levels. Correct quantities, delivery performance and reliability, and quality all play a key role in the chemical industry in particular, since the customers of this industry are usually processing companies themselves.

In addition to the aim of being ready to deliver, production also pursues the goal of minimizing costs.

The production planning process provides measures for achieving this goal, which include:

- Minimizing warehouse stocks.
- Optimizing utilization of the production resources involved and minimizing variable costs.
- Minimizing lot-size-independent costs.
- Minimizing scrap.

A number of techniques are applied in the production planning process, which facilitate these measures by:

- Creating cost-effective lots and campaigns.
- Calculating feasible deadlines.
- Reducing setup times for bottleneck resources.

In the short-term horizon from a few hours and days to a few months, the production planning process establishes a balance between demand and demand fulfillment across several production stages.

The planning horizon is geared toward capacity bottlenecks in production plants, production lead times (including maintenance times and downtimes within campaign planning), or bottlenecks in the availability of important raw materials and the corresponding planned delivery times.

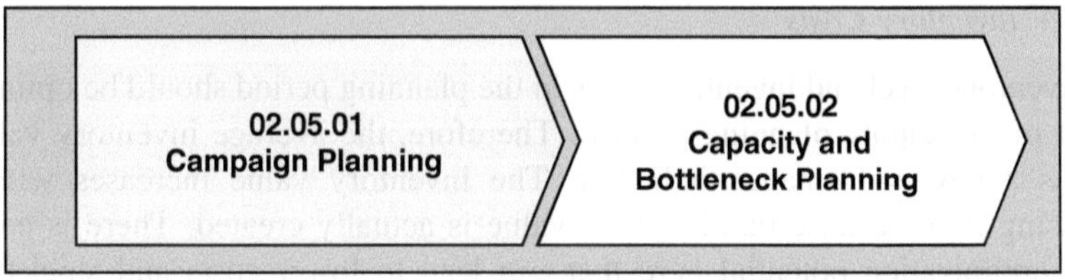

Fig. 3.20 Business processes of "Production Planning"

The main planning constraints arise from the complexity of production plants. For instance, there are numerous production stages, combined productions, subcontractors, and recursive material flows that may also involve multiple production sites. Other constraints may stem from

- Availability of important raw materials.
- Storage capacities for raw materials, intermediates, and end products.
- Uncertainties in the transportation from the supplier to the customer or subcontractor.

The result is a production plan on the basis of which quantities, quality, and delivery dates can be confirmed to customers.

The degree of reliability, however, is limited by the special aspects of chemical production because factors such as quantity, receipt date, and material quality are rarely achieved 100 %.

The production planning process is divided into the following business processes (Fig. 3.20):

- Campaign planning.
- Capacity and bottleneck planning.

3.2.6.2 Opportunities and Optimization Potential

The largest share of value creation in a manufacturing company stems from the production department. All upstream processes (such as procurement) and downstream processes (such as distribution) are directly linked to production. Production planning carries considerable optimization potential. To exploit it, however, the entire planning process must be considered as a whole. When describing the process here, we examine opportunities and optimization potential.

Campaign Planning

When the planning horizon reaches the medium-term and short-term range of production planning for production plants, campaign planning takes place. Campaign planning is carried out for both production and packing (in the event that these activities take place in different plants). It is based on a reduced bill of material to ensure that any purchases of supplies such as packing materials, labels, and so on, are scheduled in time. In the short term, campaign planning results in production, filling, and packing orders being released. At the same time, relevant procurement orders are also triggered.

Production campaign planning is particularly important in process manufacturing plants since the duration and cost of campaigns are to be optimized.

Equipment must be changed over or cleaned during production. Finished products are not just placed into final storage; they may also go into interim storage if required in a subsequent production stage, for example. Setup and cleaning processes as well as storage may be very cost-intensive. The complexity of planning is increased further in multiproduct plants in which all products and their respective constraints must be taken into account.

The main aim of campaign planning is to weigh up setup costs and storage costs. More frequent changeovers in production equipment may help reduce warehouse costs, but can also result in higher setup costs. On the other hand, if the number of changeovers is kept to a minimum, this may well bring down setup costs, but drive up warehouse costs as a result. A further consequence may be a poorer service level due to delays.

Capacity and Bottleneck Planning

Capacity planning looks at plant capacity constraints. The degree of complexity is compounded by bottlenecks at different material planning levels that are mutually dependent in the material flow. For example, a preliminary product is produced at plant 1, the follow-up product that it goes into is produced at plant 2, and both plants are bottlenecks. In this case, planned plant downtime must be taken into account. In addition, possible delays in the plants are accommodated by planning time buffers. Combined productions, recursive material flows, and lead times must also be observed.

Capacity bottlenecks in raw material procurement can arise in transportation or storage. Capacity planning means that production planning is optimized to meet requirements using these bottlenecks. This may necessitate changes in the production plan.

Legal requirements with regard to environmental protection and industrial safety must always be adhered to in production planning. Planning must therefore ensure that during both delivery and production, no material combinations occur in pipelines or containers that would pose a threat to the environment or employees. If the products are marketed by the pharmaceutical or food industries, health protection is of utmost importance.

Once the production plan has been defined, it is communicated to other units that process the planned production quantities. These may be internal filling and packing departments, subcontractors, or plants where further processing takes place, for example, to extract co-products or by-products and use them as preliminary products in their own production processes.

3.2.6.3 Success Factors and Key Performance Indicators

Overcoming the complexity of production plants and processes that have to be modeled in detail in the planning tool by production planning represents both a success factor and a challenge.

A further success factor is the ability to accommodate continuous changes in procurement and production. Both areas are constantly monitored and all changes have a knock-on effect for planning.

Production planning pursues conflicting goals of optimizing production costs, optimizing lead times throughout the entire supply chain, and attaining a defined service level. These key performance indicators have to be used, therefore, to evaluate production planning.

The conflict of goals can only be resolved by optimizing all supply chain activities with an end-to-end, process-oriented approach covering all functional areas.

Shorter Lead Times

Shorter lead times result in increased machine capacity, lower stock levels, and shorter delivery times, which contribute to customer satisfaction. Liquidity goes up because shorter delivery times generally lead to earlier payments from customers. Since shorter lead times mean that the individual orders take up less machine time, more orders can be taken on by production. In a demand market, this leads to higher sales.

Optimized Unit Costs

Unit costs are optimized through high machine utilization. By optimizing the setup stage and planning accordingly, setup costs can be reduced and the production lot optimized.

Other performance indicators include the average inventory value in a given period, inventory level, cleaning costs, and plant utilization.

The inventory value is based on the value of stocks of a given material and allows the company to select materials with high capital lockup.

The inventory level for products from the production plant is measured in days' supply. The inventory level should be kept low to reduce capital lockup. The inventory level is also relevant for raw material procurement and is also commonly measured in days' supply. Here, it is important to maintain a low inventory level for expensive raw materials in particular. However, since raw materials come at the start of the value chain, it may be beneficial to accept higher raw material stocks in favor of lower finished product stocks.

Cleaning costs are measured in relation to production costs, for example, and should be low. This indicator leads to production campaigns that are as long as possible for a product or product group. This means it stands in opposition to inventory targets, since long production campaigns result in stock build-up in order to meet delivery dates.

3.3 Sales and Marketing in the Pharmaceutical Industry

Markus Pfannschilling-Zerbe and Jürgen Schroth

3.3.1 Positioning of the Process Area of Sales and Marketing in the Value Chain of Pharmaceutical Companies

Given that products and active ingredients produced in the pharmaceutical industry are usually sold from stock, the process area of sales and marketing represents the penultimate step in the pharmaceutical value chain. This process area primarily concerns industry-specific "marketing and campaign management", the process group of "sales management", sales activities aimed at those who either prescribe the products ("indirect sales in the pharmaceutical industry") or sell the products ("direct sales in the pharmaceutical industry"), and the process group of "customer service and support", which involves handling customer inquiries, for example.

The Fig. 3.21 shows how the processes groups fit into the business process map.

In Chap. 1, we looked at the conditions and most important trends affecting the sales environment at present. Following on from this, we will now turn our attention to the process groups that fall under the process area of "sales and marketing", with particular emphasis on the process group of "indirect sales". Our main objective is to describe the business process that sees pharmaceutical

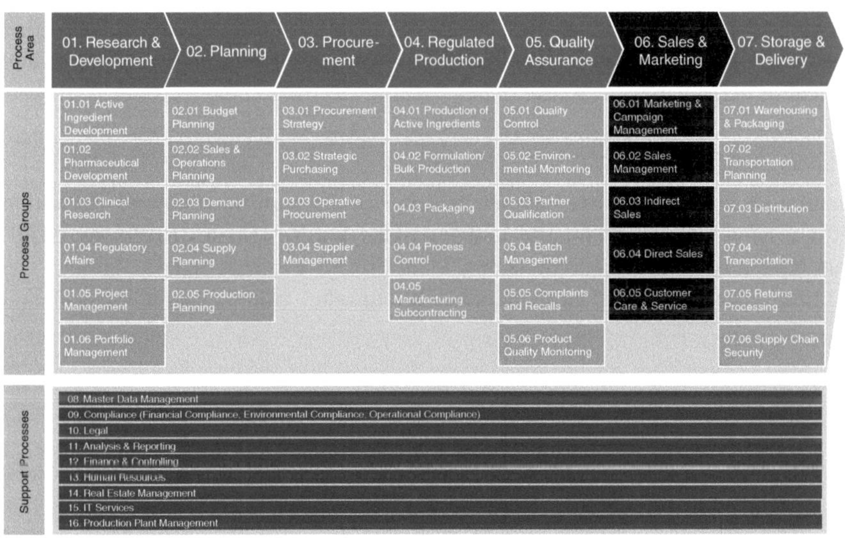

Fig. 3.21 Positioning of the process area of "Sales and Marketing" in the business process map for the pharmaceutical industry

representatives visit general practitioners, and, based on this example, illustrate how the tools presented in Chap. 2 come to use.

The trend toward forming networks, the emergence of new medical service centers as well as the need to adapt evaluations according to territory structures are the key trends changing today's sales processes.

3.3.2 Marketing and Campaign Management

3.3.2.1 Process Overview and Characteristics

The "marketing and campaign management" process centralizes all company activities whose aim it is to organize the company's ties to existing and future markets and market segments. The markets consist of the central ecosystem including the most important physicians, groups of physicians, health insurance funds, patients, competitors, distributors, and other influencers on the one hand, and the company's own product and service portfolio on the other. A commonly used definition describes marketing management as "the art and science of choosing target markets and getting, keeping, and growing customers through creating, delivering, and communicating superior customer value" (Kotler and Keller 2006). In addition to traditional marketing processes, which, of course, are also used in the pharmaceutical industry, it is worthwhile noting that the processes of key opinion leader management and event management are also commonly used in the industry. For the sake of completeness, we would also like to refer to the process of interweaving marketing and product management at this point without, however, exploring product management in detail. Figure 3.22 offers an overview of the business processes in the process group of "marketing and campaign management".

Market Research

Qualitative and quantitative market research is the starting point for marketing activities and includes all internal and external sources necessary to gain an understanding of the market situation and identify and evaluate market trends. The resulting information is then made available to other company functions. Market

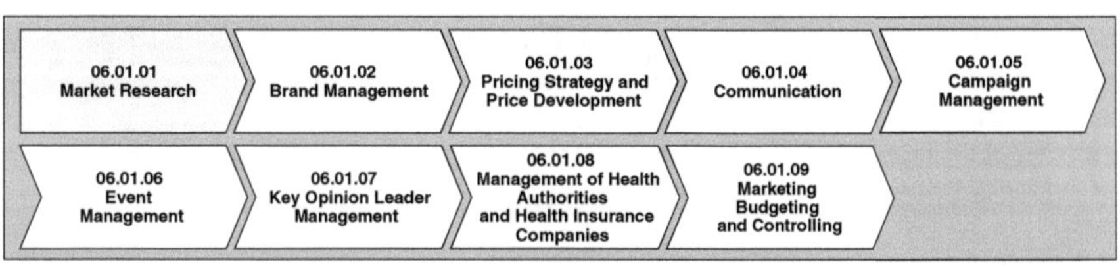

Fig. 3.22 "Marketing and Campaign Management" process overview

players are also assigned to respective market segments and groups in the ecosystem. Prominent examples of questions that marketing research seeks to answer are:

- What are the current market trends?
- How are market, sales, or price trends developing for the company's own products or relevant rival products?
- Which partners influence the success of marketing? Which partners are opinion leader and influencers?
- What characteristics describe the relevant target groups that are of interest to the company?
- Who are the competitors in our market segments and what business strategy are they following?
- What part do the statutory and private health insurance funds play in developing our business?

Brand Management

Together with product and brand management, marketing strategies are developed that account for future innovations and plan for activities to be carried out. Marketing and product management work closely together in the area of research and development to take a well-grounded approach to building up and securing the brand(s).

Pricing Strategy and Price Development

Pricing strategies and profitability considerations for the relevant market segments define the focus of this process, which is extremely important given the high investment costs associated with innovative drugs and the significance of prices for imitation products.

Communication

Marketing activities for pharmaceutical companies and their product and service portfolios must be well defined and target the main stakeholder groups, which continue to be general practitioners, clinics (and their physicians and pharmacists), and drugstores. However, the focus of activities is gradually shifting toward health authorities and health insurance funds. Furthermore, the trend of forming multi-dimensional networks of physicians, clinics, medical service centers, drugstore chains, and buying syndicates (to name but a few) calls for targeted communications to reinforce awareness of the company on the one hand, and a diversification of approaches in order to reach the relevant market players in their respective roles on the other (Hohmann and Seiter 2008, Buck-Emden and Böder 2004).

Marketing must not only identify and flesh out strategies and tactics but also operationalize them. A crucial role is played by central communication management, which is responsible for getting the message across into the markets. This aim is supported by the two key building blocks of regular communication to the markets and campaign-based communication to position particular topics and products.

Campaign Management

In the context of campaign management, existing broadly diversified communication activities are complemented by campaign-specific content and questions by means of direct and indirect distribution channels. The company's standard sales channels, such as on-site visits, telemarketing and telesales, and Internet-based communication, are adapted or enhanced as part of a campaign.

Event Management

Event management plays a vital role in marketing-oriented communication.

Event management is commonly used within the industry as an element for strategic marketing activities and a communication platform for pharmaceutical companies. From product launches to press conferences and special symposia or conferences, event management provides process-based support to help the company organize the event, manage participating partners and the event location, finalize content, and coordinate structured follow-up activities. The target group is either chosen on the basis of market research or particular groups of physicians are nominated by sales employees.

Key Opinion Leader Management

Key opinion leader management describes the process of winning over and developing key opinion leaders and interacting with them. Key opinion leaders are physicians with a strong professional reputation, usually in a particular specialty, which makes them influential when it comes to perceptions and, in some instances, prescribing policy in their specialty. Key opinion leadership can also be differentiated in terms of geographical sphere of influence, which may be regional, national, or international.

In order to benefit from this expertise, companies involve key opinion leaders in the development process for new drugs, for example. Key opinion leaders are also often engaged to author publications, conduct clinical studies, or sit on market research panels. In addition to providing extensive expertise in a consultative role, key opinion leaders act objectively, which makes them an independent authority in the public image of the company. For the reasons stated above and in the interests of both parties, overly close ties or an impression thereof are avoided.

People other than physicians can also act as key opinion leaders in the health care system. It can be concluded that regardless of their background, the strong reputation enjoyed by opinion leaders stems from their scientific expertise and their independence.

Management of Health Authorities and Health Insurance Companies

More than ever before, pharmaceutical companies are carrying out additional marketing activities aimed at organizations and contacts in health authorities and health insurance companies.

Due to regulatory requirements, it is becoming increasingly important to phrase communications carefully and manage the list of drugs being manufactured. Different countries maintain exclusion lists, prescriptions for active ingredients as opposed to dedicated products are increasingly called for and used, and contractual ties between health insurance funds and pharmaceutical companies are setting the agenda in this area of communication. As a result, the importance of this field of marketing is growing. The development of positive lists can be observed at present in a number of countries. A positive list for drugs contains products whose costs are reimbursed by the statutory health insurance funds. Products are added to the list based on their therapeutic benefits. In Germany, which does not yet have a final positive list, the Institute for Quality and Efficiency in Health Care is responsible for assessing products.

Most European Union member states and Switzerland have final positive lists (Schwabe and Paffrath 2008).

Marketing Budgeting and Controlling

The overall objectives of marketing management are indisputably to boost sales and profitability and increase the loyalty of business partners. A number of secondary objectives are derived from these, for example, to increasing the number of prescriptions, promoting ties with key opinion leaders, and expanding the market distribution of the company's own products. Sales and profitability objectives are defined regularly, as they determine budgets for marketing activities.

Budgets are monitored and adjusted by evaluating and interpreting both external market data and internal company information. Market trends are anticipated and a set of marketing-oriented objectives are defined for the entire company. These objectives influence the marketing budget, which can be twice as high as the research and development budget (Telgheder 2008b).

3.3.2.2 Opportunities and Optimization Potential

By applying marketing management processes consistently, companies can benefit from opportunities for improvements with respect to:

- Helping to define the market environment and identifying market changes and trends.
- Taking a holistic and structured approach to managing key opinion leaders.
- Improving the way innovations are evaluated in respect of current and future requirements.
- Planning and executing consistent pricing and distribution strategies.

- Establishing or improving the quality of forecasts with regard to marketing activities.
- Enabling processes to be handled across several teams by experts from brand management, controlling, sales, and finance departments as well as operational units.
- Helping to optimize labor efficiency by performing structured market analyses and exerting influence on portfolio management based on the market.
- Supporting sales organizations in key sales tasks within the scope of marketing management.

3.3.2.3 Success Factors and Key Performance Indicators

The following have emerged as the main success factors with a bearing on objectives:

- Accurate market research, above all to help identify physicians with high potential as well as long-term market trends, and to anticipate future legal conditions.
- An inside-out approach to marketing activities on the basis of knowledge obtained through accurate market research.
- Observation and protection of the interests of those involved such as patients, those who prescribe the products, influencers, health insurance funds, and state bodies.
- Dedicating available resources to creating additional value for the company.
- Standardized strategy alignment and execution of activities.
- Strict handling of the segmentation strategy (number of visits, additional services available only to those belonging to a given segment, inclusion in certain campaigns).
- Lean, standardized processes throughout the company.
- Effective and efficient support from systems and available tools.

The following key performance indicators are used to quantify goals and measure success in the area of marketing management:

- Number of campaigns.
- Response and close rate, for example, changes to prescription rates or sales orders (drugstores) during or after a campaign.
- Return on investment (ROI).
- Profitability per physician or druggist (for physicians, selling expenses compared with the assumed or analyzed prescription rate; see also the process group of "indirect sales in the pharmaceutical industry").
- Market share.
- Customer satisfaction index.

3.3.3 *Sales Management*

3.3.3.1 Process Overview and Characteristics

To drive growth and boost revenue, special efforts must be made to increase the effectiveness of sales activities with the aim of pushing up the value of sales achieved through a stable or expanding customer basis. The sales organization—and in particular the field sales force—acts as the key lever for accomplishing these goals. The task of managing this organization is a decisive part of the process group of sales management, which comprises the phases of design and planning, execution, and controlling. It is usually a recurring process executed in cycles. The results and plans that emerge from each cycle are optimized in a subsequent cycle. The following Fig. 3.23 is an overview of the processes in this process group.

The following business processes exist:

Sales Planning

To avoid unstructured market development or setting wrong priorities, sales plans are drawn up to develop markets accurately and avoid setting wrong priorities taking into account past experiences. The aim is to develop balanced and motivational target objectives and key performance indicators that apply a structure across all levels of sales activities.

After being distributed to planning dimensions such as products, sales channels, regions, and territories, these targets lead to detailed goals for the respective (groups of) employees. In addition to goals based purely on sales and profitability, key figures such as frequency of visits and the nomination of physicians for training events can be used to manage sales and subsequently measure success.

Sales Structures

The sales structure is derived from the global or company-wide go to market strategy. Depending on the characteristics of the target group(s) and the diversity of the product portfolio, a hierarchical structure is created based on region, specialty, market potential, and sales channel. The following structure can be taken as an example:

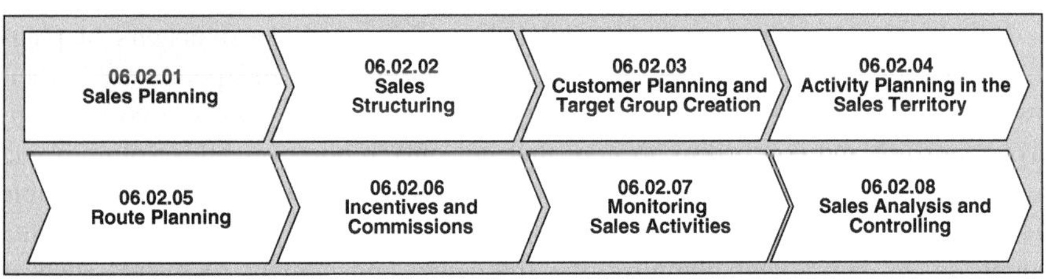

Fig. 3.23 Process overview: “Sales Management”

Level 1. Product/product line
Level 2. Business unit/division
Level 3. Sales region
Level 4. Sales territory

The structure is arranged into sales channels (general practitioners, clinics, and druggists) at different levels depending on the pharmaceutical company's size and product portfolio. Territories are restructured regularly in response to the constantly changing market environment. Restructuring might involve minimal changes such as shifting responsibility for a small number of physicians/druggists, or far-reaching changes such as completely reassigning territories and the physicians and drugstores based in them.

Customer Planning and Target Group Creation

Historical data, such as assessments made by the sales representative in the territory concerned, sales volume in the previous period, trends concerning changes to the territory's population structure, and forecast sales developments, is used as a basis to segment all of the possible contact persons in the territory. Besides financial factors, other criteria are drawn upon that describe the information needs of those in a position to prescribe the product and their role in the medical economic environment (such as opinion leaders or head physicians at hospitals). The result is the creation of segments, such as A, B, and C physicians, for example, which are assigned varying degrees of service intensity. The segmentation process also takes into account the growing number of groupings of physicians in medical service centers and the structure of clinics. The process is carried out centrally and, depending on the structure of the company, gives the territory manager the chance to diverge from the segments or exert influence on the number of members and the structure of the segments.

Activity Planning in the Sales Territory

Building on this process, both regional and national sales managers and their employees (territory managers and pharmaceutical representatives) agree on specific sales goals and define the structure and organization of daily tasks to achieve these goals. Integrated planning systems are used at the different levels of the sales hierarchy to check if goals are being achieved, thereby providing the basis for calculating the performance-related remuneration of sales employees.

Individual sales activities are usually planned by territory managers or pharmaceutical representatives themselves, who work relatively independently in their own region. To assess business developments, they have access to a comprehensive reporting and controlling system that not only reports on sales volumes and revenues but also provides non-monetary key figures. There is also a discernible trend toward centralized planning that has its roots mainly in English-speaking countries. In centralized planning, the frequency and content of events such as visits and telephone calls are defined centrally but the sales representatives remain responsible for detailed planning.

Route Planning

Process steps that help sales employees define, plan, and carry out visits are provided within the framework of route planning. This type of planning enables sales representatives to save recurring constellations of appointments as proposals for repeated reuse. This aid not only helps them regularly penetrate certain target groups but also makes it possible to reproducibly minimize travel times and travel costs in times of tight resources. Route planning takes into account both the requirements of the sales representatives and the possible visit dates of physicians and druggists. Further details of planning, carrying out, and documenting visits can be found in Sect. 3.3.4. It must be noted that route planning is not necessarily suitable for all pharmaceutical representatives. For example, it is not possible to create fixed routes in highly dynamic territories that are subject to constant change.

Incentive and Commission—Compensation Schemes in Pharmaceutical Field Sales

Defined sales targets are linked with financial incentives from the pharmaceutical company's incentive and commission scheme to provide extrinsic motivation and ensure sales activities are prioritized. Alongside standardized goals that apply to all sales employees, specific targets and incentives can be defined to reflect specific employee or sales territory situations.

All targets and incentives must be clearly defined in terms of how they are measured, where and when they apply, and what the employee receives in the event of 100 % goal achievement.

Sales and market share goals relating to general practitioners cannot be measured directly for pharmaceutical representatives in the field, but require market data, for example, from IMS Health, to be evaluated. With the introduction of legislation to promote competition between statutory health insurance funds, the extent to which data could be evaluated in the established RPM 1900 model was restricted. This model collected and provided data based on approximately 1900 territories in Germany, including competitor analyses and market share evaluations. The reduction to 250 territories is forcing a rethink both in this area and in the segmentation of physicians.

Monitoring Sales Activities

An integral part of sales management is monitoring sales activities. The aim is to be able to continuously monitor how closely defined sales goals are to being achieved across all levels of the sales hierarchy. The results of analyses can prompt corrective action to ensure success. Ideally, goal achievement reviews should be held regularly between regional managers and their sales representatives, and between sales managers and regional managers.

Today's companies are aware of the need for monitoring and, in addition to evaluating target and actual data as well as deviations, support a warning system to draw attention to exceptions uncovered by monitoring activities. Processes also support follow-up activities and help ensure the company keeps track of the effects of corrective actions.

Activities, exceptions, and corrective actions are all monitored individually or aggregated at the respective level of the hierarchy.

Sales Analysis and Controlling

Sales analysis in association with general sales controlling is in many respects an important sales management tool. Those with access to statistics not only benefit from a transparent view of their own field of activity but can also use different analyses to view their data from different perspectives. For example, a benchmark analysis is perfect for identifying top performing employees or territories. Ideally, these analyses should act as best practices, offering a recipe for success that can be copied or modified to suit a particular purpose.

Trend analyses and time series can be used to examine the impact of changes to the way the market is developed or of external influences on sales during the fiscal period.

Other company departments besides sales also have a need for analyses and evaluations. Portfolio management must be able to evaluate the sales potential of possible new products and active ingredients, for example.

Furthermore, the external need for information must also not be forgotten, whether it be sales partners, investors, or the authorities.

3.3.3.2 Opportunities and Optimization Potential

Opportunities and optimization potential result from:

- Integrating data from the sales structure, internal experiences, and external sources when creating sales segments and target groups.
- Providing well defined evaluations that allow internal and external data to be analyzed together quickly and easily.
- Using integrated sales planning, which not only adopts the goals from the company business plan but also provides input for the S&OP process (Sect. 3.2).

It is vital that the sales management process is transparent and comprehensive, allows new findings to be built into the next management round, and proactively introduces process improvements in the sales organization.

3.3.3.3 Success Factors and Key Performance Indicators

Factors that influence sales management are derived directly from the areas of activity:

- Accurate current and historical sales information from internal and external data sources
- Clearly and objectively defined targets, for example, market share, market index, and rate of visits
- Lean and standardized processes in sales and sales management.
- Support from systems and tools that are tailored to the needs of sales management.

This process group and its dependent processes can be measured using the following key performance indicators, which are aimed primarily at the operationalization of sales planning:

- Number of visits to target customers.
- Planned service intensity for defined target customers.
- Market index and comparison values of the sales territory (determined mainly from external data).
- Efficiency of sales expenses.

3.3.4 Indirect Sales in the Pharmaceutical Industry

3.3.4.1 Process Overview and Characteristics

In the pharmaceutical industry, the term "indirect sales" denotes the sales processes that are used primarily by the pharmaceutical field sales force (pharmaceutical representatives)[19] in Germany. What is special about this type of sales is that it does not lead to a direct or immediate sale of the pharmaceutical company's products/drugs to the physician.[20] Instead, the physician's final decision to make a purchase can only be evoked indirectly on the basis of samples or discussions of samples.

By visiting physicians in their place of work to provide drug samples and hold discussions, pharmaceutical representatives can introduce their company's products to physicians and encourage them to prescribe the drugs to suitable patients.

---

[19] The pharmaceutical representative may be a sales representative, regional manager, or key account manager.

[20] Depending on the field of indication, the direct contact persons may not always be the physicians but instead specialist nurses and other medical specialists. One example would be diabetes advisors, who are addressed directly by pharmaceutical representatives.

The German Medicines Act makes extensive provisions for the issuing of drug samples in Germany.

Pharmaceutical representatives in Germany also carry out non-interventional studies to obtain further information and commit physicians to their products. Here, the physician agrees to document the treatment of patients involving the product in question. Due to the monetary remuneration of physicians, non-interventional studies of this kind are not without controversy and the conduct of pharmaceutical companies in Germany is closely scrutinized by the Center for Protection against Unfair Competition, based in Bad Homburg, Germany (Telgheder 2008a).

In this sales context, pharmaceutical representatives act as information carriers, marketing instruments, and the primary link between physicians and pharmaceutical companies. They not only issue samples but also share specialist information with physicians both in practices and hospitals as well as with druggists to inform them about relevant drugs manufactured by the company.

The main products that are relevant for indirect sales in the pharmaceutical company's product portfolio are prescription drugs. Over-the-counter products and behind-the-counter products (available only from druggists), on the other hand, are predominantly marketed through the direct sales channel.

One feature that marks out the marketing of prescription drugs through the indirect sales channel is that pharmaceutical representatives and pharmaceutical companies rarely know how often their product is actually prescribed by the physician because they usually do not have direct access to this data.[21]

Therefore, an approximate approach is needed to measure success. The basis for this is the fact that Germany is divided regionally into what are known as RPM (regional pharma market) segments (in 2008 there were 250 such segments). All physicians and drugstores are assigned to these segments (their postal code and town or city determines the RPM segment to which they belong).

The success of efforts to sell prescription drugs is now measured at the level of RPM segments by analyzing the quantities sold to drugstores in each segment. When measuring success, the pharmaceutical companies assume that the majority of prescriptions submitted by patients to drugstores originate from physicians in the vicinity of the drugstore that are visited by the pharmaceutical representative. This assumption can only ever deliver approximate results, however, since patients are free to submit their prescriptions to drugstores in other RPM segments and it is not always known exactly which physician actually prescribed the product.[22]

Generally speaking, it is easier for pharmaceutical companies to measure the success of the indirect sales channel when it is used for physicians at clinics. The physicians visited by pharmaceutical representatives in clinics are predominantly those with links to the hospital's buying center, that is, the committee of medical

---

[21] Prescription data is available for individual fields of indication. However, this data is not suitable for use as the sole basis for analysis. It is therefore used only as an additional source of information. The data source we are referring to is IMS Xponent® data (IMS Health 2008a).

[22] Market data, such as that of IMS Health, is normally used to measure the success of the indirect sales channel in detail (IMS Health 2008b).

staff and pharmacists responsible for deciding which drugs are included in the hospital formulary. The motivation behind visits to these physicians is to have the pharmaceutical company listed as a drug supplier to the hospital.

Accordingly, pharmaceutical representatives who target physicians in clinics focus their efforts not on issuing samples but on providing specialist information about the drugs.

In this case, pharmaceutical companies are able to measure the indirect success of sales efforts themselves; when hospitals list drugs, their pharmacies or dispensaries place orders with the pharmaceutical company directly. Pharmaceutical representatives, however, are not usually responsible for negotiating customer-specific prices, which may be the basis for the drug being listed.

This is true in particular of pharmaceutical representatives of research pharmaceutical companies (as opposed to those of generic drug manufacturers working in hospital sales). Since the product portfolios of generic drug manufacturers are very large by comparison and are differentiated primarily on the basis of price (in addition to the actual properties of the products), their field sales representatives are mainly responsible for negotiating prices and quantities and ensuring that their drugs are ubiquitous in the market. In this respect, the activities of these pharmaceutical representatives can be more closely attributed to the direct sales channel.

3.3.4.2 Opportunities and Optimization Potential

Since sales work is essentially both consultative and influential in character, pharmaceutical representatives rely on extensive knowledge on the one hand, and offers that encourage physicians to prescribe their products on the other. Their aim is to build up relationships with physicians, transfer knowledge, and, above all, predict physicians' prescribing behavior. The tools offered by this process support relationship management of this nature by enabling sales representatives to benefit from the potential of:

- Optimized preparation of knowledge.
- Structured preparation of existing data owned by the company.
- Preparation of structured information (relating to prescriptions and drugstore sales) and unstructured information from market research companies (analyses of competitors, markets, and trends).
- Completeness of information about a balanced product portfolio.

3.3.4.3 Success Factors and Key Performance Indicators

As described in the previous chapter, the secret to the success of this process is the preparation of knowledge, which is the best possible way to ensure that pharmaceutical representatives can give expert advice. Success factors therefore include:

- Direct contact between the pharmaceutical representative and the physician to establish a foundation of trust.
- Preparation of internal and external knowledge for the pharmaceutical representative.
- Intelligent analysis of external market data and internal information about individual physicians or territories.
- A balanced product portfolio.
- Consulting know-how and customer relations expertise of the sales representative.

The key performance indicators used to measure the success of pharmaceutical field sales forces include:

- Number of visits to target customers (physicians, drugstores) for each period under review (planned, actual, and difference).
- Coverage of planned service intensity for defined target customers.
- Deviation of the market index of the sales territory (determined from external data) from the benchmark.
- Non-interventional studies arranged and carried out.
- Number of local events (for example, regular gatherings of physicians).

3.3.4.4 The Process in Detail

Other process variants besides "indirect sales to general practitioners" also exist. For the sake of completeness, these are mentioned here.

In indirect sales to hospital physicians, pharmaceutical representatives are generally not, with a few exceptions, able to predict which physicians they will see during their visit. Their preparations are therefore primarily based not on particular physicians but on departments or products. There are also links to direct sales to clinics, since the two sales employees either work hand in hand, or one sales employee takes on both roles.

The activities of the pharmaceutical representative are supported by a call center, which passes on knowledge and handles inquiries. This method is used in indirect sales primarily for B and C physicians, whom the sales representative can no longer visit personally in times of dwindling budgets. The pharmaceutical company's website rounds off its information offering by providing physicians with a means of accessing detailed information about products and their characteristics.

Interest groups constitute a further target of the indirect sales channel, which, in this case, can be structured in a number of ways and is also directly linked to marketing management as well as the management of health authorities and health insurance companies. Employees in indirect sales focus their efforts mainly on local self-help groups, medical associations, associations responsible for welfare services, and so on. At this point we refer back to the need described in Sect. 3.3.2

for consistent communication with the medical economic environment and the networks contain therein.

The following Fig. 3.24 offers an overview of possible process variants and the sub-processes of the variant of "indirect sales to general practitioners through pharmaceutical representatives".

The sub-processes cover the following activities:

Plan Visit

The sub-process of planning visits covers the process of identifying and selecting suitable physicians to be visited in the near future by pharmaceutical representatives. They are identified mainly based on geographical criteria and a number of other attributes, such as classification, practice size, and data concerning the physician's network of relationships.

The following diagram Fig. 3.25 provides an example of this sub-process.

Prepare Visit

Once visits have been planned, the relevant physicians to be visited have been identified. In preparation for the visit, the sales representative then views master data and information about past visits to establish possible content and topics to discuss.

Carry Out Visit

During this sub-process, the sales representative actually meets the physician and uses the visit mainly to provide product-related information and hand over drug samples (in the case of general practitioners).

Document Visit

In this sub-process, the sales representative records a written account of the visit to each physician, nowadays usually in a CRM system. This ensures that all relevant information is saved, such as changes to master data and any new information

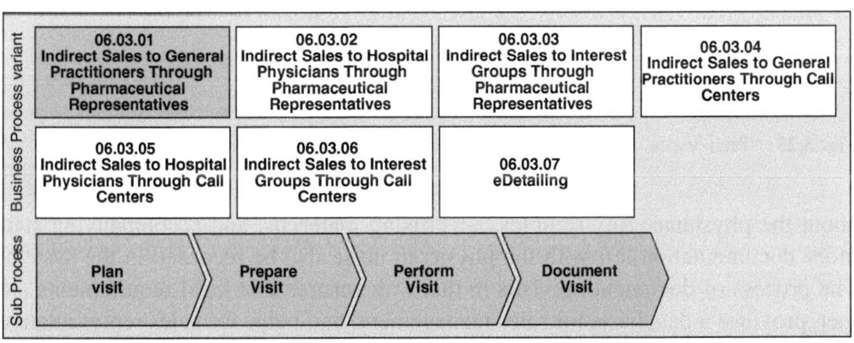

Fig. 3.24 Process overview: "Indirect Sales in the Pharmaceutical Industry"

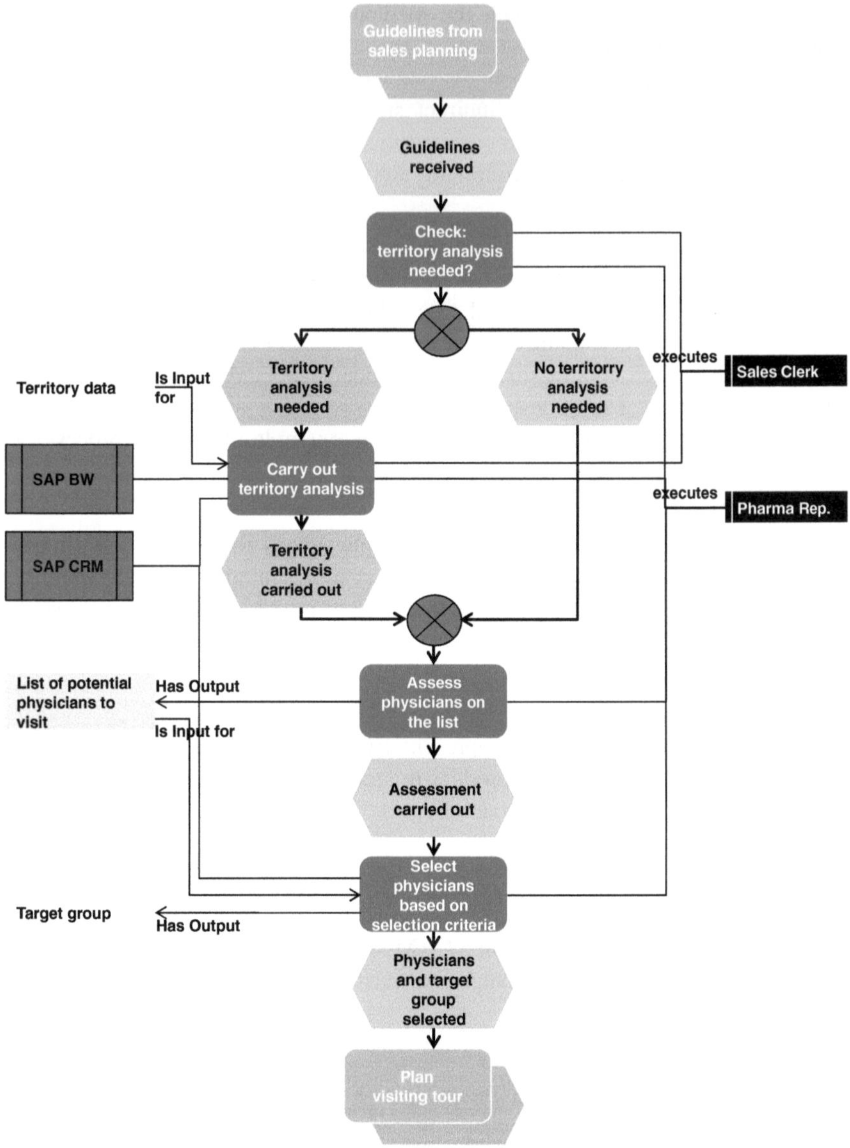

Fig. 3.25 "Plan Visits" sub-process as an event-driven process chain

about the physician. Any samples, advertising materials, and accompanying statutory documentation left with the physician must also be recorded in the system. The process of documenting visits in this way ensures that legal requirements are met, provides a data basis for sales management, and helps the sales representative prepare follow-up visits.

The "document visit" sub-process is presented in the following RACI matrix by way of example (Fig. 3.26).

The task of creating segments and target groups in the future is also aided by the availability of complete and structured documentation covering all information obtained during visits about physicians, medical practices, prescribing behavior, non-interventional studies, and the results of treatments. For this purpose, guidelines on the information to be recorded and how it should be structured are defined centrally.

	Input	Process Step	Output	Involveld Roles (also other teams or external)				Systems (old/new/manually)				
Process-ID				Physician	Pharma Rep	Sales Clerk	Manager	manually	ERP	Mobile Device	CRM	BW
06		**Sales and Marketing**			R		R					x
06.03		**Indirect Sales**										
06.03.01		**Indirect Sales with General Practicioners**										
		<...>										
		Document Visit										
06.03.01.51	current status of physician's account regarding samples, advertisings, investments	document medicine discussions, given samples, given advertisings, investments	changes are written to the physician's account		R	I				x	x	
06.03.01.52		generate sample order for physician (in case sample was not availble during visit)	Creation sample order		R	A			x		x	
06.03.01.53		create follow up activity	follow up activity is created, different responsible possible		R, I	I, R	R			x	x	
06.03.01.54		Document acknowledgements regarding non-interventional studies	New study documentation is created		R	A, I	I				x	
06.03.01.55	physician related information about study is available	Change or Closing of Study	Add information to study documentation		R	I	I				x	
06.03.01.56	physician related information about study is available	Finalize Study documentation and trigger settlement for the study	Change study status to trigger settlement		R	A, I	I		x		x	
06.03.01.57	Address or structural data of physician as changed	Start update of physicians data set	Update of respective data done		R					x	x	
06.03.01.58		Change marketing data of physician (qualitative values to describe physician in respect to segmentation)			R	I, (A)	I			x	x	
06.03.01.59		check and update visit times			R						x	
06.03.01.60		maintain campaign related information, including event management related information			R	I	I				x	

Fig. 3.26 The "Document Visit" sub-process expressed as a RACI matrix

3.3.5 *Direct Sales in the Pharmaceutical Industry*

3.3.5.1 Process Overview and Characteristics

In the pharmaceutical industry, the term "direct sales" (as opposed to indirect sales) describes the sales processes that cover the direct sale of pharmaceutical products to drugstores, hospitals, and, in some cases, also physicians (Fig. 3.27).

Pharmaceutical representatives in the field and sales employees based in the office act as sellers and constitute the primary link between business partners and the pharmaceutical company. In addition to making sales, it is also the job of both sets of sales employees to inform contact persons in drugstores, hospitals, and medical practices about relevant drugs being produced by the company.

While all of the categories in the pharmaceutical company's product portfolio are relevant for the direct sales channel, that is, over-the-counter, behind-the-counter, and prescription products, pharmaceutical representatives in the indirect sales channel sell mainly prescription drugs.

Pharmaceutical representatives also handle returns and ensure that contracts between drugstores and health insurance companies are honored. What is more, they have to sell shop displays, introduce and position promotional activities, and ensure that all associated regulations are met.

Measuring Success

In contrast to indirect sales, the success of sales activities in the direct sales channel can be measured immediately based on the orders placed by drugstores.

The success of a given field sales representative or call center employee in respect of sales to community drugstores can be measured by the pharmaceutical company itself, since sales of this nature lead to immediate orders that are either filled directly by the company itself (direct orders) or passed on to wholesalers (transfer orders).

In such instances, the data needed to measure success (sales revenue and sales volume) is available to the pharmaceutical company itself. This enables them to generate customer-specific sales statistics using internal data.

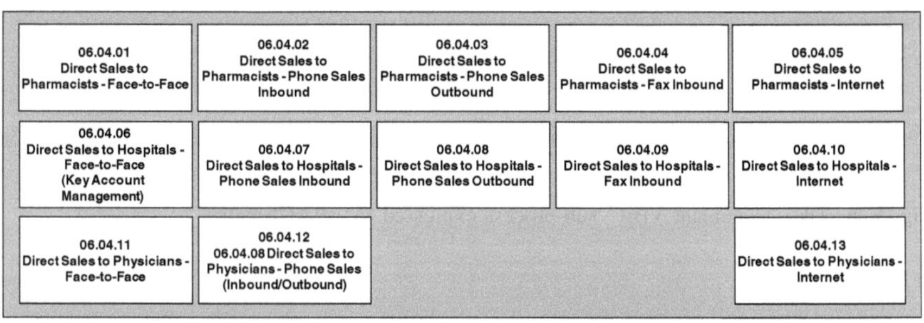

Fig. 3.27 Process variants of "Direct Sales in the Pharmaceutical Industry"

Sales Channels

On the one hand, sales orders are generated by field sales representatives, who visit the relevant drugstores in their territory and take orders during visits or have orders faxed through to them at a later date. A distinction is made between direct orders and transfer orders. The latter are handled initially by the field sales representative but then passed on directly to the pharmaceutical wholesaler to be filled on the basis of existing contracts. The inclusion of wholesale trade in the supply chain makes it easier to supply drugs promptly. However, coalitions of drugstores advocate direct deliveries from pharmaceutical companies, cutting out the pharmaceutical wholesalers (Telgheder 2008c).

On the other hand, office-based sales employees normally receive orders from drugstores by fax or telephone in call centers, or proactively call up drugstores directly to take their orders.

Direct sales are also made by field sales representatives that look after pharmacies in hospitals and clinics as well as supplying pharmacies.[23]

Due to the relatively large range of products they offer, generic drug manufacturers in particular tend to gear their clinical sales force toward sales activities.

Clinical sales activities, however, are not aimed directly at selling products; the first step in the process is to be listed as a supplier to the hospital or clinic by the committee of medical staff and pharmacists responsible for deciding which drugs are included in the hospital formulary. Inclusion in this list should be seen simply as a prerequisite for increasing business. Patients are put on certain drugs that usually continue to be prescribed after the patient leaves the hospital. In this respect, business in hospitals opens the door to subsequent prescription-based business.

Due to the comparatively large sales quantities and corresponding product bundles arranged by the pharmaceutical company, the next sales activity after being listed is to negotiate customer-specific prices and conditions for a given period as well as a set of general conditions. This applies in particular to generic drug manufacturers, since price is their key differentiator against research pharmaceutical companies.

The hospitals and clinics buying the products then obtain their orders (via their hospital or supplying pharmacy) from the pharmaceutical company directly at the conditions negotiated.[24]

[23] Supplying pharmacies supply several clinics—not all clinics have their own pharmacy.

[24] Germany does not yet have a mechanism for obtaining orders that accommodates wholesalers as a logistical link in the sales chain. As a result, there is no need to make allowance for wholesalers financially in the relationship between the hospital and the pharmaceutical company as is done in the United States, for example, with the chargeback process.

3.3.5.2 Opportunities and Optimization Potential

The main factors that shape the direct sales channel are how negotiations are handled, and reliable performance in preparing and executing sales processes. In this respect, optimization potential may be found in the following:

- Mapping and accounting for the procurement and relationship network when setting prices and conditions.
- Coordinated market and customer cultivation by including all roles involved in sales interactions.
- Benchmarking of direct sales with prescriber data so that key figures can be better assessed.
- Opportunities to automate activities associated with preparing visits (for example, notification, route planning) and carrying out visits (for example, order entry using order templates, calculation of conditions).
- Measuring the goal achievement of drugstores by comparing planned and actual sales revenue or based on other marketing measures (for example, positioning of displays).

3.3.5.3 Success Factors and Key Performance Indicators

With the emphasis on optimizing sales and revenues, the following success factors are relevant for the management of direct sales and have a bearing on the processes used:

- Stringent pricing strategy.
- Integrated order entry, also supported as a mobile application.
- Pharmaceutical representatives and key account managers with experience of negotiating.

The key performance indicators used to measure the success of sales include the following:

- Sales volume.
- Profitability (clinical sales force).
- Number of visits.
- Products included in hospital formularies for which orders exist.
- Positioning of advertisements/merchandising in drugstores.

3.3.6 Customer Service and Support

3.3.6.1 Process Overview and Characteristics

The process of "customer service and support" describes how inquiries from patients, physicians, and drugstores are handled by a central customer service team. This process also covers part of the order entry process and is closely linked with the process of "direct sales in the pharmaceutical industry". The tasks of both taking orders and providing information can take the form of inbound or outbound process variants. Inquiries are arranged in different categories depending on who they come from. The following types of inquiries exist:

- Service requests.
- Medical inquiries.
- Complaints.
- Reports of incidences of sickness/adverse reactions.

The following Fig. 3.28 provides an overview of the process variants.

Inquiries are initially received by call center employees, who attempt to provide a direct answer if at all possible. In the event of a service issue, the call center employee can, for example, confirm expected delivery dates. If the call concerns a medical matter, the employee can search a database of solutions and provide the answer directly. Customer service employees receive regular product and indication training from physicians. They also work in very close contact with pharmaceutical representatives, sales controlling, production, and marketing.

If the call center employee is unable to resolve the inquiry or lacks the experience, knowledge, or authority to make a decision, as is the case when the call relates to a complaint (either technical or medical), the inquiry is passed on to the organizational unit responsible, for example, quality management or the relevant medical department. The pharmaceutical company must ensure that it gives a full, prompt, and comprehensive reply to the inquiry both to protect its image and to meet its legal obligation to provide information and advice. Complaints of adverse reactions must be communicated to the relevant department immediately, since they must be reported without delay.

This process group also covers the initiation and—in the event of sales being affected—execution of the CAPA[25] process. In addition to receiving the initial complaint and highlighting a problem, the customer service team must also work closely with quality management to organize and execute recall campaigns.

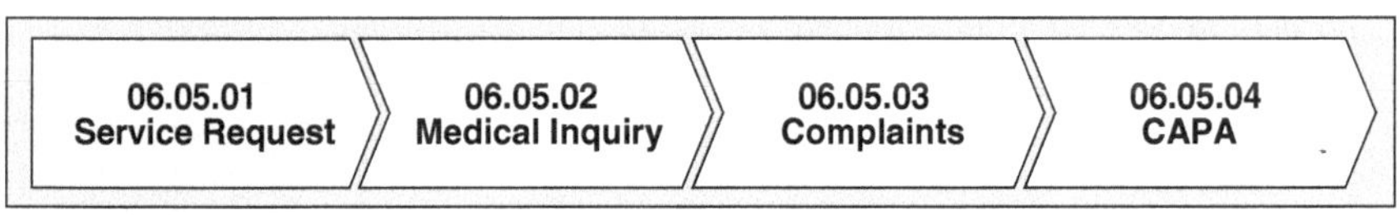

Fig. 3.28 Process variants of "Customer Service and Support"

[25] CAPA stands for corrective and preventive action.

3.3.6.2 Opportunities and Optimization Potential

To provide prompt support to service employees and therefore customers in the form of knowledge and answers, the employee must be able to identify the customer environment as soon as the call is received, comprehend the nature of the business relationship, and access a pool of knowledge directly. Ideally, all possible questions should be answered using a centralized knowledge platform. This facilitates:

- Customer inquiries to be answered quickly and directly.
- The immediate initiation of measures to resolve issues that cannot be answered directly.
- Competent telephone demeanor and direct forwarding to specialist departments where necessary.

3.3.6.3 Success Factors and Key Performance Indicators

The following factors have a key bearing on the success of this process group:

- Preparation of internal knowledge in a structured form.
- Direct access to customer data and customer history.
- The means to record and pass on both straightforward and complex inquiries rapidly and comprehensively.
- Decision-making authority and responsibilities are clearly defined.

The success of this process is measured using key performance indicators that enable customer service employees to be assessed. Bearing in mind the particular features of this industry, possible indicators include:

- Average handling time of inquiries and the solution rate of inquiries resolved directly.
- Level of satisfaction of customers with service and pharmaceutical information.
- Success of CAPA measures.
- Results of surveys among different customer groups (for example, physicians and patients) carried out regularly by independent institutes.
- Qualification of employees.

References

Andrew JP, Sirkin HL, Haanæs K, Michael DC (2007) Measuring innovation 2007: a BCG senior management survey. The Boston Consulting Group, inc., Boston, pp 10–14

Augenstein M, Alexander D (2007a) Sales and operations planning—where does forecasting fit in the S&OP process? https://www.sdn.sap.com/irj/sdn/weblogs?blog=/pub/wlg/5867. Accessed 2007 (requires registration)

Augenstein M, Alexander D (2007b) Sales & operations planning—the most important KPI's for the S&OP process. https://www.sdn.sap.com/irj/sdn/weblogs?blog=/pub/wlg/5099. Accessed 2007 (requires registration)

Augenstein M, Alexander D (2007c) The S&OP process rollercoaster? https://www.sdn.sap.com/irj/sdn/weblogs?blog=/pub/wlg/6921. Accessed 2007 (requires registration)

The Boston Consulting Group (BCG) (2008) Portfoliomatrix. http://www.bcg.de/bcg/klassiker/portfolio. Accessed 2008

Buck-Emden R, Böder J (2004) Kundenbeziehungs-management mit SAP-Branchenlösungen. Galileo Press, Bonn, p 161 et seq

Burghardt M (2001) Einführung in Projektmanagement, 3rd edn. Publicis MCD Verlag, München, pp 11–26

Cooper RG (1994) Perspective. Third-generation new product processes. J Prod Innov Manage 11:3–14

Corsten H, Gössinger R, Schneider H (2006) Grundlagen des Innovationsmanagements. Verlag Vahlen, München

Deutsches Institut für Normung (1987) DIN-Norm DIN 69901: Projektwirtschaft; Projektmanagement; Begriffe

Geschka H (1993) Wettbewerbsfaktor Zeit, Landsberg/Lech, p 182

Hauschild J (2004) Innovationsmanagement, 3rd edn. Vahlen, München, pp 501–515

Higdon B (2005) Implementing sales and operations planning. Fisher College of Business, The Ohio State University. http://www.pom.edu/mpc/MPC1/732_05_files/default.htm. Accessed 2005

Von Hippel E (1986) Lead users. A source of novel product concepts. Manage Sci 32:791–805

Hohmann J, Seiter S (2008) Neue Wege im Pharmavertrieb. In: Chemmanager 09/2008, p 12

Hopfenbeck W (2000) Allgemeine Betriebswirtschaft- und Managementlehre, 13th edn, Verlag Moderne Industrie, Landsberg/Lech, p 629

IMS Health (2008a) Xponent. http://www.imshealth.de/sixcms/detail.php/51. Accessed 2008

IMS Health (2008b) RPM. http://www.imshealth.de/sixcms/detail.php/75. Accessed 2008

Kotler P, Keller KL (2006) Marketing management, 12th edn. Prentice Hall, UpperSaddle River, NJ

Macharzina K (1995) Unternehmensführung, 2nd edn. Gabler, Wiesbaden, p 751 et seq

Montgomery DC (2001) Design and analysis of experiments, 5th edn. Wiley, Weinheim, New York

Nieschlag R, Dichtl E, Hörschgen H (1994) Marketing—Ein entscheidungsorientierter Ansatz, 17th edn. Berlin

Pleschak F, Sabisch H (1996) Innovationsmanagement. Schäffer-Poeschel, Stuttgart

Project Management Institute (PMI) (2004) A Guide to the project management body of knowledge: PMBOK guide, 3rd edn. Project Management Institute Inc., Newtown Square, PA

Porter M E (1983) Wettbewerbsstrategie. Frankfurt, p 25

Supply Chain Council (2008) SCOR™ 9.0 reference. http://www.supply-chain.org/. Accessed 2008

Schlicksupp H (1998) Produktinnovation. Würzburg, p 204

Schreyögg A, Steinmann H (1985) Strategische Kontrolle. ZfbF, H. 37: 396 et seq

Schwabe U, Paffrath D (2008) Arzneiverordnungsreport 2008: Aktuelle Daten. Kosten, Trends und Kommentare, p 2

Sheldon DH (2006) World class sales and operations planning. J. Ross Publishing, FL

Specht G, Beckmann C, Amelingmayer J (2002) F&E-management, 2nd edn. Schäffer-Poeschel, Stuttgart, pp 212–214

Telgheder M (2008a) Werbeeinsatz im Sprechzimmer. In: Handelsblatt No. 156:12

Telgheder M (2008b) Keine Qualitätskontrolle für Anwendungsstudien. In: Handelsblatt No. 156, August 13, p 12

Telgheder M (2008c) Der Fluch der billigen Pillen. In: Handelsblatt No. 181, p 12

Thom N (1980) Grundlagen des betrieblichen Innovationsmanagement, 2nd edn. Aufl., Königstein/Ts., p 53

Vahs D, Burmester R (2005) Innovationsmanagement, 3rd edn. Aufl., Schäffer-Poeschel, Stuttgart, p 284 et seq

Wallace TF (2005) Sales and operations planning. The "how-to" handbook, 2nd edn. TF Wallace & Company, Cincinnati, OH

Wildemann H (1990) Neben Kosten und Qualität kann der Faktor Zeit im Wettbewerb zum entscheidenden Element werden. In: Handelblatt, No. 195

Witt J (1996) Produktinnovation. München, p 10

Witte E (1973) Organisation für Innovationsentscheidungen. Das Promotoren-Modell. Göttingen

Zimmermann K, Obring K, Klewitz S (2003) World-class innovation. R&D management: rules for success in manufacturing industry. The Boston Consulting Group, p 5 et seq

Chapter 4
Summary

Stephanie Lockemann

This book has addressed the subject of innovative business process design in the process manufacturing sector, focusing particularly on the chemical and pharmaceutical industries.

In Chap. 1, we began by having a look at both industries. We examined the global chemical and pharmaceutical markets and substantiated our findings with examples of recent figures. We then analyzed the market environment in which process manufacturing companies operate. This environment is shaped by a number of legal and political, economic, sociodemographic, and technological factors, all of which have an impact on companies and the challenges they have to face today and in the future.

Next, we examined the market forces and their effect on process manufacturing companies. Here, too, we distinguished between a range of influencing factors, namely products, new and existing competitors, suppliers, and customers.

Finally, we transferred the market environment and market forces to the business process map, that is, the process areas and process groups in both the chemical and pharmaceutical industries. This allowed us to draw conclusions as to the processes that require particular attention and those with more of a supporting role.

In Chap. 2, we introduced SAP Consulting's business process management (BPM) methodology. After emphasizing the importance of business process management for companies, we explored SAP Consulting's approach in detail, and learned that it entails a procedure that takes us "from general to specific". The market factors examined in Chap. 1 continuously put pressure on companies to change. This pressure is manifested in business processes, which means we need a holistic overview of the company's processes. SAP's BPM methodology helps by providing a methodical approach involving four key phases, namely calibration, analysis of as-is processes, to-be process design, and implementation. This is the only way to identify and evaluate the optimization potential of a company and the individual processes it executes. Analyses can be performed at five process levels, linked to each other from levels one to five in a top-down approach.

G. Grüne et al., *Business Process Management within Chemical and Pharmaceutical Industries*, DOI: 10.1007/978-3-642-11717-6_4,

In addition to providing the methodology and executing the project, SAP Consulting offers support in the form of predefined content that helps to accelerate projects.

In Chap. 3, we presented a sample selection of this content. We investigated three process areas and the associated process groups. Specifically, these were the process area of research and development in the chemical industry with the associated process groups of ideas and requirements, bench scale trials, pilot trials and production acceptance, application technology, project management, and portfolio management. Next, we looked at the process area of planning with its related process groups (applicable within both the chemical and pharmaceutical industries) of budget planning, sales and operations planning, demand planning, supply planning, and production planning. Finally, we examined a process area very specific to the pharmaceutical industry, namely sales and marketing, together with its process groups of marketing and campaign management, sales management, indirect sales, direct sales, and customer service and support.

We provided an overview of all process groups and their characteristics and, in each case, identified opportunities and potential for optimization and described the success factors and indicators.

We studied all three process areas down to SAP BPM process level three and, by way of example, investigated one process area for each main process down to the level of process steps, that is, level five. These were the process area of bench scale trials, sales and operations planning, and indirect sales.

Author Biography

Guido Grüne is Regional Head for Mobility Services at SAP Consulting. Before joining this position he was leading SAP® 's consulting business for the process industries at SAP® Deutschland AG & Co. KG and was leading the Global Chemical Practice for SAP® Consulting. In this role he was responsible for the consulting services offered by SAP® Consulting for companies in the chemical and pharmaceutical industries. In addition to executing comprehensive implementation projects, SAP® Consulting's activities are increasingly focused on process management to optimize customer-specific processes.

Guido Grüne studied industrial engineering and business economics at the University of Paderborn, Germany.

Since joining SAP® 14 years ago, he has worked in a number of SAP® consulting roles for customers in the process manufacturing sector.

G. Grüne et al., *Business Process Management within Chemical and Pharmaceutical Industries*, DOI: 10.1007/978-3-642-11717-6,

Dr. Volker Kluy is service portfolio manager for the consulting area Process Industries at SAP® Deutschland AG & Co. KG.

He studied pharmaceutics at the Heinrich Heine University of Duesseldorf, Germany, where he obtained his doctorate at the Institute of Pharmaceutical Biology. His professional career began in the product development and quality assurance department of the Teekanne GmbH, Duesseldorf, Germany.

He joined SAP® in 2005 as consultant for the process industry in the area of logistics, with a focus on quality management and compliance topics.

Dr. Stephanie Lockemann is Vice President and Global Head for the creation of packaged solutions in the area of Supply Chain Management, Product Lifecycle Management and Manufacturing at SAP® AG.

She joined SAP® in 2000 as a consultant for process industries and was consulting manager for process industries at SAP® Consulting from 2007 to 2011.

Since 2006 she has specialized in business process management (BPM) for the process industry and used to be responsible for the industry-specific business content provided by SAP® Consulting for several years.

She holds a Ph.D. in mechanical engineering from RWTH Aachen, Germany, where she specialized in heat transfer and coal combustion.

Stefan Meinhardt is head of the SAP® Consulting practice for the Consumer Products Industries, responsible for all SAP® Consulting activities for the Consumer Products customers with special focus on Germany and the European region. Together with his team he is providing consulting services from business process management and SAP® implementation services around the Consumer Products Industry solution portfolio.

In the 1990s he worked in SAP® development as the head of Implementation, Methods and Tools, and played a key role in creating the SAP R/3® reference model with his models for business process (re)engineering.

Stefan Meinhardt is also co-publisher of the journal HMD—Praxis der Wirtschaftsinformatik and author/contributor on a wide range of topics in the field of business process management.

He received his degree in business administration at the University of Bamberg, Germany, in 1988.

Petronela Barnáková is student trainee in the consulting area Process Industries at SAP® Deutschland AG & Co. KG.

She graduated in economics and business administration from the Alexander Dubcek University of Trencin, Slovakia. Currently she is undergoing the final examination in sociology at the Ruprecht-Karls-University of Heidelberg, Germany with focus on industrial sociology and culture.

Carola Feind-Just started her career at SAP® within Business Transformation Services industry area Process Industries as Principal and Chief Consultant where she acted as strategic advisor and business process specialist for large companies in the Chemical and Life Science Industry. Today she is heading a Center of Excellence at SAP® .

Before joining SAP® in 2008, Carola worked as Principal Consultant for a global management consultancy firm and 14 years for a global chemical company. Prior she headed a division at the German-Dutch Chamber of Commerce, The Hague.

Carola holds a Master of Art in International Relations from the University of Amsterdam and a Master of Business Administration from the University of Göttingen.

Markus Pfannschilling-Zerbe is a Senior Solution Architect in the consulting area Process Industries at SAP® Deutschland AG & Co. KG.

He studied Business Administration at the University of Cooperative Education in Stuttgart, Germany followed by a sales management trainee assignment at Karstadt Warenhaus AG.

After joining SAP® as Consultant for SAP® CRM in 2002 he worked in several customer projects as solution architect to drive the implantation of industry specific solutions focusing on the process area Sales and Marketing.

He is the service owner for the industry specific implementation service "Express SAP® CRM for the Chemical Industry".

Dr. Ornulf Rexin is Senior Business Consultant for Business Transformation Services Process Industries at SAP® Deutschland AG & Co. KG.

He studied chemistry at the Albert-Ludwig University of Freiburg, Germany, where he obtained his doctorate at Freiburg Materials Research Center in collaboration with Bayer AG. He began his professional career as a group manager product development at EMS-Chemie AG, Switzerland.

In 2007 he joined SAP® as consultant for process industries with a focus on product lifecycle management, quality management and sustainability.

Klaus Schölzel works as principal consultant for the consulting area Process Industries at SAP® Deutschland AG & Co. KG.

He studied mathematics and physics at the University of Cologne, Germany, where he obtained his diploma in mathematics. His professional career began as software developer at Kienzle GmbH, Germany. He then worked for 3M Deutschland GmbH, where he was responsible for development and implementation of logistics factory applications.

Klaus joined SAP® in 1992 as consultant for the consumer products industry in the area of logistics execution and planning. His professional focus is on business process design and optimization in the area of Supply Chain Planning for process industries.

Juergen Schroth is senior project manager for the consulting area Process Industries at SAP® Deutschland AG & Co. KG.

He studied marketing and international management at the University of Mannheim, Germany, where he obtained his master in business administration. His professional career began in sales at the BASF Pharmaceuticals subsidiary Knoll AG, Ludwigshafen, Germany.

He joined SAP® in 1998 as consultant for the process industries in the area of customer relationship management, with a focus on sales management and marketing topics.

Index

G. Grüne et al., *Business Process Management within Chemical and Pharmaceutical Industries*, DOI: 10.1007/978-3-642-11717-6,

MIX
Papier aus verantwortungsvollen Quellen
Paper from responsible sources
FSC® C105338

If you have any concerns about our products,
you can contact us on
ProductSafety@springernature.com

In case Publisher is established outside the EU,
the EU authorized representative is:
Springer Nature Customer Service Center GmbH
Europaplatz 3, 69115 Heidelberg, Germany

Printed by Libri Plureos GmbH
in Hamburg, Germany